Egon Ronay's

BIRDS EYE

GUIDE TO

Healthy Eating Out

Establishment research conducted by a team of full-time professional inspectors, who are trained to achieve common standards of judgement with as much objectivity as this field allows. Their professional identities are not disclosed until they seek information from the management after paying their bills. The Guide is independent in its editorial selection and does not accept advertising, payment or hospitality from establishments covered.

Egon Ronay's Guides
Second Floor, Greencoat House
Francis Street, London SW1P 1DH

Head of editorial Moyra Fraser
Editor Alison Melvin
Copywriter Jenni Fleetwood
Editorial contributor Miriam Polunin
Publisher William Halden

Design and art direction Carole Thomas
Photographer Vernon Morgan
Stylist Janine Norris
Food stylist Janice Murfitt
Illustrations Linda Smith

Maps by GEOprojects (UK) Ltd, Henley-on-Thames
All road maps are based upon the Ordnance Survey Map with the permission of the Controller of Her Majesty's Stationery Office, Crown copyright reserved.
Town plans by Cartography Department, Automobile Association.

Distributed in the United Kingdom by the Publishing Division of the Automobile Association, Fanum House, Basingstoke, Hampshire RG21 2EA and overseas by the British Tourist Authority, Thames Tower, Black's Road, London W6 9EL.

ISBN 0 86145 508 8

AA Ref 51981

Printed in Great Britian by Hazell Watson & Viney Ltd, member of the BPCC Printing Group, Aylesbury, Bucks.

CONTENTS

INTRODUCTION

Eating Out is an activity in which we indulge for both nourishment and pleasure. By adding the adjective 'Healthy' to the phrase and using it as the title and focus of this new Egon Ronay Guide, we are not adding another 'fad' book to the bookshelves. Instead, we are demonstrating just how many farsighted chefs are already responding to the growing demand from many of us for healthy—and appetizing—food when eating out.

What our inspectors were told to look for were not self-styled 'health' restaurants, or wholefood establishments (though these have not been overlooked), but rather places that prided themselves on being willing and able to meet the demand for meals using less fat, less sugar, less salt and more fresh natural ingredients, cooked simply with competence and care. So the pub whose speciality is steak and kidney pie followed by bread and butter pudding may be included if it also offers poached salmon or grilled plaice, imaginative salads or interesting sandwiches with wholemeal bread.

Tea rooms were tops if they served tisanes and speciality teas as well as regular blends, and decaffeinated coffee alongside the filter machine. We looked at home-made breads and cakes to find wholemeal and granary loaves and scones, and low-sugar fruit bakes as an alternative to gooey gâteaux. We peered into stock pots and soup kettles, looked thoughtfully at vegetables (glad to see organically-grown produce in some establishments) and asked chefs whether sauces were served separately or as an intrinsic part of dishes we wished to highlight.

What we wanted to discover was the healthy *option*.
And that's exactly what our *Guide to Healthy Eating Out* is all about.

How To Use This Guide

THE FOLLOWING NOTES EXPLAIN THE
INFORMATION AND SYMBOLS PRINTED WITH
EACH ENTRY. THE DETAILS VARY ACCORDING
TO THE TYPE OF ESTABLISHMENT.

① YORK ② *Restaurant* ③ New Health ④ ★

⑤ 14 East Street
⑥ (0904) 20142
⑦ Map 6 D2
North Yorkshire

⑧ Lunch 12.30–2
Dinner 7.30–11
⑨ **Closed** Lunch Sat &
Bank Holidays
⑩ Vegetarian cooking
⑪ Average price £12
Set D £8.95
⑫ Credit: Amex, Diners, Visa
Luncheon Vouchers accepted

① Establishment location. London entries appear first and are in alphabetical order by establishment name. Listings outside London are in alphabetical order by location within the divisions of England, Scotland, Wales and the Channel Islands.

② Classification: *Restaurant* for full restaurant meals
Quick Bite for light meals and snacks
Pub for bar meals and snacks

③ Establishment name.

④ A star is awarded to those establishments where the cooking is outstanding.

⑤ Address.

⑥ Telephone number with STD code.

⑦ Map references are to the map section at the back of the book or to a town plan printed with the entries.

⑧ This indicates the times of first and last orders for **Lunch** and **Dinner** on Restaurant entries.

Opening hours on Quick Bite entries refer specifically to times when the snacks described are available. Many establishments have flexible hours because of their small size or remote location, and it is safest to check opening times.

Last order times on Pub entries refer to bar food.

⑨ This indicates the days of the week the establishment is closed plus any annual closures.

Pub entries indicate any restrictions on the availability of bar food.

⑩ **Type of cooking** is indicated on Restaurant and Quick Bite entries where there is a distinctly national or a wholly vegetarian menu.

Pub entries indicate whether an establishment is a free house or brewery-owned.

⑪ **Average price** on Restaurant entries refers to the approximate cost of a three-course meal for one person including service and VAT (excluding wine). The price of set lunch (L) and set dinner (D) is also given, where applicable.

Typical prices on Quick Bite and Pub entries refer to the prices of two typical dishes from the menu. Minimum charges per person are indicated in brackets.

⑫ This indicates the credit cards accepted by the establishment and if Luncheon Vouchers are accepted.

OF SALADS, MORALS, TEMPERANCE AND CHASTITY ...

'By reason of its soporifous quality, lettuse ever was, and still continues the principal foundation of the universal tribe of Sallets, which is to cool and refresh, besides its beneficial influences on morals, temperance and chastity.'

John Evelyn wrote these words three hundred years ago in his book *Acetaria: A Discourse of Sallets*, and if our research for this Guide is anything to go by this period of time has seen a decline of epic proportions in the quality of salads. Possibly matched by the decline in the salad's other claimed benefits.

When we planned our *Guide to Healthy Eating Out* two years ago, the salad was to have been its virtual centrepiece. In fact, we worried that there would be an overemphasis on the delights of British salads. Instead we found a trail of disappointments.

For the most part the salads we were presented with were dull and unappetizing and displayed the worst of British produce. One would have to be a vegetarian and a starving one at that to be tempted by some of the displays.

Even where, at a distance, displays looked colourful and eye-catching, close inspection revealed that very little effort had been made in preparation. Most consisted of very crudely prepared ingredients thrown together in an untidy haphazard manner.

Finely grated carrots left to dry out; rapidly curling slices of cucumber; half-inch thick onion wedges; whole, unwashed tomatoes; tasteless lettuce all too often greeted us.

But why? We are able to obtain all manner of interesting vegetables and herbs throughout the year, so it's really a question of a little imagination, careful planning and a modicum of supervision so that staff make sure salads remain fresh and attractive to the eye.

And must we choose sauces out of a bottle? Can no one make a decent vinaigrette dressing anymore!

NIGHT AND DAY

If salads have been a disappointment, our inspectors have been cheered by the actual number of establishments of all types and sizes that are catering for the healthy eater. One obvious sign is the number of menus offering healthy vegetarian dishes, many including a vegetarian dish of the day, and others listing chicken and fish specials that are lightly sauced or served plain.

But on behalf of vegetarians we would have liked to see more variety—lentil soup, nut cutlets and omelettes are not the only items vegetarians eat.

And we were somewhat puzzled to find more provision for the health conscious at lunch than at dinner. Healthy eaters do not go to ground at dusk!

SWEET AND SOUR

Dessert trolleys need a fresh approach. There is a weakness in us all for the rich and creamy but many of us now prefer a palate-cleansing rather then a punishing pud. Sorbets are often the only option, while fruit salad is trotted out as if it were the only fresh fruit dessert in existence.

And why is fruit salad so stereotyped? Why not a green and white version with melon, greengage, apples, grapes, kiwi-fruit and so on or a golden medley? And what about a dried fruit compote or two?

Fresh fruit plonked in a basket is all very well, but why not try more interesting combinations like papayas with litchis or fresh pineapple with cherries?

FACE TO FACE

Finally, healthy eaters, we have found, are hesitant to complain or to ask for anything out of the ordinary. Restaurateurs, pub landlords and café owners know there is a growing demand for 'the healthy option' but are still unsure how to translate that into an attractive menu. Far too many keep their healthy alternatives on the premises but out of sight, hiding the polyunsaturated margarine behind the mayonnaise and the sorbet behind the sundae.

Ask and you shall receive ...

William Halden

PUBLISHER

HEALTHY EATING PLACE OF THE YEAR

BELOW ARE THE FINALISTS FOR THE
HEALTHY EATING OUT PLACE OF THE YEAR,
CHOSEN ON THE BASIS OF OUTSTANDING COOKING
COMBINED WITH A CONCERN FOR HEALTHY EATING.

THE THREE TYPES OF ESTABLISHMENT COVERED IN THE
GUIDE ARE REPRESENTED — RESTAURANT, QUICK BITE
AND PUB; THE OVERALL WINNER WILL BE ANNOUNCED
AT THE GUIDE'S LAUNCH IN APRIL, WHEN THEY
WILL BE PRESENTED WITH A UNIQUE
WEDGWOOD FRUIT BOWL.

HENDERSONS, TIVERTON

Nevill and Elizabeth Ambler run this popular restaurant in Devon,
which admirably meets our criteria for serving good healthy food.
The menu is built around excellent prime ingredients and market-
fresh produce. Wholemeal bread and pasta are always home-made
and locally caught fresh fish is cooked simply to produce dishes that
10 are bursting with natural flavour.

Village Bakery, Melmerby

An outstanding bakery and tea room in the beautiful Lake District which is open throughout the day for a wide selection of light meals. Andrew and Lis Whitley provide all their own organically grown vegetables, fruit, milk and meat from their smallholding and bake all their own bread and cakes using only wholemeal or wheatmeal flour. Healthy eaters are spoilt for choice.

Fullers Arms, Brightling

A historic inn near Robertsbridge where the welcome is always warm and the food memorable. John and Sheila Mitchell-Sadd serve good wholesome food of a high standard and healthier dishes are always on the menu alongside a choice of vegetable side dishes. It is particularly refreshing to find a pub that caters so well for vegetarian customers.

11

Starred Entries

London

Cranks Health Food Restaurant, W1
Dorchester, The Terrace, W1
Inigo Jones, WC2

Justin de Blank, W1
Mandeer, W1
Mulford's Wine Bar, W6

England

Berkhamsted, Cook's Delight
Brightling, Fullers Arms
Brighton, Food for Friends
Chichester, Clinch's Salad House
Cockermouth, Quince & Medlar
Congleton, Odd Fellows Wine Bar & Bistro
Corse Lawn, Corse Lawn House
Coventry, Trinity House Hotel, Herbs Restaurant
Dartington, Cranks Health Food Restaurant
Eastbourne, Nature's Way
Elland, Berties Bistro
Faversham, Recreation Tavern
Great Milton, Le Manoir aux Quat' Saisons Restaurant
Ludlow, Hardwicks
Melmerby, Village Bakery
Monksilver, Notley Arms
Pitton, Silver Plough
Sheffield, Just Cooking
Skipton, Herbs Wholefood & Vegetarian Restaurant
Streatley-on-Thames, Swan Hotel Restaurant
Tiverton, Hendersons

Wales

Aberaeron, Hive on the Quay
Cardiff, Armless Dragon
Llanfihangel Crucorney, Skirrid Inn
Newport, Cnapan

12

SCOTLAND

Cullipool, Longhouse Buttery
Edinburgh, Kalpna
Edinburgh, Laigh Kitchen
Inverness, Brookes Wine Bar
Wester Howgate, Old Howgate
  Inn, Coach House

Recipes For Health

If you've always thought that healthy eating means sacrificing the appearance and flavour of your food, think again. We asked three of the Guide's establishments to share their culinary secrets with us.

Veal Kidneys with Woodland Mushroom
~and Chive Sauce~

PEBBLES RESTAURANT, AYLESBURY

2 veal kidneys, skinned and cored
salt and freshly ground black pepper
6 shallots, peeled and finely chopped
1 tsp chopped fresh thyme
225 g (8 oz) mixed wild mushrooms, washed and sliced or chopped (ceps, chanterelles or parasols for example)
300 ml (½ pint) veal or beef stock
2 tbsp snipped chives
4 tbsp natural yoghurt or soured cream
Serves 2

Season the kidneys with salt and pepper to taste. Heat a non-stick frying pan, add the kidneys and sauté, without additional fat, until golden and seared on all sides. Place in a small ovenproof dish, cover and cook in a preheated moderate oven, 180°C (350°F), Gas Mark 4, until tender but still pink, about 10–15 minutes.

Meanwhile, add the shallots and thyme to the pan and cook gently until the shallots are transparent. Add the mushrooms and cook until softened. Add the stock and cook gently, until the mixture has reduced slightly, about 5 minutes.

Thinly slice the kidneys and place on a warmed serving plate. Remove the mushroom mixture from the heat, stir in the chives and yoghurt or soured cream, blending well. Spoon over the kidneys to serve.

~Glazed Oyster Parcels with Crab~

Pebbles Restaurant, Aylesbury

800 g (1¾ lb) fresh young
  spinach leaves, washed
12 fresh oysters
75 g (3 oz) white crab meat,
  flaked
juice of ½ lemon

about 150 ml (¼ pint) fish stock
1 egg yolk
freshly ground black pepper
rock salt to serve
lemon wedges to garnish
Serves 2

Blanch the spinach leaves in boiling water for about 5 seconds, drain and refresh in cold water. Spread out on to absorbent kitchen towels to dry. Cover and set aside.

Carefully open the oysters and cut away the silvery grey muscle attaching the oyster to the shell. Reserve the oyster juices. Wash and dry 12 of the shells for serving.

Divide the crab meat evenly between the oyster shells, place on a baking tray, cover loosely with foil and keep warm.

Wrap the oysters in the spinach leaves and place in a shallow pan. Strain the reserved oyster juice, lemon juice and enough fish stock over the oysters to barely cover. Poach gently, uncovered, for about 15 seconds. Remove and place an oyster in each shell. Cover and return to the oven.

Bring the poaching liquid to the boil and reduce by about half. Remove from the heat and whisk in the egg yolk and pepper to taste. Spoon a little over each oyster. Place under a preheated hot grill and cook until golden. Serve at once on a bed of rock salt, garnished
with lemon wedges.

~CHEESE BREAD~

THE VILLAGE BAKERY, MELMERBY

15 g (½ oz) fresh yeast
pinch of sugar
about 150 ml (¼ pint) water
200 g (7 oz) wholemeal flour
½ tsp sea salt

1 tsp polyunsaturated oil
50 g (2 oz) Edam cheese,
  grated
beaten egg to glaze
Makes 8 pieces

Cream the yeast and sugar with a third of the water. Leave in a warm place for about 5 minutes, until frothy. Mix the flour with the salt, oil, yeast mixture and sufficient remaining water to mix to a smooth dough. Turn the dough on to a lightly floured surface and knead until smooth and elastic, about 10 minutes. Place in an oiled bowl, cover and leave to rise in a warm place for 30 minutes, or until doubled in size.

Turn the dough on to a lightly floured surface, knock back to release all the air bubbles, add half of the cheese and knead well to mix. Divide the dough in two and shape each into a round. Place on a greased baking tray, flatten slightly and mark into quarters with a sharp knife. Glaze with beaten egg

and sprinkle with cheese. Cover and leave to prove in a warm place until the dough has risen in size by about one-third.

Bake in a preheated hot oven, 220°C (425°F), Gas Mark 7, for about 15–20 minutes. Cool on a wire rack.

~BLACKCURRANT TART~
THE VILLAGE BAKERY, MELMERBY

For the pastry:
175 g (6 oz) plain wholemeal
    flour
½ tsp ground cinnamon
100 g (4 oz) polyunsaturated
    margarine
25 g (1 oz) light brown sugar
1–2 tbsp cold water

For the filling:
275 g (10 oz) fresh or frozen
    prepared blackcurrants
75 g (3 oz) soft light brown
    sugar
natural yoghurt or crème fraîche
    to serve
Serves 4–6

To make the pastry, mix the flour with the cinnamon. Rub in the margarine until the mixture resembles fine breadcrumbs. Stir in the sugar and sufficient cold water to bind to a firm dough. Knead lightly until smooth, cover and chill for 5 minutes. Roll out the pastry and line a 20 cm (8 inch) loose-bottomed flan tin. Prick the base with a fork. Line the flan with greaseproof paper, then fill with baking beans. Bake 'blind' in a preheated moderate oven, 180°C (350°F), Gas Mark 4, for 10–15 minutes. Remove the greaseproof paper with the beans from the flan. Return to the oven and bake for a further 5 minutes until golden. Allow to cool.

Meanwhile, to make the filling, place half of the blackcurrants in a pan with half of the sugar. Cook over a low heat until the blackcurrants are soft and pulpy. Add the remaining blackcurrants and sugar and bring to the boil, stirring constantly. Remove from the heat and leave to cool.

To serve, spoon the blackcurrant filling into the tart and level the surface. Serve with natural yoghurt or crème fraîche.

17

~Spiced Nut Lasagne~

THE TOWIE TAVERN, TURRIFF

175 g (6 oz) wholewheat lasagne
For the sauce:
4 tsp polyunsaturated oil
1 onion, peeled and chopped
1 garlic clove, peeled and
  crushed
450 g (1 lb) tomatoes, skinned,
  seeded and chopped
300 g (10 oz) mushrooms, sliced
2 tbsp tomato purée
1 tsp chopped basil
For the filling:
50 g (2 oz) each raw peanuts,
  salted cashews & almonds
½ tsp each chilli powder,
paprika & turmeric
1 garlic clove, peeled and
  crushed
175 g (6 oz) low-fat soft
  cheese
1 onion, peeled and chopped
225 g (8 oz) small broccoli
  florets, blanched
300 ml (½ pint) béchamel sauce
  (made with skimmed
  milk)
100 g (4 oz) Mozzarella cheese,
  grated
chopped fresh chervil
Serves 4–6

Cook the lasagne in boiling salted water until tender or 'al dente' according to the packet instructions. Drain thoroughly.

Meanwhile, to make the tomato and mushroom sauce heat the oil in a pan. Add the onion and garlic and cook gently until softened. Add the tomatoes, 175 g (6 oz) mushrooms, tomato purée and basil, blending well. Cook over a gentle heat stirring continuously for about 10–15 minutes until thick and pulpy.

Place the peanuts, cashews, almonds, chilli powder, paprika, turmeric and garlic in a blender and process coarsely. Mix all but about 2 tbsp of this spiced nut mixture with the soft cheese.

Line a large lightly oiled ovenproof dish with lasagne. Cover with half of the tomato and mushroom sauce. Top with another layer of pasta and half of the cheese and nut mixture. Top with another layer of pasta and half of the chopped onion, remaining mushrooms and broccoli. Repeat all these layers again and finish with a layer of pasta. Spoon over the béchamel sauce, top with the Mozzarella and sprinkle with the reserved spiced nut mixture. Bake in a preheated hot oven, 200°C (400°F), Gas Mark 6, until golden and cooked, about 20–30 minutes. Sprinkle with chopped chervil and serve hot with a crisp salad.

~CHICKEN MERATI~
THE TOWIE TAVERN, TURRIFF

2 × 100 g (4 oz) boneless
chicken breasts, skinned
½ tsp each ground coriander,
cumin & paprika
pinch of chilli powder
150 ml (¼ pint) natural yoghurt
2 tbsp chopped fresh coriander
50 g (2 oz) carrot, peeled
50 g (2 oz) spring onions,
trimmed

50 g (2 oz) fresh pineapple,
peeled and cored
50 g (2 oz) French beans,
trimmed (optional)
2 tsp polyunsaturated oil
1 garlic clove, crushed
40 g (1½ oz) long-grain brown
rice, cooked
25 g (1 oz) salted cashew nuts
Serves 2

Slice the chicken breasts into thin julienne strips. Mix the ground coriander with the cumin, paprika and chilli. Add the chicken and toss to coat. Cover and chill for 15 minutes. Mix the yoghurt with the coriander, cover and chill until required. Cut the carrot, spring onions and pineapple into thin julienne strips. Blanch the carrot, spring onions and French beans (if used) in boiling water for 1–2 minutes. Drain and refresh under cold running water.

Heat the oil and garlic in a large frying pan or wok. Add the chicken pieces in batches, and sauté quickly until golden. Remove with a slotted spoon. Stir fry the vegetable mixture for 2–3 minutes until just tender. Add the chicken, pineapple, rice and cashew nuts and cook until hot, about 1–2 minutes. Serve with the yoghurt
and a green salad.

The Birds Eye View of
HEALTHY

You are what you eat! It is an old saying open to interpretation, although there can be little dispute that what we eat can make all the difference between feeling fit and healthy, or feeling really second rate. It is our view that what and when we eat is a matter of personal choice; however, it is important that each of us has good advice with which to make sound choices about our diet. On this Birds Eye and Egon Ronay Guides think alike. Just as Birds Eye provide a wide range of balanced, nutritious food from which you can prepare healthy meals for you and your family at home, this Guide will help you select an eating establishment for healthy eating out.

The Right Balance

Where once the family always sat down to eat together, now mealtimes are fragmented and formal meals are rare. But now as then the desire is still for good, nutritious, wholesome food, with variety and interest of utmost importance, whether meals are for the family eating together, separately or for just one person.

No single food alone is unhealthy, and there is no such thing as the 'perfect diet'. It is how we combine the myriad of different foods available to us, and the quality of their ingredients, that is the key to our nutritional well being.

Frozen foods are so familiar to us they are often taken for granted, yet their nutritional value

Nature provides its own sugar, liquid, colouring, preservatives, additives and flavouring.

So we add nothing

BIRDS EYE

is far from being appreciated. Frozen foods are as nutritionally valuable as fresh foods, more so in some cases. Freezing keeps food closest to its natural state, retaining the natural nutrients. The quality of the food you take out of a well run freezer is the same as the quality you put in. A great deal depends on the quality of the ingredients used by frozen food producers.

Birds Eye pride themselves on the quality of their products, their concern for quality starting as far back as at the seed stage in the growing of, for example, peas, but always at the point where the raw materials and ingredients are selected.

Food Processing and Additives

We have in recent times all been made aware of the importance of diet to our health. Additionally, attention has been given to the subject of additives.

Consider, for example, how a steak and kidney pie is made. The gravy needs to be thickened and coloured, the pie needs to be

EATING

seasoned with salt and pepper and perhaps some herbs. This improves the flavour and colour of the pie and gives a good consistency. In most household food preparation vital extra ingredients are added to enable recognisable products to be made and to give characteristic appearance and flavour. For example, pickling onions requires vinegar and salt and sugar, making a cake calls for baking powder and perhaps colouring and spices. The food manufacturer also needs to use such ingredients, but now the term used is food additives. Some are found in most kitchens, and some have been used for centuries – acetic acid which is used for pickling is one of the oldest methods of preservation. Some additives are of natural origin such as the green colouring chlorophyll, and others are synthetic such as the antioxidant propyl gallate. But whether an approved food additive is extracted from a natural source or is made synthetically, is of no consequence to the body. The body only distinguishes between whether an additive has nutritive value or not.

Nevertheless, Birds Eye's policy is only to use an additive where strictly necessary, and from a natural source where possible. In fact, many of Birds Eye's products contain no additives at all.

Freezeline Service

Our 'Freezeline' service is always available to answer questions you have about our products, on freezing, microwaves and nutrition, supported by a selection of literature. One such booklet, 'A Birds Eye View of Healthy Eating' offers advice on nutrition and additives, and 'Freezing, Freezers and Microwaves' covers all you need to know about owning and using to advantage these appliances.

Healthy and Convenient

We need no reminder of how busy we all seem to be these days. All too often we have little time to eat a meal and even less to prepare one. Yet it is important that we should try to make sure we eat well-balanced, wholesome meals at some time during the day.

Frozen food is a very convenient way of buying and storing food in today's busy world, making it possible to prepare, with ease, a variety of meals and snacks to suit individual needs and tastes, at any time.

The Birds Eye menu offers an extensive selection of recipe meals and meal ingredients, each prepared from the highest quality produce. Whether your fancy is a tasty meat or fish dish, simply fish fingers, a vegetable meal, some international flavour or a tasty grilled beefburger, the choice is yours.

With most of our products also suitable for microwave preparation, it need take only a matter of minutes before you are enjoying your own choice from our menu, and your family enjoying their own personal preference if it differs.

We take great care to ensure we offer a range to meet all individual tastes. We also take care to provide full information on our products, information on nutrition and storage, and advice on traditional and microwave cooking.

In the interests of healthy eating we work out the nutritional information for you and put it on all our frozen food packs. The Food Facts panel tells you how much protein, fat, carbohydrate and how many calories are in a certain amount of food.

FOOD FACTS			
Each Steak provides at least one fifth of the protein recommended daily for most people; to keep the fat and calorie content down, simply grill.			
A cooked Steak contains:	Grilled	Shallow Fried	Deep Fried
Protein	14g	14g	14g
Fat	9g	12g	14g
Carbohydrate	13g	13g	13g
Calories	185	210	230
Calories per ounce	51	64	84

THE CAPTAIN'S TABLE

The Birds Eye View of
HEALTHY

Health from the sea

'fresh' fish. Much of the Birds Eye fish is frozen at sea while that caught closer to shore is landed and frozen within hours. This ensures the texture and taste are at their best. In fact, even if you catch fish yourself, it can hardly be fresher than the Birds Eye range.

Now, in addition to the classic Fish Finger, there are a number of interesting variations, using different species of fish, wholemeal crumbs and several types of light batter which can be selected according to taste and desired cooking method.

Loaves and fishes – the ingredients of Birds Eye Fish Fingers – are still the important staple foods that they were in biblical times.

Fish Fingers, however, present these ingredients in the most convenient possible form – fish fillet with a light, crisp breadcrumb coating.

Invented in 1955, the popularity of Fish Fingers is widespread and several generations have enjoyed this delicious and convenient way of eating fish.

The freezing process has taken the messiness out of buying and preparing

EATING

Balanced meals in minutes

When life becomes really hectic we need good square meals more than ever, but unfortunately these are the times when we are most likely to seize a 'stodgy' snack which, chosen without care, may well be high in calories yet low in nutrients.

It is a daunting prospect to start preparing an interesting and appetising meal from scratch after a long day at work or when you're in a hurry to go out.

Using MenuMaster prepared meals, however, means that at these busy times you can enjoy a proper, square meal in minutes rather than in hours. The use of microwave ovens means this is now easier than ever before.

Some of the dishes in the range are 'meal centres' which act as the basis of the meal to which vegetables can be added. Others are complete meals which are carefully balanced to ensure a good proportion of protein, carbohydrate, fat and fibre.

More and more people are enjoying and experimenting with vegetarian-style

dishes – whether they are confirmed vegetarians or not. So some of the latest introductions to the MenuMaster range include vegetable-based dishes, from simple ones like Cauliflower Cheese, to more complex international recipes like Vegetable Chilli with Mexican Rice or Sweet & Sour Vegetables with Wild Rice.

The Birds Eye View of
HEALTHY

Vegetables for vitamins, minerals and fibre

When Clarence Birdseye discovered the process of quick freezing he provided us with the means of enjoying an endless harvest of high quality foods throughout the year, regardless of season.

Freezing effectively stops the clock, suspends time, so that vegetables harvested in the summer can be enjoyed in the same prime condition all year round.

But how do frozen vegetables compare with 'fresh' ones? More often than not, most favourably. Take, for example, Birds Eye Peas from the Country Club range. They are selected and frozen within 2½ hours of being picked. This ensures the minimum loss of vitamins and retains all the freshness, flavour and quality. The peas are virtually 'suspended in

time' in the freezer. Compare this with so-called 'fresh' peas that may well have taken days just to arrive at the greengrocers from the fields – losing valuable vitamins on the way.

All Birds Eye vegetables are carefully selected and speedily frozen to keep them in prime condition, and now there is a wide variety to choose from.

Many may want their families to adopt a healthier diet by eating more vegetables, but cannot afford the time-consuming preparation involved in serving them in interesting ways. The Birds Eye range includes interesting mixtures of vegetables, with little or no preparation and certainly no waste.

Prepared vegetable dishes like Cauliflower Cheese or Ratatouille conveniently make meals more interesting, while introducing valuable nutrients.

EATING

Meat for protein

Protein is needed for growth and repair of body tissues and, like carbohydrate, is also a source of energy. Meat is for many people the favourite part of a meal and it provides a valuable source of that protein.

We are now more conscious of the fat content of foods, trying to ensure that our diets do not contain excessive fat, so we now look for leaner cuts of meat and aim to grill rather than fry.

The Birds Eye Steakhouse range uses top quality ingredients and the low fat burgers and grills contain less fat than standard products.

The important thing to remember is that there is no such thing as an unhealthy food – but there is such a thing as an unhealthy diet if the mixtures of foods do not provide a healthy balance. The odd helping of burger and chips, for instance, need cause no concern.

Schweppes ®...
the essential accompaniment

An essential for the enjoyment of any meal is the drink that accompanies it. Time was when a pint of foaming ale or a bottle of favourite wine, served at the correct temperature, were the preferred companions to any order given in restaurant, bistro, or pub.

The tide of opinion has changed, however. Many diners eschew the wine list or beer tap, and seek drinks which refresh ... leaving a clear head and a clean palate.

For them, Schweppes provides the answer. With Tropical Spring, Appletise, Malvern Water, plus Slimline and the widest range of pure fruit juices.

This portfolio blends tradition and innovation.

Tropical Spring is a new, totally natural, soft drink developed specially to appeal to the young and health conscious. Its unique appeal lies in a blend of nine fruit juices (orange, apple, grape, pineapple, passionfruit, mango, banana, peach and apricot) and naturally sourced spring water. It is the first totally natural citrus-base carbonated drink, and contains no artificial sweetener, colour, or preservatives, or any added sugar.

Appletise is satisfyingly sparkling, with a clean taste that complements meals perfectly.

Appletise is made from the pure juice of several green apple varieties, blended together and carbonated to add sparkle. Like Tropical Spring, no sugar, preservatives or colouring are added.

Its introduction five years ago created a demand for a totally new type of soft drink, and it remains best seller within its class.

Schweppes was the first company to introduce low calorie drinks to the British public when the Slimline range was brought on to the market 22 years ago. Since then, Schweppes Slimline Tonic Water, Bitter Lemon and Ginger Ales have proved firm favourites, and Slimline has become a byword for low-calorie.

Malvern, England's best known Natural Spring Water has been bottled from a source in Worcestershire's Malvern Hills since 1850. Both still and sparkling varieties have a light, pleasantly natural taste that matches the popular demand for mineral water perfectly.

Lastly, there are Schweppes complete range of fruit juices.

Only Schweppes can offer the healthy drinker such a mix of the new and the traditional, drawing on over two centuries of expertise to meet the needs of today.

Coca-Cola & Schweppes Beverages Ltd.
St. Albans Herts. AL1 3AD

MENU GUIDELINES FOR THE HEALTHY EATER

HOW TO PLEASE YOUR PALATE
—HEALTHILY—

When you go out for a meal, you want to choose your favourite food, not what's 'good for you'. But what if you find the menu includes dishes that are tempting, delicious—*and* healthy? You can eat, be merry and not need to count calories, cholesterol or antacid tablets next day.

What should you look for? A healthy meal doesn't have to mean melon, grilled fish and no pudding. Although experts still wrangle over the right way to eat, there's wide international agreement on five clear targets to give you a healthier style of eating—and drinking.

The targets set out in the NACNE (National Advisory Committee on Nutritional Education) and COMA (Committee on Medical Aspects of Food Policy) reports can give you confidence that it is worthwhile to change your eating habits if you want to feel your best. You may not need to change your meals dramatically to benefit.

1. Look for dishes that are low in fat.

Eating less fat isn't advised only to benefit your heart. Because fat contains more than twice as many calories per ounce as either protein or carbohydrate, a meal with less fat is likely to be lower in calories in total. It will also be easier to digest.

Most of the fat in restaurants comes from four food items: pastry, sauces, frying fats and cheese. All can push a dish into astronomic fat levels of 30 to 50 per cent. Oh, and peanuts in the bar (around 50 per cent fat).

Eating *less* fat doesn't mean you can't eat *any* of these foods. You can achieve a reduction by eating smaller portions, or by choosing only one higher-fat item in an otherwise lean meal. The simplest way is to avoid fried food, and ask for sauces to be omitted or served separately so you can limit how much you take. Remember that an extra dollop of hollandaise or mayonnaise often contains as much fat and as many calories as the salmon steak or beef salad it adorns.

Many chefs are now cooking with less fat, and the influence of 'cuisine naturelle' in butter-free sauces made with natural stock and purées helps. But watch out for two pitfalls: 'nouvelle cuisine' dishes presented in pools of conventional rich sauces, and the assumption that 'vegetarian' always means healthy.

28

If you enjoy cheese with a meal, think of it as a main course item, to team with a lighter entrée.

2. Choose the right carbohydrate.

The days of 'bran with everything' have passed, but the message stays that we can benefit by eating more of what used to be damned as 'stodge'. Bread, rice, pasta all give us fibre in a gentle way—together with an important part of our B vitamins and minerals. The 'whole' versions of each give us more nutrients than the white, but even these are preferable to foods high in fat and sugar, which satisfy little of our food needs. Eating 1 ounce less fat and 1 ounce less sugar in a meal releases an astonishing 360 calories which translate into a more nourishing extra potato or spoonful of pasta, with calories to spare. Don't spoil it by piling on butter: a real advantage of the 'whole' versions is that they have more flavour of their own without being dowsed in extras.

3. Eat less sugar.

The average Briton gains 1 in 5 of his calories from sugar—if you include the sugar in alcohol. That's a fifth of our calories from a food that provides none of the vitamins and minerals we need. The contribution of sugar to tooth decay is another reason to avoid eating a lot of sweet foods. However, a little sugar won't hurt you, if a little means a teaspoonful or two in a main meal. But you *don't* need it for energy, and the less you eat, the more appetite you'll have for other foods—any of which will provide more goodness per calorie. On restaurant dessert trolleys sugar is the main ingredient in anything made with caramel, meringue or syrup. Chocolate is over half sugar (and almost a third fat).

4. Eat more fresh vegetables and fruit.

The better the cooking, the easier it will be to follow this advice. Aim to include both foods in a meal, whether it's crudités, pineapple with Kirsch, bananas flambés or ratatouille. Vegetables and fruit are a good source of fibre and provide a wide range of vitamins and minerals—lost, along with their flavour, if overcooked.

5. Limit alcohol, especially if you're a woman.

Over 24 drinks a week is a drinking problem—and women can damage their health by less, current thinking suggests. It's also safer for your liver not to drink either in huge binges, or spread over seven days a week. Have alcohol-free days and try drinking mineral water or spritzers—a mixture of white wine and mineral water—when eating out. More restaurants now offer non-alcoholic or low-alcoholic cocktails, beer and wine. 29

<u>Decaffeinated coffee & herb teas</u> Increasingly available, and helpful for those who want to avoid caffeine. Decaffeinated coffee can be ground and indistinguishable except by lack of after-effects; good herb teas include peppermint, chamomile, fennel (helps digestion) and mixed fruit. If necessary, take your own tea bags and ask for boiling water.

<u>Salt</u> The benefit of eating less salt is less well established than other factors governing a healthy diet. But even if your blood pressure doesn't call for salt reduction, using less may help you uncover more satisfying flavours in food.

<u>Cholesterol</u> It's now thought that only a few people on special medical advice need avoid cholesterol, which is often high in otherwise healthy foods such as shellfish and liver. Instead, it's thought that the best way to counter cholesterol build-up via diet is to eat less saturated (hard) fat in general. So eggs, for instance, are not considered unhealthy for cholesterol reasons, provided you don't eat more than an average one per day (the typical Briton eats 3-4 per week), and don't eat large amounts of animal or hardened vegetable fat as well.

<u>Special dietary needs</u> If you have any special dietary requirements, allergies to certain foods, perhaps, do mention this when booking as most establishments will be happy to prepare a suitable meal.

Keep these guidelines in mind and you'll find that you can pick a healthy meal from most menus. And do remember to ask for what you want—from sauce served separately to skimmed milk with your coffee. Most establishments will be only too happy to oblige.

HEALTHY ALTERNATIVES

The following list gives examples of healthy dishes to look out for when choosing a meal at a restaurant or pub.

FIRST COURSES

<u>Soups</u> Any, provided they aren't based on butter and cream. Good examples, apart from obvious consommés, are minestrone, gazpacho, split pea or lentil soups and cock-a-leekie. Ask if the soup contains cream.

<u>Artichoke</u> Choose vinaigrette dressing rather than melted butter or hollandaise, and ask for it to be served separately so you can limit how much you add.

<u>Asparagus</u> As above, or ask for some lemon to squeeze over.

<u>Caviar</u> Beluga or lumpfish, healthy if rather salty. Eat with unbuttered wholemeal bread or salad.

30 <u>Crab</u> Excellent provided it isn't mixed with mayonnaise.

Crudités Ask for some cottage or curd cheese instead of the mayonnaise-based dips.

Grapefruit Skip the cherry if you dislike artificial colours; ask the waiter for an unsugared half.

Melon Don't write it off as boring—it can be wonderful. Ask for it not to be sugared. Ginger is good for you.

Moules marinière Very healthy, provided the mussels are.

Oysters Ideally healthy food, oozing with minerals. Ask for the brown bread to be unbuttered or meagrely spread.

Pâté Ask for wholemeal toast and hope it's a lean-ish pâté. Team with a light main course.

Prawn cocktail Ask for dressing to be served separately, or for a wedge of lemon instead.

Smoked fish Fine, provided the bread is lightly buttered.

Terrines Fish or vegetable, they often contain a little cream, but are still basically very light. Surrounding sauces may be rich but many establishments now use light purées or yoghurt-based sauces.

MAIN COURSES

Fish Most fish is very lean (under 4 per cent fat) provided it isn't fried (in batter or otherwise), or bathed in a rich sauce. If you find plain grilled fish boring, look out for fish casseroles, kebabs, pies topped with potato (but not with pastry) or pickled fish, such as gravad lax.

Meat Lowest in fat are poultry and game, but lean lamb, beef and veal if you fancy it are low-fat, provided they aren't fried, richly sauced or accompanied by pastry in any form. Pick pies topped with sliced or mashed potatoes. If in doubt about how something has been cooked, ask before ordering rather than be disappointed. Avoid farmed duck, goose and pork unless it's the leanest fillet or trimmed breast.

VEGETARIAN DISHES

Bean cuisine Generally low in fat, unless it's carrying a lot of cheese. Don't neglect the possibilities of pease pudding or bean soups, which are solid enough to act as main courses alongside salads or light vegetable dishes.

Pasta Healthy (especially if wholewheat), provided the sauce isn't loaded with butter, cream or bacon bits.

Pizza Surprisingly well balanced, provided topping isn't heavy on the salami or extra olive oil.

Stir-fries No longer only from Far Eastern restaurants. Nuts, tofu, peas or sweetcorn all provide protein.

Gratin dishes Surprisingly rich unless the restaurant has made an effort to make sauces less fatty by using less butter or margarine and low-fat milk or stock.

Salads Shaking off their rabbit-food image, with imaginative mixtures. Salads featuring noodles, rice, burghul wheat, 31 beans, nuts, sunflower seeds, cheese or avocado pears are all excellent.

Risottos Healthy, with same reservations as for pasta.

Soufflés Featuring watercress, mushrooms, cheese or vegetables can be very light.

Vegetable platters Vegetables cooked with care and prettily served are a first-class option: ask for a platter of vegetables of the day. If you are concerned about lack of protein, team with cheese for dessert, but most of us don't need large amounts of protein at every meal.

ETHNIC DISHES

Japanese An excellent choice unless you pick the deep-fried dishes like tempura or wash your food down with too many calories from lager.

Chinese Varies from the delightfully healthy stir-fries, soups, casserole-style meat, steamed fish, steamed rice and crisp-roasted meat to the fat-laden sweet-and-sour, spare ribs, fried spring rolls and fried rice (though this can be barely fried if well prepared). Choose the non-deep-fried range, and you won't go far wrong.

Indian Curries will only be as greasy as their main ingredient, so chicken, seafood, vegetable or fish varieties will generally be leaner than meaty ones. Accompaniments are generally low-fat and nourishing enough to make a tasty meal on their own: lassi (yoghurt drink), raitas (yoghurt with vegetables), chapatis (healthier than the fried puris or poppadoms), dhal, (spiced bean or lentil purées). Tandoori and tikka (small kebabs) are especially healthy forms of cooking, where no extra fat is added and existing fat in meat is grilled off. Indian restaurants can always cater for vegetarians and are the best choice for vegans.

Italian Although pasta and pizza are generally considered ultra-fattening, both can be healthy if authentic, i.e., plenty of the pasta or pizza base, compared to the richer toppings.

SNACKS AND PUB FOOD

Sandwiches Have been vindicated as a perfectly healthy food provided they aren't heavily buttered or laden with high-fat fillings such as peanut butter, cream cheese, liver paté or fatty bacon. Many establishments making sandwiches to order will be happy to use low-fat spread or polyunsaturated margarine, if requested. Wholemeal breads are healthiest, but white bread still makes a healthier dish than other snacks. Good fillings are lean meat, fish, eggs (boiled, and without mayonnaise), cottage cheese, bananas, occasionally hard cheese and, of course, salads provided they don't wallow in oily dressings.

32 **Pies** Among the least healthy foods, because pastry is around

a third fat. A modest pork pie can use up a third of the average daily calorie requirements.

Baked potatoes Neck and neck with sandwiches for good health, *provided* you don't pile on butter or hard cheese. Good fillings include cottage cheese, *small* amounts of sour cream plus tomatoes or other salad vegetables, sweetcorn, ratatouille mixtures or yoghurt with chopped herbs.

Cakes & buns Pastry and sponge mixtures are all about a third fat, but items made with yeast, such as currant buns, malt loaf, or fruit bread, will be far lighter on fat and on sugar. Wholemeal scones and wholemeal banana sandwiches are good alternatives for a sweet tooth.

Burgers Much of their fat lies in the accompanying mayonnaise, fries, coleslaw, fruit pies or battered items. The best choice is a plain burger, along with a plain bun, undressed salad and perhaps beans or corn-on-the-cob without butter.

Quiches & pizzas Vary considerably in health level. Wholemeal quiche will be lower in fat if the filling is vegetable-based, rather than the traditional bacon and cheese variety. Pizza is lower in fat than quiche, provided the base is not pastry but authentic yeast dough. Wholemeal pizzas are worth watching out for.

Kebabs Generally low-fat, and pitta bread with plain doner kebab and salad makes a healthy balance, although it's a pity wholemeal pitta is not more widely available.

Shepherd's pie, Lancashire hot pot & meat-with-two-veg Generally leaner and lower in calories than 'fast food' meals such as pies and chips, sausages or fry-ups.

DESSERTS

Ice cream Unless a super-creamy variety, will be one of the least rich puddings offered on a dessert menu. Sorbets are better: although they have just as much sugar, they have virtually no fat.

Fruit dishes Healthiest, provided the fruit hasn't been made into fritters and isn't served in a pastry case. Summer pudding, fruit crumbles (eat the fruit rather than the topping), fruit pancakes (ask them to omit sugar), pineapple, orange slices, stewed figs and fresh fruit salad are good examples, but beware of 'fools'—unless yoghurt is specified, they'll be laden with cream (double cream is about half fat).

Custards Can be a good choice, provided it's not crème brûlée. As you get the food value of milk for your calories, this teams well with a light main course.

Yoghurt Natural unsweetened makes an ideal topping for many desserts instead of cream.

Cheese Lower fat cheeses include Edam, Gouda, Brie, Camembert and reduced-fat 'Cheddars'. Eat after light main courses and aim for small portions.

NEW FRUIT CUISINE

Bright electric green and refreshingly piquant, the Kiwifruit or 'Chinese gooseberry' grown in New Zealand's temperate and fertile climate since the turn of this century has become a firm favourite in Britain. Alexander Allison was the first recorded nurseryman in New Zealand to have propagated the seeds successfully and encourage its cultivation.

Appealingly furry and humble on the outside, New Zealand Kiwifruit has quite a remarkable and delightful surprise inside—a vivid green fragrant flesh with violet-ringed inner sunburst, strikingly attractive. Its taste almost defies description but the flavour and aroma are akin to melon, strawberries or bananas, yet uniquely delicious.

Low in calories yet high in nutrients it makes a healthy addition to any meal. Few other fruits, let alone grains and vegetables, on a calorie for calorie basis have such a high vitamin C content (105 mg per 100 g—almost twice that of an average orange). It also contains significant amounts of vitamin E (twice that of the avocado with only 60% of its calories), valuable dietary fibre and essential minerals like potassium, chromium and folic acid in a concentrated and easily digestible form.

'New Zealand Kiwifruit provides colour, nutrition and visual appeal in preparing special dishes such as our Tulip Ston Easton Park.'
MARK HARRINGTON, HEAD CHEF, STON EASTON PARK HOTEL

Easily prepared, New Zealand Kiwifruit can simply be cut in half across, then scooped out with a spoon, or peeled and cut into slices, cubes or wedges. Totally edible, the flesh does not require any laborious 'freeing' from inedible stones or pips. Hold onto the skin too—it makes an effective meat tenderiser because of the enzymes it contains. Simply place, cut side down, on the meat, fish or poultry and allow to stand for 30 minutes.

Mature and hand-harvested in May, New Zealand Kiwifruit are available fresh and in peak condition from June to January. They are ripe when slightly soft to the touch or when there is a little 'give' beneath the skin (although even the firmest fruit will quickly ripen if placed in a plastic bag with an apple or banana). Store in the refrigerator and it will keep in good condition for 2–3 weeks.

The culinary uses of New Zealand Kiwifruit are many and 34 varied—its brilliant colour and delightful tangy taste makes it perfect for the fruit bowl and ideal for both hot and cold desserts like sorbets, ice creams, fools, fruit salads, yoghurts or a filling for pan-hot crêpes. Its sunny fragrant and piquant flesh also makes it a natural partner to richer foods in savoury dishes like skewered brochettes, meat, fish and poultry, main course salads, pasta dishes, and stir-fried or rice-based favourites. Thinly-sliced, generously-cubed or cut into eye-catching wedges, it also gives that unmistakable attractive garnish or zesty lift to year-round salads and cold table buffets. Delicious with lower-fat soft cheese like Camembert, it will also make a welcome addition, or perhaps introduction, to the traditional cheeseboard. And, if you prefer a light start to the day, try it for breakfast in an egg cup with a yoghurt side dressing or as a fruity topping for a crunchy muesli cereal.

It is true to say that the only limit to the use of New Zealand Kiwifruit is your own imagination—experiment with its striking colour, exquisitely flavoured flesh and versatile nature for truly creative and memorable meals.

'Come and discover for yourself at our Terrace Garden Restaurant the nutritious and exciting flavour offered by New Zealand Kiwifruit.'
DAVID CHAMBERS, EXECUTIVE CHEF, LE MERIDIEN PICCADILLY

BEAUTIFUL BEGINNINGS

New Zealand Kiwifruit can make a starter special. Colourful, versatile and deliciously different, it adds flavour and interest to fish cocktails and savoury starter salads.

'With over 25 different fish varieties on our menu
New Zealand Kiwifruit always provides an interesting
and eye-catching accompaniment and garnish.'
RAYMOND DU SOULIER, HEAD CHEF, CAFÉ FISH DES AMIS DU VIN

~NEW ZEALAND KIWIFRUIT MOUSSÉ~

Perfect for a hot summer's evening, New Zealand Kiwifruit filled with paprika cheese in a sweet sharp dressing.

4 New Zealand Kiwifruit	1 tsp white wine vinegar
50 g (2 oz) low-fat soft cheese	4 tbsp salad oil
¼ tsp ground paprika	salt and freshly ground black
1 tbsp lemon juice	pepper

Remove both ends of each Kiwifruit with a sharp knife. Using an apple corer, carefully remove the centre and reserve.

Mix the cheese with the paprika and black pepper to taste, blending well. Stuff the hollowed centres of the Kiwifruit with this mixture and chill until firm.

Finely chop the reserved Kiwifruit centres. Add the lemon juice, vinegar, oil and salt and pepper to taste, blending well.

To serve, peel the filled Kiwifruit carefully and cut each into 4 thick slices. Arrange on individual serving plates with a little of the dressing. Serve lightly chilled. SERVES 4.

'As one of the new wave of vegetarian restaurants, we use
New Zealand Kiwifruit regularly as a main ingredient in our
imaginative range of salads and desserts.'
KEITH CHRISTIE MURRAY, PROPRIETOR, CHRISTYS HEALTHLINE

SMOKED TROUT AND NEW ZEALAND KIWIFRUIT
~HORS D'OEUVRE~

Fruity and piquant, New Zealand Kiwifruit is the ideal partner
to smoked trout in this delicious starter.

4 New Zealand Kiwifruit
4 smoked trout fillets, weighing
   about 125–150 g (4–5 oz) each

1 tbsp low-fat soft cheese
3 tbsp thick-set natural yoghurt
freshly ground black pepper

Peel and slice the Kiwifruit. Cut the trout fillets into strips
about 1 × 3.5 cm (½ × 1½ inches). Arrange 3 slices of
Kiwifruit and a quarter of the smoked trout on each individual
serving plate or scallop shell.
   Blend the cheese with the yoghurt until smooth. Coarsely
chop the remaining Kiwifruit and fold into the yoghurt mixture
with pepper to taste. Spoon over the sliced Kiwifruit and serve
lightly chilled with wholemeal bread. SERVES 4.

37

VEGETARIAN & WHOLEFOOD RESTAURANTS

—— LONDON ——

Beehive, SW9
Chequers, NW1
Cherry Orchard, E2
Christys Healthline, W1
Country Life, W1
Cranks, WC2
Cranks Health Food
    Restaurant, W1
Di's Larder, SW11
Dining Room, SE1
Diwana Bhelpoori House, NW1
    & W2
Earth Exchange, N6
East West Restaurant, EC1
Fallen Angel, N1
First Out, WC2
Food for Health, EC4
Food for Thought, WC2
Govindas, W1
Harrods Health Juice Bar, SW1
Mandeer, W1
Manna, NW3

Millwards, N16
Neal's Yard Bakery & Tea
    Room, WC2
Neal's Yard Bakery at the
    Ecology Centre, WC2
Nuthouse, W1
Raj Bhelpoori House, NW1
Rani, N3
Ravenscourt Park Tea House,
    W6
Ravi Shankar, NW1
Raw Deal, W1
Sabras, NW10
Slenders, EC4
Suruchi, N1
Wholemeal Vegetarian Café,
    SW16
Wilkins Natural Food, SW1
Windmill Wholefood
    Restaurant, SW6
Woodlands Restaurant,
    W1 & SW1

—— ENGLAND ——

Altrincham, Nutcracker
    Vegetarian Restaurant
Ambleside, Harvest
Ambleside, Zeffirellis
Ashtead, Bart's
Avebury, Stones
Aylesbury, Wild Oats
Barnard Castle, Priors
    Restaurant
Berkhamsted, Cook's Delight
Birmingham, Gingers
Birmingham, La Santé
Birmingham, Wild Oats
Bournemouth, Flossies
Bournemouth, Salad Centre
Bowness-on-Windermere,
    Hedgerow
Brighton (Hove), Blossoms
Brighton, Food for Friends
Brighton, Saxons

Bristol, Wild Oats II
Bury St Edmunds, Beaumonts
Cambridge, Nettles
Castle Cary, Old Bakehouse
Cauldon Lowe, Staffordshire
    Peak Arts Centre
Chester, Abbey Green
Chichester, Clinch's Salad
    House
Chichester, St Martin's Tea
    Rooms
Christchurch, Salads
Cockermouth, Quince &
    Medlar
Coventry, Trinity House Hotel,
    Herbs Restaurant
Croydon, Hockneys
Croydon, Munbhave
Dartington, Cranks Health
    Food Restaurant

Derby, Lettuce Leaf
Eastbourne, Ceres Health Food
　Restaurant
Eastbourne, Nature's Way
Glastonbury, Rainbow's End
　Café
Gosforth, Girl on a Swing
Grantham, Knightingales
Hastings, Brant's
Hereford, Fodder
Hereford, Marches
Hythe, Natural Break
Ipswich, Marno's Restaurant
Kendal, Eat Fit
Kendal, Waterside Wholefoods
Lancaster, Libra
Leicester, Blossoms
Ludlow, Olive Branch
Newcastle-upon-Tyne,
　Madeleine's
Norwich, Café La Tienda
Nottingham, Ten
Penrith, Bluebell Tearoom
Poole, Inn à Nutshell
Portsmouth (Southsea),
　Country Kitchen
Preston, Eat Fit

Richmond, Richmond Harvest
Richmond, Wildefoods
　Wholefood Café
Ryton-on-Dunsmore, Ryton
　Gardens Café
Salisbury, Mainly Salads
Sandford Orcas, Holway Mill
Shrewsbury, Delany's
Skipton, Herbs Wholefood &
　Vegetarian Restaurant
Stockport, Coconut Willy's
Stroud, Mother Nature
Swindon, Acorn Wholefoods
Tiverton, Angel Foods
Totnes, Willow
Tunbridge Wells, Pilgrims
Ware, Sunflowers
Wareham, Annies
Warley, Wild Thyme
Warminster, Jenner's
Wells, Good Earth
Worcester, Natural Break
Worthing, Hannah
Worthing, Nature's Way Coffee
　Shop
Yeovil, Trugs
York, Gillygate Wholefood Café

—— Scotland ——

Edinburgh, Country Kitchen
Edinburgh, Helios Fountain
Edinburgh, Henderson's Salad
　Table

Edinburgh, Kalpna
Falkirk, Healthy Life
Peebles, Sunflower
St Andrews, Brambles

—— Wales ——

Cardiff, Sage
Carmarthen, Waverley
　Restaurant
Machynlleth, Centre for
　Alternative Technology

Machynlleth, Quarry Shop
Newport, Cnapan
Newport, Happy Carrot
　Bistro
Newtown, Jays

SUNDAY EATING

(L) & (D) are indicated where an establishment is only open for lunch or dinner

—— LONDON ——

Aspava, **W1**
Azami, **WC2** (D)
Benihana, **NW3**
Café Fish des Amis du Vin, **SW1**
Camden Brasserie, **NW1**
Le Caprice, **SW1**
Carriages, (Wine Bar), **SW1**
Chequers, **NW1**
Chiang Mai, **W1**
Delhi Brasserie, **SW7**
Diwana Bhelpoori House, **NW1 & W2**
Draycott's (Wine Bar), **SW3**
Earth Exchange, **N6**
East West Restaurant, **EC1**
English House, **SW3**
Equatorial, **W1**
Fallen Angel, **N1**
Good Earth, **NW7 & SW3**
Govindas, **W1**
Grosvenor House, Pavilion Espresso Bar, **W1**
Gurkhas Tandoori, **W1**
Hilton Kensington, Market Restaurant, **W11**
Hoults (Wine Bar), **SW17**
Laurent, **NW2**
London Hilton, Roof Restaurant, **W1** (L)
Lou Pescadou, **SW5**
Manna, **NW3**
Maxim (Wine Bar), **W7 & SW1**
Memories of India, **SW7**
Le Meridien Piccadilly, Terrace Garden Restaurant, **W1**

Millwards, **N16**
Mogul, **SE10**
Mulford's (Wine Bar), **W6**
Nakamura, **W1**
Nouveau Quiche, **SE14**
Old Poodle Dog Restaurant, **SW1**
Parsons, **SW10**
Pasta Undergound, **NW1**
Le Petit Prince, **NW5** (D)
Pollyanna's, **SW11**
Raj Bhelpoori House, **NW1**
Rani, **N3**
Ravenscourt Park Tea House, **W6**
Ravi Shankar, **NW1**
Royal Festival Hall, Riverside Café, **SE1**
Sabras, **NW10**
Sagarmatha, **NW1**
Shaheen of Knightsbridge, **SW3**
Suruchi, **N1**
Swiss Centre, **W1**
Topkapi, **W1**
Tui, **SW7**
Victoria & Albert Museum, New Restaurant, **SW7**
Village Delicatessen & Coffee Shop, **W14**
Wholemeal Vegetarian Café, **SW16**
Windmill Wholefood Restaurant, **SW6** (D)
Woodlands Restaurant, **W1 & SW1**
Youngs, **N1**
Zen **W3, NW3**

—— ENGLAND ——

Ambleside, Harvest
Ambleside, Zeffirellis
Ashburton, Ashburton Coffee House
Ashford-in-the-Water, Cottage Tea Room
Atherstone, Cloisters Wine Bar & Bistro
Avebury, Stones
Bath, Canary
Bath, Moon & Sixpence (D)
Beaulieu, Montagu Arms Hotel Restaurant
Belbroughton, Coffee Pot
Berkhamsted, Cook's Delight
Birmingham, Dynasty
Bishop's Waltham, Casey's
Boot, Brook House Restaurant
Bowness-on-Windermere, Hedgerow
Bradford, Pizza Margherita
Brighton (Hove), Blossoms
Brighton, Gar's
Bristol, Wild Oats II
Broadway, Collin House Hotel Restaurant
Broadway, Lygon Arms Restaurant
Canterbury, Il Vaticano Pasta Parlour
Canterbury, Sweet Heart Patisserie
Chagford, Teignworthy Restaurant (D)
Chenies, Bedford Arms Thistle Hotel Restaurant
Chester, Chester Grosvenor Restaurant
Cockermouth, Wythop Mill
Congleton, Odd Fellows Wine Bar & Bistro
Corse Lawn, Corse Lawn House
Croydon, Munbhave
Cuckfield, Ockenden Manor Hotel Restaurant
Elland, Berties Bistro
Esher, Good Earth
Faversham, Recreation Tavern
Grange-in-Borrowdale, Grange Bridge Cottage
Grasmere, Wordsworth Hotel, Prelude Restaurant

Great Dunmow, Starr (L)
Great Milton, Le Manoir aux Quat' Saisons Restaurant (L)
Halstead, Halstead Tandoori
Harrogate, Bettys
Helmsley, Black Swan Hotel Restaurant
High Lorton, White Ash Barn
Hungerford, Bear at Hungerford Restaurant
Jevington, Hungry Monk
Kendal, The Moon
Keswick, Mayson's
Keswick, Underscar Hotel
Leamington Spa, Ropers
Ledbury, Applejack Wine Bar (L)
Leighton Buzzard, Swan Hotel, Mr Swan's Restaurant
Lewes, Mike's Wine Bar
Long Melford, Chimneys (L)
Looe, Talland Bay Hotel Restaurant
Lower Beeding, South Lodge Restaurant
Lyndhurst, Parkhill Hotel Restaurant
Manchester, Yang Sing
Marlborough, Polly
Marlow, Compleat Angler Hotel, Valaisan Restaurant
Mawnan Smith, Meudon Hotel Restaurant
Melmerby, Village Bakery
Midhurst, Spread Eagle Hotel Restaurant
Oakham, Oakham Gallery
Oxford, Randolph Hotel, Spires Restaurant
Richmond, Richmond Harvest
Richmond, Wildefoods Wholefood Café
Ryton-on-Dunsmore, Ryton Gardens Café
St Michael's Mount, Sail Loft
Salisbury, Mo's (D)
Sandford Orcas, Holway Mill
Shrewsbury, Cornhouse Restaurant & Wine Bar
South Woodford, Ho-Ho
Stockport, Coconut Willy's (D)
Streatley-on-Thames, Swan Hotel Restaurant

England contd...

Studley, Peppers (D)
Sturminster Newton, Plumber
  Manor Restaurant
Thame, Mallards
Tideswell, Horsmans Poppies
Trebarwith Strand, House on
  the Strand
Wallingford, Brown & Boswell

Wells, Cloister Restaurant
Whitby, Magpie Café
Wilmslow, Stanneylands Hotel
  Restaurant (L)
Woodstock, Brothertons
  Brasserie
Yeovil, Little Barwick
  House (L)

—— SCOTLAND ——

Achiltibuie, Summer Isles
  Hotel Restaurant (D)
Arisaig, Old Library Lodge &
  Restaurant
Edinburgh, Brasserie Saint
  Jacques
Edinburgh, Lune Town (D)
Edinburgh, Verandah Tandoori
Eriska, Isle of Eriska
  Restaurant
Gullane, Greywalls Restaurant
Invergarry, Inn on the Garry
  Restaurant (D)
Inverness, Brookes Wine Bar
  (summer only)
Inverness, Dunain Park Hotel
  Restaurant

Kildonan, Three Rowans Tea
  Shop & Restaurant
Kingussie, Wood 'n' Spoon
Kinlochbervie, Kinlochbervie
  Hotel
Longformacus, Horn House
  Hotel
New Abbey, Abbey Cottage
St Andrews, Pepita's Restaurant
Tayvallich, Tayvallich Inn (L)
Troon, Piersland House Hotel
  Restaurant (L)
Turnberry, Turnberry Hotel
  Restaurant
Ullapool, Ceilidh Place
Wester Howgate, Old Howgate
  Inn, Coach House

—— WALES ——

Cardigan, Rhyd-Garn-Wen
  (D)
Crickhowell, Cheese Press
Hay-on-Wye, Granary
Keeston, Keeston Kitchen

Machynlleth, Centre for
  Alternative Technology
Newport, Cnapan
Talsarnau, Maes-y-Neuadd
  Hotel Restaurant

RESTAURANTS WITH DISTINCTLY NATIONAL COOKING

—— LONDON ——

CHINESE
Good Earth, NW7 & SW3
Maxim (Wine Bar), W7 & SW1
Poons, WC2
Youngs, N1
Zen W3, NW3

ENGLISH
English House, SW3

FRENCH
Dorchester, The Terrace, W1
Frederick's, N1
Inigo Jones, WC2
London Hilton, Roof
    Restaurant, W1
Lou Pescadou, SW5
Peacheys Restaurant, NW3

GREEK
Nontas, NW1

INDIAN & PAKISTANI
Delhi Brasserie, SW7
Diwana Bhelpoori House,
    NW1 & W2
Gurkhas Tandoori, W1
Kensington Tandoori, W8
Mandeer, W1
Memories of India, SW7
Mogul, SE10
Raj Bhelpoori House, NW1
Rani, N3
Ravi Shankar, NW1
Sabras, NW10
Sagarmatha, NW1
Shaheen of Knightsbridge, SW3
Shezan, SW7
Suruchi, N1
Woodlands, W1 & SW1

ITALIAN
La Barca, SE1
Gran Paradiso, SW1

JAPANESE
Ajimura, WC2
Asuka, NW1
Azami, WC2
Benihana, NW3
City Miyama, EC4
Defune, W1
Hokkai, W1
Ikeda, W1
Ikkyu, W1
Ipphei, NW3
Kitchen Yakitori, W1
Koto, NW1
Matono, W1
Nakamura, W1
One Two Three, W1
Saga, W1
Yumi, W1

KOREAN
Arirang, W1
Arirang House, SW1

SOUTH-EAST ASIAN
Equatorial, W1

SWISS
Swiss Centre, W1

THAI
Chaopraya, W1
Chiang Mai, W1
Tui, SW7

TUNISIAN AND
NORTH AFRICAN
Laurent, NW2
Le Petit Prince, NW5

TURKISH
Aspava, W1
Topkapi, W1

—— ENGLAND ——

CHINESE
Birmingham, Dynasty
Brighton, Gar's
Esher, Good Earth
Manchester, Yang Sing
South Woodford, Ho-Ho

ENGLISH
Broadway, Collin House Hotel
  Restaurant
Grimsthorpe, Black Horse Inn
  Restaurant

FRENCH
Birmingham, Michelle
Botley, Cobbett's
Brampton, Tarn End
Chester, Chester Grosvenor
  Restaurant

Great Milton, Le Manoir aux
  Quat' Saisons Restaurant
Manchester, Truffles
Marlow, Compleat Angler
  Hotel, Valasian Restaurant

INDIAN
Birmingham, Rajdoot
Bristol, Rajdoot
Croydon, Munbhave
Halstead, Halstead Tandoori
Manchester, Rajdoot
Studley, Peppers

ITALIAN
Basingstoke, Franco's

—— SCOTLAND ——

CHINESE
Edinburgh, Lune Town

INDIAN
Edinburgh, Kalpna
Edinburgh, Verandah Tandoori

Our inspectors never book in the name of
Egon Ronay's Guides; they disclose their
identity only after paying their bills.

LATE NIGHT EATING IN LONDON

—— LONDON ——

Aspava, W1
Le Caprice, SW1
Diwana Bhelpoori House, NW1
First Out, WC2
Gurkhas Tandoori, W1
Jeeves Wine Cellar, W1
Kensington Tandoori, W8
London Hilton, Roof
   Restaurant, W1
Lou Pescadou, SW5

Matono, W1
Le Meridien Piccadilly, Terrace
   Garden Restaurant, W1
Millwards, N16
Parsons, SW10
Pollyanna's, SW11
Shaheen of Knightsbridge, SW3
Swiss Centre, W1
Topkapi, W1
Youngs, N1

—— 🍽 ——

Changes in data may occur in establishments
after the Guide goes to press. Prices should
be taken as indications rather than firm
quotes.

—— 🍽 ——

OPEN AIR EATING

—— LONDON ——

Aspava, W1
Bubbles Wine Bar, W1
Chequers, NW1
Di's Larder, SW11
Earth Exchange, N6
Frederick's, N1
Govindas, W1
Gran Paradiso, SW1
Justin de Blank at General
   Trading Company, SW1

Lou Pescadou, SW5
Manna, NW3
Memories of India, SW7
Peacheys Restaurant, NW3
Pollyanna's, SW11
Ravenscourt Park Tea House,
   W6
Raw Deal, W1
Twenty Trinity Gardens, SW9
Wilkins Natural Foods, SW1

—— ENGLAND ——

Ambleside, Zeffirellis
Ashtead, Bart's
Avebury, Stones
Bakewell, Green Apple
Bath, Moon & Sixpence
Berkhamsted, Cook's Delight
Berwick-upon-Tweed, Wine
   Bar
Birmingham, La Galleria Wine
   Bar
Bishops Lydeard, Rose Cottage
Bishop's Waltham, Casey's
Boot, Brook House Restaurant
Bridgnorth, Sophie's Tea
   Rooms
Bristol, Wild Oats II
Bury St Edmunds, Beaumonts
Canterbury, Il Vaticano Pasta
   Parlour
Canterbury, Sweet Heart
   Patisserie
Castle Cary, Old Bakehouse
Cheltenham, Retreat
   (Wine Bar)
Chester, Abbey Green
Chester, Pierre Griffe Wine Bar
Chichester, St Martin's Tea
   Rooms
Chichester, Savourie
Chipping Norton, Nutters
Congleton, Odd Fellows Wine
   Bar & Bistro

Corse Lawn, Corse Lawn House
Dartington, Cranks Health
   Food Restaurant
Derby, Lettuce Leaf
Devizes, Wiltshire Kitchen
Easingwold, Truffles
Emsworth, Cloisters
Faversham, Recreation Tavern
Frome, Settle
Glastonbury, Rainbow's End
   Café
Grange-in-Borrowdale, Grange
   Bridge Cottage
Grantham, Knightingales
Hastings, Brant's
Hereford, Fodder
High Lorton, White Ash Barn
Hope, Hopechest
Kendal, The Moon
Kendal, Waterside Wholefoods
Lancaster, Libra
Lewes, Mike's Wine Bar
Ludlow, Hardwicks
Newark, Gannets
Penrith, Bluebell Tearoom
Richmond, Wildefoods
   Wholefood Café
Romsey, Latimer Coffee House
Totnes, Planters
Totnes, Willow
Trebarwith Strand, House on
   the Strand

50

Wareham, Annies
Warminster, Jenner's
Wells, Good Earth

Worcester, Natural Break
York, Gillygate Wholefood Café

—— SCOTLAND ——

Aberfeldy, Country Fare Coffee
   House
Arisaig, Old Library Lodge &
   Restaurant
Colbost, Three Chimneys
Dirleton, Open Arms Hotel
   Lounge
Edinburgh, Laigh Kitchen
Edinburgh, Waterfront Wine
   Bar

Falkirk, Healthy Life
Kildonan, Three Rowans Tea
   Shop & Restaurant
Longformacus, Horn House
   Hotel
New Abbey, Abbey Cottage
Tayvallich, Tayvallich Inn
Ullapool, Ceilidh Place
Wester Howgate, Old Howgate
   Inn, Coach House

—— WALES ——

Chepstow, Willow Tree
Hay-on-Wye, Granary
Keeston, Keeston Kitchen

Machynlleth, Centre for
   Alternative Technology
Newport, Cnapan

———————— ᵞ◻◖ ————————

If you are unsure of what to order, do
remember to ask the staff for advice on food
choices. Many restaurants will adapt dishes
to suit your requirements or prepare special
meals if given prior notice.

———————— ᵞ◻◖ ————————

HEALTHY EATING OUT
—IN—
LONDON

LONDON

LONDON

LONDON

LONDON

LONDON

LONDON

LONDON

LONDON

GUIDE TO ESTABLISHMENTS

LONDON*Restaurant*Ajimura

51 Shelton Street, WC2
01-240 0178

Map 11 C3

Lunch 12–3 Dinner 6–11 (Sun
   6–10.30)
Closed Lunch Sat & Sun & Bank
   Holidays
Japanese cooking

Average price £18
Set L & Set D from £9
Credit: Access, Amex, Diners, Visa

The discriminating diner will find plenty to please both palate and purse at this friendly Japanese restaurant. The extensive menu carries a full description of every dish so the wary need not worry about encountering that delicacy, raw fish, unless they order sushi, sashimi or su-no-mono. There is plenty for the vegetarian—for example seaweed salad, mixed vegetable hors d'oeuvre, hijiki with tofu quick-fried in sake sauce with carrots and noodles and avocado sashimi. Both white and brown rice are available and there is a wide range of vegetables and fresh fruits.

LONDON*Quick Bite*Almeida Theatre
Wine Bar

la Almeida Street, N1
01-226 0931

Map 11 D1

Open 10.30–2 & 5.30–11
Closed Sun & Bank Holidays

Typical prices: Cheese & lentil
   flan £2.95 Pasta, mushroom &
   shoyu salad 85p

Part of the Almeida Theatre complex, this popular wine bar is particularly busy on theatre nights and has plenty for the health conscious. Lunch might be wholemeal pasta with mushrooms, or cheese and lentil flan. There is always a choice of five salads, starters include a soup, guacamole and houmus and there is fresh fruit salad for dessert. From time to time a single nation is put under the spotlight, Portuguese food perhaps, when tuna soup might precede chicken casserole with almonds and red peppers.

54

LONDON · *Restaurant* · Arirang

31 Poland Street, W1
01-437 6633

Map 11 C3

Lunch 12–3 Dinner 6–11
Closed Sun, January 1, Easter
  Monday & December 25 & 26
Korean cooking

Average price £15
Set L from £3.95
Set D from £10
Credit: Access, Amex, Diners, Visa

A meal in a Korean restaurant is always a flexible feast. Soup may be a starter, a mid-meal refresher or drunk like a beverage throughout the meal. The helpful staff will happily make suggestions as to suitable combinations and the healthy eater might build a meal around shikumchee (spinach with sesame seeds), bulgogi (marinated thinly sliced beef), steamed rice and shin-sol-lo (fish and meat soup). There is also a choice of set meals that makes selection of dishes even simpler. Fresh fruits to follow—or try the ginseng tea.

LONDON · *Restaurant* · Arirang House

3 Park Close, SW1
01-581 1820

Map 12 B4

Lunch 12–3 Dinner 6–10.30
Closed Sun, January 1 & 2 &
  December 25 & 26
Korean cooking

Average price £16
Set meals from £25 for two, also
  Set L £5
Credit: Access, Amex, Diners, Visa

Considerate and helpful service, coupled with consistently good food, is the hallmark of this Korean restaurant in Knightsbridge. Prices are reasonable. Appetisers cost £1 or less, and the most expensive item, whole spring chicken stuffed with ginseng root, nuts and rice, is under £10. Fresh vegetables are presented in exciting ways. The marrow, crisply fried in a featherlight batter, is highly recommended. Many predominantly vegetable dishes have a small meat content—vegetarian versions are available.

LONDON — *Quick Bite* — Aspava

19b Trebeck Street,
  W1
01-491 8739

Map 12 B4

Open noon–midnight
Closed December 25

Typical prices: Shish kebab £3.85
  Houmus £1.35
Luncheon Vouchers accepted

There's an astonishingly extensive menu at this tiny corner restaurant. The food is Mediterranean with some Middle Eastern influence and raw materials are of good quality. Don't miss the Turkish thinly sliced cured fillet steak, grilled with tomato and lemon. Starters range from stuffed aubergines or vine leaves to yoghurt and cucumber or feta and olive salad. Main courses include lots of healthy kebabs served with Basmati rice. Salads and grills are also available, with some vegetarian dishes. Sorbets and fresh fruit for afters.

LONDON — *Quick Bite* — Asuka

209a Baker Street,
  NW1
01-486 5026

Map 11 B2

Open 12–2.30 & 6–11
Closed Lunch Sat, all Sun, Bank
  Holidays & 10 days Christmas
Japanese cooking

Typical prices: Tekamaki sushi
  £6.50 Assorted sushi £10
Credit: Access, Amex, Diners, Visa

This typical Japanese restaurant with its rice paper screens has none of the discomfort associated with fold-on-the-floor feasting. You'll find high-backed chairs in the dining room and comfortable upholstered stools at the sushi bar, where you can watch the sushi chef sculpting mackerel, tuna, prawns, sea bass, salmon and yellowtail in wafer-thin slices with consummate skill and artistry. On the main menu you might choose sui-mono, a delicate clear soup, and then sample a sizzling asuka steak or king prawns.

LONDON *Restaurant* Azami

13 West Street, WC2
01-240 0634

Map 11 C3

Lunch 12–2.30 Dinner 6–9.30
Closed Mon, Lunch Sat & Sun &
 Bank Holidays
Japanese cooking

Average price £25
Set D £30
Credit: Access, Amex, Diners, Visa

The food in this Japanese restaurant has a definite Western bias in deference to the majority of the diners, but truly authentic dishes are there for the asking. Healthy eaters have a wide choice. Starters include several clear soups such as dobin mushi (with prawns and chicken), plus appetizers like yakitori and a superbly flavoured salmon teriyaki. The main course might be beef fillet or fish, vegetables and soybean curd traditionally cooked at your table. Sushi is served at the table or at the sushi bar and the set dinner also provides a well-balanced meal.

LONDON *Restaurant* La Barca

80 Lower Marsh, SE1
01-261 9221

Map 12 D4

Lunch 12–2.30 Dinner 7–11.30
Closed Lunch Sat, all Sun, Bank
 Holidays & 4 days Christmas
Italian cooking

Average price £18
Credit: Access, Amex, Diners, Visa

Theatregoers throng to this cheerful Italian restaurant very close to the Old Vic. Competently cooked and well-flavoured Italian favourites are served by friendly and efficient staff. You could start with chargrilled sardines or Parma ham. There's pasta aplenty but also a good selection of meats and simple grills including lamb cutlets, lean steaks and veal chops cooked to taste. The vegetables are all beautifully cooked and very fresh. Various desserts and fresh fruit salad as a finale.

LONDON *Quick Bite* **Beehive**

11a Beehive Place,
SW9
01-274 1690

Map 10 C6

Open 11–4 & 7–10.30 (Sat 10–5 &
7–11)
Closed Sun & Bank Holidays
Vegetarian cooking

Typical prices: Lentil lasagne
£1.35 Satay with sesame seed
rice £3.75
Luncheon Vouchers accepted

The buzz around town is that this vegetarian restaurant is a good place to eat, so arrive early to be sure of a table. Lunchtimes are simple, with soups and specials like lentil lasagne and mushroom tagliatelle listed on a blackboard, as well as a counter display of salads and organic breads. There's an Oriental influence in both furnishings and food, which intensifies after 7pm. The evening menu is more elaborate, offering a choice of four starters, four main courses and four desserts, all carefully prepared from first-class ingredients.

LONDON *Restaurant* **Benihana**

100 Avenue Road,
NW3
01-586 9508

Map 9 B3

Dinner only 5.30–11, (Sun from 7)
also Sun Lunch 12–3
Closed December 25
Japanese cooking

Average price £25
Set L from £8.25
Set D from £15.25
Credit: Access, Amex, Diners, Visa

Hibachi-cooking in a high-tech environment. That's the story at this ultra-modern and very spacious restaurant, tastefully decorated in shades of grey and black. Tables seat eight and are almost always fully booked. Traditional lunches and dinners centre on chicken, steak, prawns, scallops or salmon, all grilled at speed on the stainless steel hotplate at the teppan-yaki bar. The set dinner includes a prawn appetizer, soup, salad, rice and vegetables, and green tea. Sorbet or fresh fruit salad to follow.

LONDON   *QuickBite*   Bentley's Wine Bar
& Oyster Bar

11 Swallow Street, W1
01-734 0401

Map 11 C3

Open 12–3 & 5.30–9
Closed Sun & Bank Holidays

Typical prices: Grilled whole
   plaice £3.75 Vegetables with
   Eastern spiced sauce £3.40
Credit: Access, Amex, Diners, Visa
Luncheon Vouchers accepted

Two choices here: you can eat at the ground floor oyster bar, or step downstairs to the attractive cellar wine bar. At the former you perch on stools at the marble-topped counter to down oysters or cold dishes; the wine bar offers well-spaced tables where you can enjoy an extended repertoire including salmon and several salads for starters, followed perhaps by grilled plaice or rump steak. There's a regular vegetarian dish such as vegetables with Eastern spiced sauce, and a good platter of low and medium fat cheeses to round off your meal.

LONDON   *QuickBite*   Bubbles Wine Bar

41 North Audley
   Street, W1
01-499 0600

Map 11 B3

Open 11–3 & 5.30–11
Closed Dinner Sat, all Sun & Bank
   Holidays

Typical prices: Salmon steak &
   salad £5.50
   Spinach & ricotta pie £2.75
Credit: Access, Amex, Diners, Visa
Luncheon Vouchers accepted

Effervescent owners David and Susan Nichol have made Bubbles one of the most exciting wine bars in London. Whether you dine on the level or descend to the basement bistro, the food is superb. Susan's salads are crisp and fresh, ideal accompaniments to the cold pink-roast lamb, coated with mustard and fresh herbs, that is one of the house specialities. Hot dishes served downstairs include vegetarian choices like vegetable risotto. Sorbet is a sensible sweet for those able to resist the Pavlova.

LONDON

Quick Bite

Café Fish des Amis du Vin

39 Panton Street, SW1
01-839 4880

Map 11 C3

Open 11.30am–11.30pm
Closed Sun

Typical prices: Steamed hake
£5.75 Grilled Dover sole £8.95
Credit: Access, Amex, Diners, Visa

Fish is treated with respect at this restaurant, where the only starter (included in the cover charge) is a small portion of fish pâté with French bread so that the main course fish dishes can be perfectly cooked to order. Healthy eaters will find it easy to make a selection from a menu that categorises dishes by cooking method. Concentrate on the grills, salads, omelettes and baked or steamed fish. The accompaniments, new potatoes and crisply cooked vegetables, will be served without sauce on request. Desserts include fromage blanc with fresh fruit.

LONDON

Quick Bite

Camden Brasserie

216 Camden High
  Street, NW1
01-482 2114

Map 11 C1

Open 12–3 & 6.30–11.30 (Sun
  6–10.30)
Closed December 24–January 2

Typical prices: Monkfish brochette
£5.50 Avocado & raw vegetable
salad £3.95

There's atmosphere aplenty at this popular brasserie, with its wooden floors and open fire. The charcoal grill provides some good choices for healthy eaters, including monkfish brochette, chicken Oriental and calf's liver. There is always a fresh pasta dish suitable for vegetarians, and a couple of composite salads such as niçoise or avocado with carrots, celery, mushrooms and lettuce. Starters might be smoked trout or grilled sardines and simple sweets include kiwi and lemon sorbet.

LONDON *Restaurant* Le Caprice

Arlington House,
  Arlington Street, SW1
01-629 2239

Map 12 C4

Lunch 12–2.30 (Sun 12–3) Dinner
  6–12 (Sat & Sun 7–12)
Closed Lunch Sat, Bank Holidays
  & 1 week Christmas

Average price £20
Credit: Access, Amex, Diners, Visa

Sunday brunch is a speciality of this hugely popular '30s-style restaurant near Piccadilly. Try a jog in Hyde Park, then a healthy meal of crudités rafraîchies and monkfish brochette and perhaps treat yourself to a Bloody Mary or Buck's Fizz. During the week Le Caprice is where the film set feeds so be sure to book a table. The cooking is competent, the ingredients of good quality and the French-influenced menu includes plenty of salads and fresh vegetables. Vegetarian and vegan meals are regularly on offer.

LONDON *Quick Bite* Carriages (Wine Bar)

43 Buckingham
  Palace Road, SW1
01-834 8871

Map 12 C4

Open 11.30–2.30 & 5.30–10.30
Closed Sat & Sun in winter & Bank
  Holidays

Typical prices: Smoked chicken
  salad £4.75 Salade niçoise £4.95
  (Minimum lunchtime charge £4)
  Credit: Access, Amex, Diners, Visa

Opposite the Queen's Gallery at Buckingham Palace, this contemporary wine bar and restaurant provides imaginatively conceived and well cooked food with some satisfying healthy choices. The menu changes every week but always includes starters such as soup, fish mousse, cheese flan and avocado salad; and main dishes like mixed cheese platter (four cheeses, salad and wholemeal bread), smoked chicken salad, and smoked salmon served with scrambled egg. Grilled fish or steak is also offered.

LONDON · *Restaurant* · Chaopraya

22 St Christopher's
  Place, W1
01-486 0777

Map 11 B3

Lunch 12–3 Dinner 6.30–11
Closed Lunch Sat, all Sun & Bank
  Holidays
Thai cooking

Average price £16
Set L & Set D £12
Credit: Access, Amex, Diners, Visa

Authentic Thai cooking is extremely tasty, thanks to careful seasoning and subtle use of fresh spices. At this smart restaurant there are over a hundred dishes to choose from. Enlist the aid of the helpful staff if in doubt. Perhaps a bowl of hot and sour soup with lemon and chilli, followed by grilled prawns or steamed fish with preserved plums and ginger. Vegetables include tasty stir-fries such as broccoli with oyster sauce, and there is a range of Thai composite salads such as tuna with lemon juice and onion. Lots of noodle and rice dishes, too.

LONDON · *Quick Bite* · Chequers

18 Chalk Farm Road,
  NW1
01-485 1699

Map 9 C3

Open 10am–12.30am
Closed December 25
Vegetarian cooking

Typical prices: Lentil soup with
  bread £1.35 Pasta with mint,
  tomato & onion 85p

Chess is the name of the game that is played in the front section of this vegetarian café. Towards the back moves are all in one direction—towards the superb salads set out on a side table. At least 17 varieties are produced every day, including mushrooms with coriander, beetroot with dill and various bean medleys. Make a meal of these by starting with a bowl of thick lentil soup and a hunk of wholemeal bread or try one of the selection of hot main dishes. There's always fresh fruit salad for afters.

241 Globe Road, E2
01-980 6678

Map 9 D3

Open 12–9.30 (Thurs till 2.30)
Closed Sun, Mon, 1 week August
  & 1 week Christmas
Vegetarian cooking

Typical prices: West Indian beans
  £1.45 Pasta con spinaci £1.75
Luncheon Vouchers accepted

This well-established pretty restaurant is run by a Buddhist cooperative and attracts a large clientele. As the staff work a rota the menu changes frequently, but the food is consistently imaginative and well cooked. A soup such as cream of watercress or mushroom and dill could be followed by a tofu burger with vegetables or a succulent flavoursome nut roast. There is a colourful selection of salads, and excellent wholemeal bread. Drinks include a good range of herbal teas including a hibiscus blend. Vegans are catered for.

48 Frith Street, W1
01-437 7444

Map 11 C3

Open 12–3 & 6–11.30 (Sun till 11)
Closed January 1, 3 days Easter &
  2 days Christmas
Thai cooking

Typical prices: Sweet & sour
  vegetables £3.50
  Hot & sour beef ball salad £3.50
Credit: Access, Amex, Visa

If you've never tried Thai food, head for this smart modern restaurant, where over a hundred dishes await discovery. Described on the menu as 'somewhere between Chinese and Indian cookery', Thai meals generally consist of several dishes, some mild and some spicy, served with rice. Assemble a healthy repast from dishes like grilled marinated chicken, steamed eggs and quick-fried seasonal vegetables or choose from vegetarian specialities such as hot and sour vermicelli salad.

LONDON *Quick Bite* Christys Healthline

122 Wardour Street,
W1
01-434 4468

Map 11 C3

Open 8am–11.30pm (Sat from 10);
Wine bar 11–3 & 5.30–11
Closed Sun & Bank Holidays
Vegetarian cooking

Typical prices: Healthline salad
£3.50 Mushroom, nut & beer
pâté £1.95
Credit: Access, Amex, Diners, Visa
Luncheon Vouchers accepted

Get the day off to a healthy start at this smart new vegetarian restaurant complex. Breakfast, from 8–10am includes free-range eggs, wholemeal cereals and breads, low-fat spreads, additive-free preserves, fresh fruit juices and yoghurts. For lunch you might start with lentil, tomato and basil pâté with sesame crispbread. To follow, there are imaginative salads, pizzas and always a pasta dish and savoury specials like vegetable casserole with brown rice. Organic vegetables are used wherever possible and there's plenty of choice for vegans.

LONDON *Restaurant* City Miyama

17 Godliman Street,
EC4
01-489 1937

Map 11 D3

Lunch 12–2.30 Dinner 6–10
Closed Sat, Sun & Bank Holidays
Japanese cooking

Average price £25
Set L from £5.60
Set D from £11
Credit: Access, Amex, Diners, Visa

Located in a quiet street not far from St Paul's Cathedral, this Japanese restaurant is smart and sophisticated. A striking black and white marbled entrance hall leads to the ground floor teppan-yaki bar and sushi counter. Only sushi and lighter cooked fish dishes are available at the counter—the selection is freshness itself and it is a joy to watch the food being prepared. In the mirrored restaurant downstairs you can have the full menu from zensai (appetisers) through soups and savoury dishes to fresh fruit.

1 Heddon Street, W1
01-434 2922

Map 11 C3

Open 11.30–2.30
Closed Sat, Sun, Bank Holidays &
  3 days Christmas
Vegan cooking

Typical prices: Soup & salad £2.50
  Lentil pilaff £1.99
(Minimum charge £1.99)
Luncheon Vouchers accepted

Anyone who thinks vegan food lacks variety should visit this basement restaurant off Regent Street, where a feast costs less than a fiver and an extensive range of delicious dishes proves there is life after dairy produce. Everything on the menu is freshly prepared. There are two salad bars, one for vegetables and the other for fruit and nuts. Try eggplant 'Parmesan' (made with tofu and sunflower pimento cheese) or baked potatoes stuffed with mushrooms, and one of the four types of wholemeal bread always available. Desserts include fresh fruit and light, nut creams.

17 Great Newport
  Street, W1
01-836 5226

Map 11 C3

Open 8–7.30 (Sat from 10)
Closed Sun & Bank Holidays
Vegetarian wholefood cooking

Typical prices: Minted split pea &
  tomato soup £1.25 Wholewheat
  pasta & brown nut sauce £1.75
Luncheon Vouchers accepted

Another Cranks! That these places proliferate so freely is proof of their huge popularity. This newest branch is just off Charing Cross Road, close to Leicester Square tube station, and offers a similar bill of fare to that available at the Marshall Street and Tottenham Street establishments. Plenty of wholesome bakes, filled wholemeal baps, soups, hot savouries and earthenware bowls piled high with crisp salads. Don't miss the desserts, which make excellent use of fresh fruit and yoghurt.

65

LONDON

LONDON — *Quick Bite* — Cranks

9 Tottenham Street,
W1
01-631 3912

Map 11 C2

Open 8am–8pm (Sat from 9)
Closed Sun & Bank Holidays
Vegetarian wholefood cooking

Typical prices: Savoury rice salad
£1.45 Macaroni in tomato
sauce £2.75
Luncheon Vouchers accepted

Cranks' famous formula is as successful as ever at these light and spacious premises, where bold white walls are softened by masses of greenery. The day begins with breakfast, when there is a choice of four cereals or soy, millet or sunflower seed porridge, followed by poached or scrambled eggs and scones. Lunch, detailed on a blackboard menu beside the self-service counter, might be cauliflower and broccoli soup, followed by lentil bake. There's a choice of five hearty salads and healthy eaters can tuck into a sugar-free carob cake.

LONDON — *Quick Bite* — Cranks in Covent Garden

Unit 11, Covent
Garden Market, WC2
01-379 6508

Map 11 C3

Open 10–8
Closed Sun & Bank Holidays
Vegetarian wholefood cooking

Typical prices: Tofu & lentil
quiche £1.35
Kidney bean salad £1.45
Luncheon Vouchers accepted

Queues are as common as quiches in this tiny Covent Garden snack bar and wholefood shop. Customers who know a good thing when they eat it are happy to wait or share a table in the somewhat cramped conditions of the cellar café beneath the takeaway shop. Cranks classics, prepared in their Marshall Street kitchens, are the order of the day—lovely light wholemeal quiches, splendid salads, soups, pizzas and tasty wholemeal baps. Lots of cakes and bakes too, right through to closing time.

LONDON   *Quick Bite*   **Cranks Health ★**
Food Restaurant

8 Marshall Street, W1
01-437 9431

Map 11 C3

Buffet open 8–7; Dine & Wine
  6.30–11
Closed Sun & Bank Holidays

Typical prices: Wholemeal
  pancake £4.25 (Dine & Wine)
  Lentil & mushroom patties £1.25
Credit: Access, Amex, Diners, Visa
Luncheon Vouchers accepted

Many healthy eaters have a soft spot for this restaurant, the original Cranks, and the place which has arguably done more to promote vegetarian eating in London than any other establishment. Daytime dishes are much the same as those offered at other branches but an innovation is the candlelight dinner, providing a wide choice of dishes at very reasonable prices. You might try melon salad followed by Brazil and cashew nut roast with steamed vegetables, and round off your meal with fresh fruit salad.

LONDON   *Quick Bite*   **Daly's Wine Bar**

46 Essex Street, WC2
01-583 4476

Map 11 D3

Open 8.30–5.30
Closed Sat, Sun & Bank Holidays

Typical prices: Dover sole from
  £8.10 Chicken salad £1.75
Credit: Access, Amex, Diners, Visa
Luncheon Vouchers accepted

Legal eagles fly to this popular establishment when not at the Bar. The early morning continental breakfast gives way to a lunchtime buffet just before noon and the freshly made salads on the salad bar are well worth sampling together with the excellent home-made wholemeal bread. Also on the buffet table are succulent cold meats. Grilled halibut, Dover sole and oysters are regularly on the menu, and simpler hot dishes include soup, pasta, cauliflower cheese, barbecued chicken and jacket potatoes.

LONDON *Restaurant* Defune

61 Blandford Street,
 W1
01-935 8311

Map 11 B3

Lunch 12–2.30 Dinner 6–10.30
Closed Sun, Bank Holidays,
 1 week August & 1 week from
 December 31
Japanese cooking

Average price £26
Credit: Amex, Diners

Space is at a premium in this tiny Japanese restaurant. A small upper room eases the situation a little but it is still essential to book. There are no set meals but each dish is fully described on the menu, so it is easy to put together a healthy repast. Sushi may be a starter or full meal—consult the illustrated menu in the foyer for details. Several refreshing soups are served, including suiwan and misho-shira, and main courses include teriyaki and sakanachiri, a hearty meal-in-a-pot consisting of fish and vegetables in simmering stock. Fresh fruit to follow.

LONDON *Restaurant* Delhi Brasserie

134 Cromwell Road,
 SW7
01-370 7617

Map 12 A5

Lunch 12–2.30 Dinner 6–11.30
Closed December 25
Indian cooking

Average price £14
Credit: Access, Amex, Diners, Visa

The chef of this restaurant was formerly to be found at a leading hotel in India, and his expertise and flair are evident. The menu includes several rice and pulse dishes, a range of breads, including wholewheat and the irresistible peshwari nan, stuffed with ground almonds and sultanas. Guests who prefer their food grilled will enjoy the tandoori quails or king prawns, cooked over charcoal to tender perfection. Indian desserts are notoriously sweet but fresh mango or a bowl of lychees make a good finale.

62 Lavender Hill,
   SW11
01-223 4618

Map 10 C6

Open 10–6
Closed Sun, Bank Holidays, 3 days
   Christmas & 2 weeks August
Vegetarian wholefood cooking

Typical prices: Tabbouleh 95p
   Vegetarian pastitsio £1.80

The 'larder' is a little wholefood shop-cum-café where Di
Kilpatrick cooks simple but wholesome vegetarian snacks
and light meals. The friendly back-of-the-store atmosphere
is sustained by the comfortingly well-stocked shelves that
surround the tables. The blackboard menu changes daily—
come early for the best choice. A hot or cold soup could be
followed by spinach and mung bean bake or wholewheat
noodles with aubergine, ground nuts and béchamel sauce.
There's always a selection of salads like marinated chick
peas with raw vegetables and puds include carob mousse.

Winchester Walk, off
   Cathedral Street, SE1
01-407 0337

Map 10 D4

Open 12.30–2.30 & 7–10
Closed Sat, Sun, Mon & Bank
   Holidays
Vegetarian wholefood cooking

Typical prices: Wakame & tofu
   salad £2 Chinese-style spicy
   aubergines £4.50

Tucked away behind the vegetable market, this wholefood
restaurant is not easy to find but once located is likely to
become a favourite eating place. The owners, William
English and Sandra Cross, produce healthy food of a high
standard and both menus and individual dishes are
carefully balanced. You could start with wakame and tofu
salad with sesame dressing, proceed to a mushroom and
cheese pancake with green bean and garlic sauce, and
conclude with Greek yoghurt, honey and strawberries.

114 Drummond Street, NW1 01-388 4867	114 Drummond Street open 12–10 Closed December 25
Map 11 C2	
121 Drummond Street, NW1 01-387 5556	121 Drummond Street open noon– midnight Closed December 25
Map 12 C2	
50 Westbourne Grove, W2 01-221 0721	50 Westbourne Grove open 12–3 & 6–11 (Sat & Sun 12–11) Closed Mon & December 25
Map 11 A3	Indian vegetarian cooking
	Typical prices: Thali £3.75 Deluxe dosa £2.75 Credit: Access, Diners, Visa Luncheon Vouchers accepted

You can take a culinary cruise around the Indian sub-continent thanks to the varied vegetarian menu at these simply appointed restaurants. Start at Chowpaty beach with pooris, chick peas and sour sauce, then move to Madras for one of the region's famous dosas. Unsure of what to choose? Ask the friendly obliging staff about the delicious Gujerati-style thalis (set meals)—an excellent way of sampling several different dishes. Desserts are rich and generally very sweet but mango water ice or passion fruit sorbet are healthy alternatives.

Our inspectors never book in the name of
Egon Ronay's Guides; they disclose their
identity only after paying their bills.

LONDON　*Restaurant*　Dorchester, ★
The Terrace

Park Lane, W1
01-629 8888

Map 11 B4

Dinner only 6–11.30
Closed Sun

Average price £30
Set D £29, also £66 for two
Credit: Access, Amex, Diners, Visa

Many of the dishes on Anton Mosimann's exciting menu have the suffix 'CN'. This denotes 'cuisine naturelle', a cooking technique that eschews cream, butter, oil and alcohol and limits sugar and salt. Seasonally changing menus feature a wide selection of the finest and freshest produce available from the markets. The cooking is of the highest calibre. The healthy eater might dine on marinated salmon with yoghurt dressing, followed by poached fillet of beef or steamed sea bass with strips of pork. Citrus fruits with sorbet make a fitting finale.

LONDON　*Quick Bite*　Draycott's (Wine Bar)

114 Draycott Avenue,
　SW3
01-584 5359

Map 12 B5

Open 12.30–2.45 (Sun 11–2.30 &
　7–10.30)
Closed January 1 & 3 days
　Christmas

Typical prices: Grilled chicken
　breast £4.95
　Vegetable Stroganoff £4.25
Credit: Access, Amex, Diners, Visa

Sunday morning joggers break for brunch at this popular wine bar, where from 11am to 2.30pm simple delights include wholemeal rolls, smoked salmon with scrambled eggs and fresh fruit with yoghurt and honey. Weekday winebibbers can take solid nourishment in the form of healthy dishes like brochettes of seafood or grilled chicken breast with a touch of herb butter. Meat-lovers favour grilled steak and vegetarians have various choices, such as mild vegetable curry or vegetable Stroganoff.

213 Archway Road, N6
01-340 6407

Map 9 C2

Open 12–3 (Sun till 4) & 6–10.30
Closed Wed, Thurs, some Bank
  Holidays & December 24–31
Vegetarian wholefood cooking

Typical prices: Tofu lasagne £3.20
  Butter bean pie £3.20

Jugs of iced water with lemon slices on every table make an excellent first impression at this basement restaurant, as do the fresh flowers. The healthy approach to eating is much in evidence. Vegetables are organically grown where possible, eggs are free-range, organic brown rice is always used and desserts are sugar-free. Yoghurt (dairy and soya) is used in cooking and to top desserts and many salads are served without dressings. A simple meal might be miso soup, nut and carrot roast with rice or a choice of salads and apple crumble.

LONDON *QuickBite* **East West Restaurant**

188 Old Street, EC1
01-608 0300

Map 9 D3

Open 11–10 (Sat & Sun till 3pm)
Closed Bank Holidays & 10 days
  Christmas
Macrobiotic cooking

Typical prices: Savoury flan £1.10
  Mixed salad £1.20
Luncheon Vouchers accepted

There's more to macrobiotics than mere sustenance. It has been defined as balancing an individual's food with his physical and mental state and environment. Harmony is therefore at the heart of this restaurant and ingredients are combined in the ratio of 50% grains, 30% cooked vegetables, 15% beans and 5% seaweed and raw vegetables. Such food is naturally very good for you; it is also extremely tasty. Very reasonably priced set meals offer delicacies like scrambled tofu and nori seaweed.

3 Milner Street, SW3
01-584 3002

Map 12 B5

Lunch 12.30–2.30 (Sun till 2)
  Dinner 7.30–11.30 (Sun till 10)
Closed Good Friday & December
  25 & 26
English cooking

Average price £25
Set L £10.50 (Sun £11.50)
Set D £17.50 (Sun only)
Credit: Access, Amex, Diners, Visa

Recipes at the English House are culled from English country cookery books and make the most of some of England's finest ingredients. Dishes include poached salmon trout on a sorrel blanket, calf's liver with bacon and sage, and delicately pink roast rack of lamb with leeks. Both natural yoghurt and polyunsaturated margarine are used where appropriate in sauces that enhance rather than mask flavours and there are regular vegetarian dishes. The weak-willed should pass up the sweets trolley!

37 Old Compton
  Street, W1
01-437 6112

Map 11 C3

Open 12–3 & 6–11.15 (Sat
  12–11.15, Sun 12–11)
Closed December 24–26
South East Asian cooking

Typical prices: Satay £3
  Gado gado £2.60
Credit: Access, Amex, Diners, Visa

At this modest two-roomed restaurant you can make the acquaintance of at least 79 South East Asian dishes, from traditional Indonesian satay to gado gado. Some might be termed acquired tastes, such as the fish head curry, but healthy eaters will find plenty of simple dishes with new and exotic flavours. One of the best of these (for two or more) is the famous 'Steamboat', a sort of fondue where meats, fish, bean curd, eggs, noodles and vegetables are cooked in hot broth.

LONDON — *Restaurant* — L'Escargot

48 Greek Street, W1
01-437 2679

Map 11 C3

Lunch 12.30–2.30 Dinner 6–11.15
Closed Lunch Sat, all Sun, Bank
Holidays & 1 week Christmas

Average price £20
Credit: Access, Amex, Diners, Visa

Martin Lam cooks with style for both the elegant restaurant and the more informal brasserie downstairs. The varied menu offers an excellent choice based upon French recipes and 'cuisine nouvelle'. Healthy eating is intrinsic in dishes such as spinach fettuccine with fresh tomato and basil sauce or pasta salad with salmon, scallops and squid served with a ginger and soy dressing. There are several vegetarian dishes on the menu, including aubergine charlotte with tomato and yoghurt, and cottage cheese and farmhouse Cheddar salad with banana, mango and almonds.

LONDON — *Quick Bite* — Fallen Angel

65 Graham Street, N1
01-253 3996

Map 11 D1

Open 12.30–9 (Sat & Sun till 10)
Vegetarian cooking

Typical prices: Lentil bake £2.25
Poppy seed cake 70p
Luncheon Vouchers accepted

Space is at a premium at this lively vegetarian café-bar, so be prepared to share a table at peak times. The short but varied menu changes daily and includes plenty of choice for vegans. You might start with vegetable and barley soup or mushroom and tofu pâté, then sample the vegetable curry with brown rice, or wholemeal pasta with spinach and corn. All meals are offered with a selection of three salads. In the afternoon cakes and bakes are served with refreshing tisanes and freshly-squeezed orange juice.

52 St Giles High Street,
  WC2
01-240 8042

Map 11 C3

Open 11 am–midnight
Closed Sun & Bank Holidays
Vegetarian cooking

Typical prices: Mushroom bisque
  £1.20 Greek bean salad £1.20
Luncheon Vouchers accepted

In the lee of Centre Point, this lively vegetarian restaurant is always well patronised. The decor is contemporary, the atmosphere informal and the cooking capable. From about 12.30 hot soups and savouries are served. Stuffed cabbage rolls, maybe, or a vegetable moussaka. Don't miss the nut rissoles. Perfectly seasoned and with a little lemon to lift the flavour, these are excellent, and so is the barbecue sauce that accompanies them. Wholemeal quiches have hearty vegetable fillings like spinach, mushroom and onion, and three salads are offered daily.

13 Blackfriars Lane,
  EC4
01-236 7001

Map 11 D3

Open 8–3
Closed Sat, Sun, Bank Holidays &
  2 weeks Christmas
Vegetarian cooking

Typical prices: Moussaka £2.45
  Home-made yoghurt 50p
Luncheon Vouchers accepted

Visit this cavernous health-food counter-service restaurant at lunchtime and you may have to share a table, such is its popularity. The food is healthy, hearty, satisfying and very reasonable if not sophisticated. There are many changes on the menu daily. Start with a soup or grapefruit cocktail, then try one of the chef's specials, which might be a vegetarian moussaka or spinach soufflé with tomato sauce. Super salads, carefully balanced in terms of nutrition, and tasty sweets including home-made yoghurt and sorbets.

LONDON *QuickBite* .Food for Thought

31 Neal Street, WC2
01-836 0239

Map 11 C3

Open 12–8
Closed Sat, Sun, Bank Holidays &
December 22–January 10
Vegetarian cooking

Typical prices: Fresh spinach &
mushroom tagliatelle £1.30
Stir-fried vegetables with brown
rice £1.30
Luncheon Vouchers accepted

For proof positive that vegetarian food is excellent value you need look no further than at this immensely popular restaurant. There isn't any question about the freshness of the ingredients—they are prepared in full view of the customers, providing a culinary cabaret of controlled chaos. Soup and stir-fries top the bill, together with savoury dishes such as cauliflower cheese, macaroni al forno, West Country casserole and courgette quiche with excellent wholemeal pastry. Super puds include crumbles, a selection of yoghurts and a chunky fresh fruit salad.

LONDON *Restaurant* Frederick's

Camden Passage, N1
01-359 2888

Map 11 D1

Lunch 12–2.30 Dinner 7–11.30
Closed Sun & Bank Holiday
Mondays
French cooking

Average price £20
Set L £7.50 (Sat only)
Credit: Access, Amex, Diners, Visa

The menu at this classic restaurant includes an invitation to inspect the kitchens, so confident is the management that the high standard of care and consideration displayed in the restaurant is maintained below stairs. The same willingness to please is apparent on the menu. Dishes cooked without butter or cream such as grilled lamb cutlets with fresh herbs are set alongside richer fare, and every menu carries at least two vegetarian dishes. A favourite is a trio of vegetable mousses with a mixed salad.

14 Frith Street, W1
01-439 3370

Map 11 C3

Lunch 12–2.30 Dinner 6–11.30
(Pre-theatre menu 6–7.30)
Closed Lunch Sat, all Sun &
  December 25 & 26

Average price £20
Set L & Set D £16
  (Pre-theatre menu £9.50)
Credit: Access, Amex, Diners, Visa

Chef Carla Tomasi's imaginative cooking has earned this contemporary Soho restaurant a considerable following. The fixed-price menu changes monthly and includes such treats as triple mousse of broccoli, tomato and parsley with cucumber and herb dressing, and ravioli filled with watercress and wild rice. It is intriguing to find samphire on the menu in a dish that also includes sea trout and lemon grass. There is always a choice of excellent vegetarian dishes as well as delectable desserts and an exciting selection of cheeses.

————————— 🍴📖 —————————
If you are unsure of what to order, do
remember to ask the staff for advice on food
choices. Many restaurants will adapt dishes
to suit your requirements or prepare special
meals if given prior notice.
————————— 🍴📖 —————————

LONDON

143 The Broadway, NW7
01-959 7011

Map 9 A1

143 The Broadway Lunch 12–2.30
(Sun 12.30–3) Dinner 6–11
Closed 4 days Christmas

233 Brompton Road, SW3
01-584 3658

Map 12 B5

233 Brompton Road meals 12–11
(Sun 12.30–11)
Closed 4 days Christmas

91 King's Road, SW3
01-352 9231

Map 12 B5

91 King's Road meals 12.30–11.45
Closed 4 days Christmas

Chinese cooking

Average price £15
Set L & Set D from £10.50
Credit: Access, Amex, Diners, Visa

Chinese cuisine is rich and varied and is well represented at these three London restaurants (another in Esher, see page 197). Start with chicken wrapped in rice paper, or steamed Pacific prawns, or try one of ten soups including the very tasty hot and sour soup from northern China. There is a wide selection of seafood including steamed sea bass and Dover sole. Shredded beef mandarin or poached chicken are good main course choices. Steamed bean curd served with a soy sauce is a speciality and there are plenty of vegetable and rice or noodle dishes.

LONDON *QuickBite* Govindas

9 Soho Street, W1
01-437 3662

Map 11 C3

Open 11.30–8 (Thurs–Sat till 9,
Sun 12.30–3.30)
Closed December 25 & 26
Vegetarian cooking

Typical prices: Spinach pie with
vegetables £3.50
Vegan fruit slice 95p
Luncheon Vouchers accepted

The cooking at this pleasant self-service vegetarian restaurant follows the rules of the Hare Krishna movement, so no eggs, mushrooms or onions are used, and soy is kept to a minimum. Despite these restrictions, the food is tasty, varied and very enjoyable. The selection might include a quiche, made with cheese and an egg substitute, samosas, jacket potatoes with cottage cheese and pizzas and vegeburgers. There is always a soup—with wholemeal bread—and a vegan dish such as five bean pot. Five different salads extend the range and there is fresh fruit salad to follow.

LONDON *Restaurant* Gran Paradiso

52 Wilton Road, SW1
01-828 5818

Map 12 C5

Lunch 12–2.30 Dinner 6–11.15
Closed Lunch Sat, all Sun, Bank
Holidays & 2 weeks August
Italian cooking

Average price £15
Credit: Access, Amex, Diners, Visa

At least eight fresh vegetables are on the menu every day at this charming Italian restaurant. Dine on the garden terrace in summer and enjoy such dishes as fresh trout and salmon salad, grilled veal chops with herbs, young whole roasted chicken with herbs or chicken casseroled with wild mushrooms. The pasta dishes such as pasta fagioli or borlotti beans with pasta are fresh and tasty and wholewheat pasta will be provided on request. Wholemeal bread is served and salads are made without dressing if preferred.

79

LONDON *Quick Bite* Grosvenor House, Pavilion Espresso Bar

Park Lane, W1
01-499 6363

Map 11 B3

Open 7 am–10 pm (Sat & Sun till 10.30

Typical prices: Smoked turkey sandwich £4.75
Freshly squeezed fruit juice £2
Credit: Access, Amex, Diners, Visa

For freshly-squeezed orange or vegetable juice and a healthy light snack at any hour of the day between breakfast and bedtime, make a beeline for this stylish espresso bar. The choice is limited to tempting sandwiches and light meals but everything is fresh and tasty. Try the smoked salmon and soft cheese sandwich on olive bread, or the more substantial aubergine, tomato and mozzarella layer. Sliced cold meats are available too, and there's a fresh fruit platter with yoghurt dressing. The pick-me-ups are delicious—try the mixed vegetable juice cocktail.

LONDON *Quick Bite* Gurkhas Tandoori

23 Warren Street, W1
01-388 1640

Map 11 C2

Open 12–3 & 6–12
Closed December 25 & 26
Nepalese cooking

Typical prices: Tandoori king prawns £5.95
Vanita tarkara £1.65
Credit: Visa
Luncheon Vouchers accepted

Military memorabilia serve as decor in this unpretentious Nepalese restaurant named after those famous fighting Nepalese, the Gurkhas. The food is unfailingly delicious, using fresh spices such as coriander, and there is plenty to please the health-conscious diner. The wide menu covers not only Nepal: there are dishes from all over the Indian subcontinent. Try the subtly-flavoured lentil soup, followed perhaps by chicken tikka or tandoori king prawns. Fresh fruit such as guavas, lychees or mangos to follow.

LONDON *Quick Bite* Harrods
Health Juice Bar

Knightsbridge, SW1
01-730 1234

Map 12 B4

Open 9–4.45 (Wed 9.30–6.45, Sat
9–5.45)
Closed Sun & Bank Holidays
Vegetarian cooking

Typical prices: Tagliatelle with
aubergine, onion & tomato £3.25
Sweet & sour salad £1.50
Credit: Access, Amex, Diners, Visa

Healthy eating in Harrods is in sparkling clean smart surroundings in the basement. Early morning shoppers can start the day with pick-me-ups like orange juice with egg, banana, milk and honey, or enjoy muesli or fresh fruit salad. Pure fruit juices, like orange, grapefruit or tomato, are served in generous tumblers, and milk by the glass includes fresh goats' milk. Lunch might be tagliatelle with aubergine, onion, tomato and basil, or a fresh crisp salad such as celery, nuts and sultanas or mixed bean. Fruit salad or dried fruit compote to follow.

LONDON *Restaurant* Hilton Kensington,
Market Restaurant

179 Holland Park
Avenue, W11
01-603 3355

Map 10 B4

Lunch 12.15–3 Dinner 5.30–10.45

Average price £18.50
Set L & Set D from £9
Credit: Access, Amex, Diners, Visa

Businessmen and women occupy many of the tables at this stylish restaurant, where the carvery's rib of beef with jacket potato and lightly cooked vegetables or salads makes a good lunchtime choice. All items on the menu are served without sauces if preferred, and grilled sole, poached turbot and corn-fed chicken are all popular. Vegetarian dishes make interesting use of pulses as in the Caribbean medley of black-eyed beans, red peppers and coconut sauce or the chilli sin carne made with soya mince.

59 Brewer Street, W1
01-734 5826

Map 11 C3

Lunch 12.30–2.30 Dinner 6–10.30
Closed Sun & Bank Holiday
  Mondays
Japanese cooking

Average price £15
Set L from £6.50
Set D from £13.50
Credit: Access, Amex, Diners, Visa

This Japanese restaurant's select menu is tailored to tourists as well as regular customers, and dishes regarded as acquired tastes coexist happily with more familiar items. Lunch might be a set meal such as tempura with sashimi, also including soup, pickles, rice and fruit. Similar but slightly more elaborate set meals are served at night, each based upon a main dish such as beef teriyaki or hokkai nabe (a one-pot stew with fish and vegetables in miso). With your choice you will receive an appetizer, clear soup, yakitori or grilled fish, rice and fresh fruit.

LONDON *Quick Bite* Houlls (Wine Bar)

20 Bellevue Road,
  Wandsworth
  Common, SW17
01-767 1858

Map 10 C6

Open 12.30–2.45 & 6.30–10.45
  (Sun 7–10.30)
Closed 5 days Christmas

Typical prices: Lentil & split pea
  soup £1.50
  Poached salmon trout £6.95
Credit: Access, Amex, Visa

An atmospheric wine bar, Houlls makes a commendable contribution to this catalogue of healthy eating establishments. Start, perhaps, with grilled chicken kebab with yoghurt, or try a summer salad consisting of diced fresh vegetables with hazelnuts and a fromage blanc dressing. Seekers after simplicity may order grilled sirloin steak, poached salmon trout or grilled sole from a main course selection that also includes a vegetarian dish. Vegetables are cooked until just tender and well presented.

30 Brook Street, W1
01-629 2730

Map 11 B3

Lunch 12.30–2.30 Dinner
  6.30–10.30
Closed Sat, Sun, Bank Holidays &
  10 Days Christmas
Japanese cooking

Average price £22
Set L from £8.50
Set D from £22
Credit: Access, Amex, Diners, Visa

Light, nourishing soups form an integral part of a Japanese meal, and at Ikeda you can enjoy yasai sui-mono—vegetable broth with carrots, spring onions, bamboo shoots and Japanese mushrooms—or the popular miso soup with tofu. This well-patronised restaurant offers an imaginative selection of traditional Japanese dishes, including interesting delicate hors d'oeuvre and simmered specialities like chawan mushi—a combination of prawns, chicken, mushrooms and other vegetables with savoury egg custard. Fresh fruit is always available.

LONDON *Restaurant* Ikkyu

67 Tottenham Court
  Road, W1
01-636 9280

Map 11 C2

Lunch 12.30–2.30 Dinner 6–10.30
  (Sun from 7)
Closed Lunch Sun, all Sat & 8 days
  Christmas
Japanese cooking

Average price £16
Set meals from £4.50
Credit: Access, Amex, Diners, Visa

The food served in Japanese restaurants is so fundamentally healthy that it is difficult to put together a meal that is actually bad for you. Provided you go easy on the few deep-fried dishes such as tempura, you can relax and order anything that takes your fancy. At this busy basement restaurant, the choice is wide. Many customers find the meltingly tender sushi irresistible while others are happy to start with chicken and spring onion yakitori and progress to a fish dish such as grilled sea bream.

LONDON *Restaurant* Inigo Jones ★

14 Garrick Street, WC2
01-836 6456

Map 11 C3

Lunch 12.30–2.30 Dinner 5.30–
11.30 (Pre-theatre menu 5.30–7)
Closed Lunch Sat, all Sun & Bank
Holidays
French cooking

Average price £35
Set L & Set D £16.25
Credit: Access, Amex, Diners, Visa

Inigo Jones is a restaurant of quality. Chef Paul Gayler devises exciting menus, cooks and presents food beautifully and is sensitive to a growing public demand for healthier dishes. Wholemeal bread is always available. Vegetables are lightly cooked and supplied sans sauce on request. Rice, pasta and pulses all make regular appearances in innovative guises. Cream and butter are lavishly used but you will also find sauces made with skimmed milk or yoghurt. The vegetarian set menu includes marinated vegetable kebabs on braised pimento couscous.

LONDON *Restaurant* Ipphei

253 Finchley Road,
NW3
01-435 8602

Map 9 B2

Lunch 12.30–3 Dinner 6–10.30
Closed Tues, Bank Holidays &
1 week New Year
Japanese cooking

Average price £16
Set L from £6
Set D from £12
Credit: Access

The ambience is informal at this small Japanese restaurant. Sit at polished pine tables or make a booking for one of only four stools at the sushi bar. Set meals give customers the opportunity to try a variety of dishes. Dinner might start with a selection of chef's appetizers, followed by sashimi, then grilled fish, tempura, sukiyaki with rice, and pickles. Dessert will be fresh fruit or a water ice. The à la carte menu features favourites like tonkatsu (pork cutlet served with salad) and unadon (rice with broiled eel).

LONDON *Quick Bite* Jeeves Wine Cellar

139 Whitfield Street,
 W1
01-387 1952

Map 11 C2

Open 11.30–3.30 & 5.30–12
Closed Sun, some Bank Holidays
 & 1 week Christmas

Typical prices: Fettuccine
 carbonara £4.35
 Vegetarian crêpes £4.25
Credit: Access, Amex, Diners, Visa
Luncheon Vouchers accepted

Help yourself to a healthy lunch or dinner at the below-stairs buffet of this attractive wine bar. Cold roast beef, ham and turkey are carved to order and accompanied by a choice of up to a dozen very good salads. Daily hot dishes include lasagne, chilli con carne and the like—but the small restaurant section around the corner has some rather more adventurous dishes. Try the tagliatelle scampi or the grilled lamb steak with rosemary. Desserts include a beautifully fresh fruit salad.

LONDON *Quick Bite* Justin de Blank ★

54 Duke Street, W1
01-629 3174

Map 11 B3

Open 8.30–3.30 (Sat from 9) &
 4.30–9
Closed Dinner Sat, all Sun & Bank
 Holidays

Typical prices: Lamb & apricot
 casserole £4.10 Turmeric rice,
 pepper & hazelnut salad £1.80
Credit: Access, Visa
Luncheon Vouchers accepted

The flowers are fresh and the food simple and delicious at this self-service restaurant. Blackboards list lots of healthy dishes. Start, perhaps, with a delicately-flavoured cucumber, courgette and fennel soup, or try Justin's light and tangy mushroom mousse with granary bread. There are light quiches and pâtés and a good selection of salads, including a wonderful yellow rice, hazelnut and pepper mixture. Also hot specialities such as mushroom risotto.

85

LONDON *QuickBite* Justin de Blank at General Trading Company

144 Sloane Street,
SW1
01-730 6400

Map 12 B5

Open 9–5.15 (Sat till 2.30)
Closed Sun, Bank Holidays, Sat
preceding Bank Holiday Monday
& 1 week Christmas

Typical prices: Chicken, avocado
& pecan salad £4.35 Three
mushroom & olive risotto £4.30
Luncheon Vouchers accepted

Shoppers and local glitterati alike know this garden restaurant, whose pretty patio becomes a favourite meeting place on fine days. In summer, a suitably light menu offers poached salmon or cold rare roast beef with generous and well-constructed salads. In winter, hot soups and warming dishes make a welcome appearance. Vegetarian specialities, served daily, are interesting and imaginative. The spinach and celeriac roulade with green salad is an excellent choice. Pasta, rice and pulses appear regularly.

LONDON *Restaurant* Kensington Tandoori

1 Abingdon Road, W8
01-937 6182

Map 10 B4

Meals noon–midnight
Closed December 25
Indian cooking

Average price £15
· Credit: Access, Amex, Diners, Visa

Long opening hours are by no means the only attribute of this attractive Indian restaurant, but they are an asset worth mentioning in an area so close to Kensington High Street. The Kensington Tandoori offers a range of tikkas, biryanis and curries based on chicken, lamb, prawns and vegetables. Vegetarians might like to try the vegetable thali which includes mattar paneer, aloo gobi, tarka dal, raita, pilau rice and nan. Succulent chicken and lamb tikkas served with crisp salad are both recommended.

12 Lancashire Court,
New Bond Street, W1
01-629 9984

Map 11 C3

Open 12–2.30 & 6–9.30
Closed Dinner Sat, all Sun, Bank
Holidays & 10 days Christmas
Japanese cooking

Typical prices: Natto lunch £4.80
Yakitori lunch £3.80
Luncheon Vouchers accepted

This tiny Japanese restaurant fills quickly. Set lunches are simplicity itself and ideal for the healthy eater eager to experience new tastes. A starter such as seaweed with fresh octopus will be followed by miso soup. Then there's a choice of six main courses, including grilled fish with salads and rice, and barbecued chicken. Eel is a speciality here—try it barbecued for a tasty treat. Alternatively, sample Mr Takabayashi's exquisitely fresh sashimi. Fruit provides the finale. Evening meals are more elaborate but equally interesting.

LONDON *Restaurant* **Koto**

75 Parkway, NW1
01-482 2036

Map 11 B1

Lunch 12.30–2.30 (Sat from 12)
Dinner 6–10.30
Closed Sun & Bank Holidays
Japanese cooking

Average price £15
Set L from £4.30
Set D from £12.50
Credit: Access, Amex, Diners, Visa

Zensai—Japanese hors d'oeuvre—whet the appetite at this attractive restaurant near Regent's Park. The menu is explicit, and includes sashimi and sushi, simple grills and a selection of rolled vinegared rice dishes collectively called makizushi. Healthy eaters in search of new experiences might enjoy the nabe-mono. This is the Orient's answer to the fondue, with hot broth in place of oil. Try salmon and fresh vegetables cooked in soya bean broth, or monkfish or sea bream.

LONDON   *Quick Bite*   **Laurent**

428 Finchley Road,
  NW2
01-794 3603

Map 9 B2

Open 12–2 & 6–11
Closed Dinner Sun, Bank Holidays
  & August
Tunisian cooking

Typical prices: Vegetable
  couscous £4
  Couscous complet £5.50
Credit: Access, Visa

This friendly little restaurant specialises in couscous, a semolina-based dish from North Africa. Made by an expert, Tunisian Laurent Farrugia, it is everything a good budget dish should be—robust, filling and full of flavour. There are three versions: one vegetarian, another with the addition of lamb and spicy sausage and the 'Royal', which adds a lamb chop and brochette. Mint tea to follow, or choose a sorbet from the small international menu that sits alongside the Tunisian specialities, offering grilled sole or steak for more conservative customers.

LONDON   *Quick Bite*   **Lincoln's Inn Wine Bar**

49a Lincoln's Inn
  Fields, WC2
01-242 0058

Map 11 D3

Open 11.30–3 & 5.30–10.30
Closed Sat, Sun & Bank Holidays

Typical prices: Smoked chicken
  salad £3.50 Suprême of chicken
  stuffed wth asparagus £6.50
Credit: Access, Amex, Diners, Visa
Luncheon Vouchers accepted

Just a step away from the Old Curiosity Shop, this pleasantly informal wine bar offers a good selection of soundly prepared foods, including a ground floor cold counter which will appeal to the healthy eater. Choose from tuna and sweetcorn salad, home-cooked ham, peppered mackerel, smoked chicken, rare roast beef and smoked salmon salad. Some like it hot and will choose, instead, a hearty soup or steaming savoury dish. In the basement below waitresses serve an extended choice.

LONDON — *Restaurant* — London Hilton, Roof Restaurant

22 Park Lane, W1
01-493 8000

Map 12 B4

Lunch 12.30–2.30 (Sun 10.30–2.45) Dinner 7.30–1.30
Closed Lunch Sat and Dinner Sun
French cooking

Average price £30
Set L from £15.75 (Sun £15.90)
Credit: Access, Amex, Diners, Visa

Doing justice to one of the finest views in London is not an easy task but chef Sebastian Badia has proved more than equal to the challenge. His buffet is a gastronomic tableau with more than 50 different dishes. Heartier wholefoods such as brown rice, wholemeal bread and pulses have not yet reached these lofty heights but the menu includes delicate fish dishes, superb salads and lightly cooked vegetables. An imaginative vegetarian menu offers such treats as warm vegetable salad with tarragon dressing, and sliced artichoke hearts glazed with coriander.

LONDON — *Restaurant* — Lou Pescadou

241 Old Brompton Road, SW5
01-370 1057

Map 12 A5

Lunch 12.30–3 Dinner 6.30–12

Average price £15
Credit: Access, Amex, Diners, Visa
Luncheon Vouchers accepted

Fish has pride of place at this friendly French restaurant. The choice is varied and includes grilled lemon sole, skate, monkfish, turbot, cod, Dover sole and red mullet. Oysters are a speciality and you'll also find mussels, crab, squid and coquilles on the menu. If nothing in the net appeals, try a pizza, an omelette or a dish of al dente pasta with fresh and very tasty tomato and basil sauce. Meat-lovers are not forgotten—steaks are available and can be simply grilled if required—and there are regular vegetarian dishes.

LONDON

89

LONDON — *Quick Bite* — Mandeer ★

21 Hanway Place,
  Tottenham Court
  Road, W1
01-323 0660

Map 11 C3

Open 12–3 & 6–10.15
Closed Sun & 1 week Christmas
Indian vegetarian cooking

Typical prices: Lentil soup with
  vegetables £2.20
Thali Mandeer £7.25
Credit: Access, Amex, Diners, Visa
Luncheon Vouchers accepted

The thalis (set meals) at this excellent Indian vegetarian restaurant are very good value. In addition to the regular and de luxe thalis, there are specials tailored to those unable to tolerate garlic or onion, and another for vegans. Everything is carefully prepared in spotless kitchens to a high standard. From the main menu, you might try yoghurt or lentil soup, then a special vegetable dish like spiced spinach or sweet and sour yellow dried peas, with brown rice, nuts and raisins. As a finale there are lots of fresh fruit desserts, sorbets and lassis.

LONDON — *Quick Bite* — Manna

4 Erskine Road, NW3
01-722 8028

Map 11 B1

Open 6.30–12
Closed Bank Holidays
Vegetarian wholefood cooking

Typical prices: Manna hot pot
  £3.95 Spinach pancakes with
  cheese & rice £4.10

The salads are extra-special at this deservedly popular restaurant just off Regent's Park. It is obvious that raw materials are selected with care and combined to produce both an interesting flavour and stunning composite picture. The varied menu includes a soup such as Chinese vegetable, served with a wonderful home-baked wholemeal roll. Alternatively try the arame seaweed salad for a sensational taste. Main courses like black-eyed bean casserole with peppers and rice are very enjoyable.

Quick Bite

Matono

25 Brewer Street, W1
01-734 1859

Map 11 C3

Open 12–2.30 & 6–12
Closed Lunch Sun
Japanese cooking

Typical prices: Oshizushi from £7
  Assorted sushi from £10
Credit: Access, Amex, Diners, Visa

There's a tranquil atmosphere at this Japanese restaurant, created in part by a water garden in the sushi bar opposite the entrance. The fish fillets are set out in a glass display case and you may watch the talented sushi chef at work behind a high wooden counter. Oshizushi is available with salmon, sea eel or mackerel, and they also serve the beautifully boxed chirashizushi—fish fillets arranged on a bed of vinegared rice with sculpted vegetables. The à la carte menu includes items like sea urchin, salmon roe and cuttlefish.

7 Boston Parade,
  Boston Road, W7
01-567 9708

Map 10 A5

143 Knightsbridge,
  SW1
01-225 2553

Map 12 B4

7 Boston Parade open 12–3 &
  5.30–11 (Sun 12–2 & 7–10.30)
Closed some Bank Holiday
  Mondays, January 1 & December
  25 & 26

143 Knightsbridge open 11–3 &
  5.30–11 (Sun 11.30–2.30 &
  6.30–10.30)
Closed 1–2 days Christmas

Chinese cooking

Typical prices: Szechuan 'sea-
  spices' aubergine £2.50
  Vegetarian set meal £8.90 (for
  two)
Credit: Access, Amex, Diners, Visa
Luncheon Vouchers accepted

Chinese cooking and classical music combine to make
these wine bars decidedly different from any others. The
menu at both is extensive but not explicit so consult the
helpful staff when attempting to select the most healthy
dishes. Start with a soup, perhaps, then try one of the chef's
specialities such as lemon chicken or king prawn fu-yung.
Vegetarians who visit Boston Parade are catered for with
noodle and rice specialities while the newer Knightsbridge
restaurant offers a vegetarian set dinner for two. Lychees
make a refreshing dessert.

Changes in data may occur in establishments
after the Guide goes to press. Prices should be
taken as indications rather than firm quotes.

Restaurant **Memories of India**

18 Gloucester Road,
  SW7
01-589 6450

Map 12 A4

Lunch 12–2.30 Dinner 5.30–11.30
Closed December 25 & 26
Indian cooking

Average price £15
Set L & Set D £10.50
Credit: Access, Amex, Diners, Visa

Skilful cooking, helpful service and attractive surroundings
have established this smart restaurant as a popular place
on London's culinary carousel. The detailed menu gives
healthy eaters plenty of choice. Tandoori chicken, diced
lamb or king prawns, lightly charred on the outside, moist
and succulent within, are ideal dishes. Add very good
Basmati rice from Pakistan—and a crisp green salad or
mixed raita. There are plenty of vegetable dishes, any one
of which will be served as a main course on request, and
mangoes and lychees to follow.

LONDON *Restaurant* **Le Meridien Piccadilly,
Terrace Garden Restaurant**

Piccadilly, W1
01-734 8000

Map 11 C3

Meals 7am–midnight (Sun from
  8am)

Average price £15
Set L £12.50
Credit: Access, Amex, Diners, Visa

Escape from the hubbub of city streets to this green oasis
above Piccadilly. Under a canopied glass roof, a profusion
of plants creates a light airy ambience. This lightness of
touch is evident in the menu, which provides several
healthy dishes such as steamed angler fish with basil and
tomato and grilled fillets of Dover sole. There are always
exciting salads such as smoked chicken breast with mango
and grapefruit and vegetarian dishes are available on
request. Exotic fruit salads give sweet satisfaction.

93

97 Stoke Newington
  Church Street, N16
01-254 1025

Map 9 D2

Open noon–midnight
Closed 1 week Christmas
Vegetarian cooking

Typical prices: Lentil pâté £1.45
  Brochette de légumes £4.20
(Minimum mealtime charge)

Watching all the world go by from the large windows of this vegetarian corner restaurant makes eating here fun and informal. The evening menu changes daily but always includes about half a dozen starters, main courses and desserts. A typical meal might be houmus with pitta bread or gazpacho soup, followed by vegetable brochette or broccoli and almond strudel, with fresh fruit salad for afters. You could sample most of the dishes on the menu in a composite called 'Tastie Maisie'. A simplified menu operates at lunchtime offering salads and light snacks.

LONDON *Restaurant* **Mogul**

10 Greenwich Church
  Street, SE10
01-858 6790

Map 10 D5

Lunch 12–2.30 Dinner 6–11.30
  (Sat till 11.45)
Closed December 25 & 26
Indian cooking

Average price £12
Set meals from £5.50
Credit: Access, Amex, Diners, Visa

Biryanis are a speciality of the North Indian (Mogul) style of cooking found at this comfortable restaurant. The skilful handling of spices results in such enjoyable dishes as prawn biryani. Simple dishes include a good range of tandooris grilled in a charcoal-fired, clay oven. Try the sizzler special or tandoori chooza, or pick a mixture of dishes from the vegetable specialities. Choose from six different breads, including wholemeal parathas and chapatis. Round the meal off with mango or lychees.

LONDON *QuickBite* Mulford's Wine Bar ★

127 Shepherd's Bush
   Road, W6
01-603 2229

Map 10 B5

Open 12–3 & 5.30–11 (Sat 6–11,
   Sun 7–10.30)
Closed Bank Holidays &
   December 24–January 1

Typical prices: Nouvelle terrine
£1.70 King prawns & salad £4.75
Credit: Access, Amex, Diners, Visa

Fresh, interesting and wholesome food sets this wine bar apart from some of its rivals. The short blackboard menu changes every day but a typical meal for a healthy eater might consist of carrot and avocado timbale or nouvelle terrine, followed by home-baked ham and salad, or prawn and courgette tagliatelle. Lovers of red meat will find grilled rump steak always on the menu and there is usually a vegetarian dish. Everything is made on the premises by redoubtable cook Rebecca Allen, and owners Peter and Venetia Mulford create a comfortable atmosphere.

LONDON *Restaurant* Nakamura

31 Marylebone Lane,
   W1
01-935 2931

Map 11 B3

Lunch 12–2.30 Dinner 6–10.30
Closed Lunch Sun, all Sat & Bank
   Holidays
Japanese cooking

Average price £18
Set L from £6.50
Set D from £21
Credit: Access, Amex, Diners, Visa

Prime raw materials are prepared with considerable care at this Japanese restaurant in Marylebone Lane. A colourful poster in the sushi bar illustrates the wide range of fish available, from mackerel, cuttlefish and scallops to salmon roe (considered a speciality). The general menu has plenty for the healthy eater, including grilled salmon, cod, eel or prawns, and beef teriyaki with salad. Vegetable dishes make much of mushrooms and nori and light soups may be drunk throughout the meal to cleanse the palate.

LONDON   *QuickBite*   Nanten

6 Blandford Street, W1
01-935 6319

Map 11 B3

Open 12–2 & 6–10
Closed Lunch Sat, all Sun, Bank
  Holidays & January 1–3
Japanese cooking

Typical prices: Yakitori lunch
  £7.20 Sashimi £5.00
Credit: Access, Amex, Diners, Visa

Booking is advised at this very popular Japanese restaurant and yakitori bar. Space is limited to a few tables, with most customers opting to sit on stools at the bar behind which the food is prepared and served. Yakitori—bamboo skewers on which marinated food is cooked over a charcoal fire—are slimmer and less substantial than the kebabs they resemble, and are ideal for healthy eaters. Varieties include chicken, beef, asparagus, spring onion and mushroom. Add clear soup, grilled salmon, noodles and mixed vegetable salad for a delicious and nutritious meal.

LONDON   *Restaurant*   Neal Street Restaurant

26 Neal Street, WC2
01-836 8368

Map 11 C3

Lunch 12.30–2.30 Dinner 7.30–11
Closed Lunch Sat, all Sun, Bank
  Holidays and 1 week Christmas–
  New Year

Average price £25
Credit: Access, Amex, Diners, Visa

This chic modern restaurant is popular all the year round and no more so than in autumn when Mr Antonio Carluccio, the managing director, imports white truffles and black chanterelle mushrooms especially for gastronomes. The menu, which changes every month, is the same for lunch and dinner and includes a number of interesting fish dishes such as pink trout with chives and ginger, and monkfish with fennel and saffron sauce. There are well chosen vegetables of good quality and a selection of salads.

Quick Bite

Neal's Yard Bakery & Tea Room

6 Neal's Yard, Covent
   Garden, WC2
01-836 5199

Map 11 C3

Open 10.30–8 (Wed till 3.30, Sat
   till 4.30)
Closed Sun, Bank Holidays &
   Christmas–New Year
Vegetarian cooking

Typical prices: Vegetarian pizza
   £1.30 Stuffed pitta bread 90p
Luncheon Vouchers accepted

For a snack or early evening meal that's as nutritious as it is delicious, try the fare at this vegetarian tea room in Covent Garden. Everything here is baked with 100% wholemeal stoneground flour. The appetising cakes owe their sweetness to dried fruits and honey—no sugar is used in their preparation. Savouries, available after midday, include soups, pizzas, stuffed pitta bread and salads. Vegan dishes such as vegetable pasties are also on offer together with a tempting selection of wholemeal breads. There is a good range of teas, tisanes and fruit juices, plus coffee.

LONDON

Quick Bite

Neal's Yard Bakery at the Ecology Centre

45 Shelton Street, WC2
01-379 4324

Map 11 C3

Open 10–5
Closed Sun & Bank Holidays
Vegetarian cooking

Typical prices: Soup & wholemeal
   roll £1.20
   Pizza & mixed salad £2.10
Luncheon Vouchers accepted

The salads deserve special mention at this cheerful café on the ground floor of the London Ecology Centre. Crisp, complex and well dressed, they make a meal on their own, or can be enjoyed in the company of vegetarian favourites like vegetable pâté, bean burgers or houmus with salad. Hot food is available from noon and includes soup such as spicy lentil, minestrone or tomato and savoury dishes like ratatouille with brown rice and mixed salad. No puds as such but a good range of wholesome sugar-free bakes.

LONDON *Quick Bite* Nontas

16 Camden High
  Street, NW1
01-387 4579

Map 11 C1

Open 12–2.45 & 6–11.30
Closed Sun, Bank Holidays &
  2 days Christmas
Greek cooking

Typical prices: Charcoal-grilled
  red mullet £4.50
  Chicken kebab £3.25
Credit: Access, Amex, Diners

Good honest Greek cooking is the hallmark of this friendly and unfussy neighbourhood bistro. A healthy meal might include a starter like yoghurt and cucumber salad or mixed green salad with feta and olives. Charcoal-grilled red mullet is a must whenever it is on the menu; alternatively try the grilled king prawns, or any of the fish or meat kebabs. Good salads, but no hot choice for vegetarians. A platter of fresh fruit makes a fine ending, with yoghurt and honey or rosewater ice as appetising alternatives.

LONDON *Restaurant* Nouveau Quiche

301 New Cross Road,
  SE14
01-691 3686

Map 10 D5

Dinner only 6–11 (Sun 12–2.30 &
  7–11)
Closed 2 weeks August & 1 week
  Christmas

Average price £10
(Minimum charge £5 after 7 pm)
Credit: Access, Visa

This cooperative venture opposite Deptford Town Hall has become a popular meeting place thanks to food that is healthy, hearty and highly imaginative. The menu changes twice a month but always includes one or two finely balanced soups such as miso and vegetable or parsnip and almond. The majority of main courses are vegetarian specialities such as Ghanaian nut stew or walnut-stuffed aubergines but meat-lovers can enjoy healthy dishes like baked chicken breast with fresh tarragon and lime.

26 Kingly Street, W1
01-437 9471

Map 11 C3

Open 10–7 (Sat 10.30–5)
Closed Sun
Vegetarian wholefood cooking

Typical prices: Wholewheat, lentil
& vegetable hot pot £2.25
Mixed grains & pasta £2.25
Luncheon Vouchers accepted

Simple, well-seasoned and capably cooked food has long been the hallmark of this modest self-service vegetarian restaurant at the back of a small shop. A blackboard lists the dishes of the day: always a soup, several hot dishes and about a dozen different salads with wholemeal bread. You might choose mixed bean casserole or vegetable lasagne, or settle for a snack such as a chilli bean pancake roll with tomato sauce and natural yoghurt. Filled baked potatoes are always available and desserts include fruit salad, hot fruit crumble and wholesome cakes.

130 Regent's Park
Road, NW1
01-586 5486

Map 11 B1

Open 12.30–2.30 & 7–11
Closed Sun, Bank Holidays &
10 days Christmas

Typical prices: Bacon, apple &
celery salad £2.95 Cold salmon
trout with cucumber salad £4.25
Credit: Access, Amex, Diners, Visa

Imaginative, appetising and well-prepared food makes Odette's a pleasant place to while away a few hours. Starters include minted pear vinaigrette and a delicious light textured carrot soup served with good granary bread. To follow, select a simple main course such as the vegetarian moussaka. Jacket potatoes are always available and there's a good selection of salads prepared from crisp, fresh, raw ingredients. Desserts include fresh fruit salad or fruit sorbets.

LONDON · *Restaurant* · Old Poodle Dog Restaurant

Royal Court Hotel,
Sloane Square, SW1
01-730 1499

Map 12 B5

Lunch 12–2.30 Dinner 6–10.30

Average price £20
Set L & Set D £9.95
Credit: Access, Amex, Diners, Visa

Sloane rangers with discerning taste patronise this elegant restaurant in the Royal Court Hotel. A healthy meal could commence with crudités, go on to grilled Dover sole and finish with fresh fruit. The menu also includes dishes like grilled calf's liver, traditional roasts and interesting salads such as salade japonaise with its orange and grapefruit segments tossed with peach, apple, nuts and yoghurt. Vegetarians are exceptionally well catered for with a separate menu that includes main courses like yam, bean and beet casserole.

LONDON · *Restaurant* · One Two Three

27 Davies Street, W1
01-409 0750

Map 11 B3

Lunch 12–2.30 Dinner 6.30–10.30
Closed Sat, Sun, Bank Holidays &
    Christmas-early January
Japanese cooking

Average price: £25
Set L from £7.50
Set D from £25
Credit: Access, Amex, Diners, Visa

First-class Japanese cooking depends upon the highest-quality raw materials, and these are in evidence at this simple but stylish restaurant in the heart of Mayfair. Dishes are categorised by cooking method, making selection simple for the healthy eater. Simmered foods include spring greens with scrambled egg, for instance, and there is a long list of grilled items including yakitori, and teriyaki steaks and fish dishes. Sashimi is a good choice, thanks to perfectly fresh fish. Selection of fruit to follow.

LONDON   *QuickBite*   **Palings Wine Bar**

25 Hanover Square,
  W1
01-408 0935

Map 11 C3

Open 11.30–3 & 5.30–11
Closed Lunch Sat, all Sun, Bank
  Holidays & 3 days Christmas

Typical prices: Smoked mackerel
  & salad £2.85
  Cold chicken & Waldorf salad £3
Credit: Access, Amex, Diners, Visa
Luncheon Vouchers accepted

Arrive early to be sure of a table at this smart basement wine bar in Hanover Square. The cold buffet, available noon and night, provides plenty of healthy choices, including good rare roast beef, barbecued chicken and smoked mackerel, and a choice of four or five simple salads like spinach and mushroom, and red cabbage and horseradish, with wholemeal bread. There are composite salads too. Try the chicken and pasta in yoghurt dressing. At lunchtime there are hot dishes, including at least one vegetarian item. Only light snacks after 9.30 and at weekends.

LONDON   *QuickBite*   **Parsons**

311 Fulham Road,
  SW10
01-352 0651

Map 12 A6

Open noon–12.30am (Sun till
  midnight)
Closed December 25 & 26

Typical prices: Tuna fish & pasta
  salad £4.10
  Vegetarian burritos £3.35
Credit: Access, Amex, Diners, Visa
Luncheon Vouchers accepted

The fans turn at Parsons from midday to midnight, keeping the air—and the customers—circulating. The service is informal and friendly and a varied menu provides plenty of choice. Hot from the charcoal grill come tender steaks or marinated kebabs, served with a jacket potato or mixed salad. Composite salads include niçoise, tuna and pasta and a vegetarian fruit and cottage cheese platter. For lighter bites there are soups and sandwiches. For desserts, try the lemon water ice or fresh mango sorbet.

LONDON   *QuickBite*   Pasta Fino

27 Frith Street, W1
01-439 8900

Map 11 C3

Open 12–11.30
Closed Sun, Bank Holidays &
1 week Christmas

Typical prices: Spaghetti marinara
£2.75
Tagliatelle giardiniera £3.25
Credit: Access, Visa

Home-made pasta is the raison d'être of this eating place which is so popular at lunchtime that it is best to get there early. Sauces tend to be on the rich side but healthy eaters might try pasta giardiniera, with market-fresh vegetables, or marinara, a simmered tomato sauce flavoured with fresh basil. All the pasta is produced on the premises in one of three colours, thanks to the introduction of tomato and spinach to some of the dough. Wholewheat spaghetti is also available.

LONDON   *QuickBite*   Pasta Underground

214 Camden High
Street, NW1
01-482 0010

Map 11 C1

Open 12–3 & 6–11
Closed Lunch Sat, Dinner Sun &
Bank Holidays

Typical prices: Chicken brochette
£3.60 Feta salad £3.50

Fresh pasta, made daily on the premises, is the particular attraction of this cheerful basement restaurant. There are seven different varieties to choose from. Try penne with tomatoes, tuna and olives, or the house speciality— spaghettini with pesto and sliced potatoes. Other delicious choices include grilled marinated chicken with ginger, lime, orange and soy sauce, and tempura king prawns with vegetables. The salads include a popular Mediterranean medley with feta cheese. Excellent fruit sorbets.

205 Haverstock Hill,
  NW3
01-435 6744

Map 9 C3

Lunch 12–2.30 (Sun till 2) Dinner
  7–11.30
Closed Lunch Sat, Dinner Sun &
  Bank Holidays
French cooking

Average price £20
Set L & Set D £8.95
Credit: Amex, Diners, Visa

Peacheys is as popular as ever and booking is advisable for one of their closely grouped tables. The large menu includes a variety of modern and more classical French dishes. You might start with grilled goats' cheese coated in walnuts and breadcrumbs and served with a spinach and chicory salad, and choose for your main dish poached sea bass with a fresh coriander and tomato sauce. Guests who prefer simple unsauced food can usually be accommodated. Vegetarians are not specifically catered for but suitable dishes can be supplied upon request.

LONDON *Quick Bite* Le Petit Prince

5 Holmes Road, NW5
01-267 0752

Map 9 C3

Open 12–2.30 & 7–11.30
Closed Lunch Sun & Mon, also
  Lunch June–September & 1 week
  Christmas
North African cooking

Typical prices: Vegetable
  couscous £3.30
  Royal couscous £7.20

Take a hearty appetite to this very relaxed restaurant in Kentish Town, where light, refreshing starters leave plenty of room for the mainstay of the meal, couscous. This North African dish, comprising steamed semolina grains and vegetables in broth, can be served solo or with the meat of your choice—lamb kebab, braised chicken or home-made meatballs maybe. A small bowl of hot pepper paste adds fire to the fuel. Alternatively there is a range of salads or simple grills. Sweets include sorbet.

LONDON — *Restaurant* — Pollyanna's

2 Battersea Rise,
 SW11
01-228 0316

Map 10 C6

Lunch (Sun only) 1–3 Dinner 7–12
Closed Sun eve, January 1 &
 4 days Christmas

Average price £20
Set L £9.95
Set D £10.95
Credit: Access, Amex, Visa

Eamonn Connolly cooks with a light touch and one has the impression that every dish on the menu has been carefully constructed with much skill and imagination. There are lots of healthy starters such as marinated salmon, and smoked turkey salad, and main courses include grills and fish which will be served plainly if requested. The vegetarian items are inviting and unusual. Try a red and green pepper mousse followed by a salad of baby vegetables. Salads include tabbouleh, cucumber and orange, and a combination of dried fruit and nuts.

LONDON — *Quick Bite* — Poons

4 Leicester Street,
 WC2
01-437 1528

27 Lisle Street, WC2
01-437 4549

Map 11 C3

Open 12–11.30
Closed Sun (Leicester Street), Mon
 (Lisle Street) & 3 days Christmas
Chinese cooking

Typical prices: White cooked
 prawns with ginger £4
 Steamed chicken £2.90
Set Meals from £10 for two (Lisle
 Street)

It takes time to peruse the menu common to both these modest restaurants—there are 200 items listed. Although frying is a popular method of cooking, healthy eaters will find a good selection of braised and steamed dishes, including steamed fresh scallops, steamed mushrooms with minced prawn stuffing and braised prawns with fresh ginger. Wind-dried foods are a speciality, and sweets include almond-flavoured bean curd. Staff are friendly and helpful. Booking recommended.

LONDON *Quick Bite* Raj Bhelpoori House

19 Camden High
Street, NW1
01-388 6663

Map 11 C1

Open 12–11.30
Indian vegetarian cooking

Typical prices: Aloo chana chat £1
Raj thali £3.70
Credit: Access, Amex, Diners, Visa
Luncheon Vouchers accepted

Drink sweet or salted lassi with your judiciously spiced meal at this friendly vegetarian restaurant. The cooking, South Indian in origin, includes some tasty treats for healthy eaters. Start, perhaps, with a vegetable kebab with salad, and then try one of the pancakes, or dosas. The paper dosa, wafer-thin and served with a separate vegetable filling, is a good choice. Extras include Indian breads and traditional side dishes like raita—chopped cucumber and carrot in spiced yoghurt. Sweets are extra rich and sugary so have another glass of lassi instead.

LONDON *Quick Bite* Rani

3 Long Lane, N3
01-349 4386

Map 9 B1

Open 12.30–2 & 6–10.30
Closed December 25
Indian vegetarian cooking

Typical prices: Plain dosa £2.50
Special thali £6
(Minimum evening charge £4)
Credit: Access, Visa

There's a different curry every day of the week at this bright and lively Indian vegetarian restaurant. On Monday the choice is gram flour vermicelli cooked with tomatoes and onions; on Friday the principal ingredient is baby cucumber; and Sunday's suggestion is a dry mixed vegetable curry with toasted wholemeal baps. There are three thalis—ranging from the simple to the super—and dosas, breads and rice dishes. An unusually extensive list of desserts includes a range of five fresh-fruit sorbets.

Quick Bite

Ravenscourt Park Tea House

Ravenscourt Park, W6

Map 10 A5

Open 10–5 (Sun till 6)
Closed Good Friday & 9 days
  Christmas
Vegetarian cooking

Typical prices: Red bean goulash
£1.20 Vegetarian burger £1
Luncheon Vouchers accepted

All the food, with the exception of the ices, is prepared on the premises at this unpretentious little café slap bang in the centre of Ravenscourt Park. Food is displayed on a counter or detailed on the blackboard. They offer two soups, perhaps barley broth and green pea—with good wholemeal bread. Dish of the day might be mushroom and vegetable slice with sauce, and there's a range of bakes and simple cakes, plus filled wholemeal rolls for healthy eaters in a hurry. Organic vegetables are used where possible and cheeses are vegetarian.

LONDON

Quick Bite

Ravi Shankar

135 Drummond Street,
  NW1
01-388 6458

Map 11 C2

Open 12–11
Indian vegetarian cooking

Typical prices: Mysore thali £3.95
  Samosa £1.10
Credit: Access, Amex, Diners, Visa
Luncheon Vouchers accepted

Conveniently placed for Euston Station, this Indian vegetarian restaurant offers satisfying food at reasonable prices. Long opening hours and a seven-day week make it a popular venue for staff from the nearby radio and television centres and, whether you pop in for a glass of freshly-squeezed orange juice or talk business over a thali, the staff will make you welcome. Try an uthappam—a sort of lentil pizza topped with a spicy tomato, onion and coconut mixture—teamed with a raita.

107

LONDON

Quick Bite

Raw Deal

65 York Street, W1
01-262 4841

Map 11 B2

Open 10–10 (Sat till 11)
Closed Sun, Bank Holidays &
1 week Christmas
Vegetarian cooking

Typical prices: Wholemeal ravioli
provençale £2.30 Chick pea &
aubergine savoury £2.50
(Minimum charge £1.75)
Luncheon Vouchers accepted

The secret of success for this vegetarian restaurant is its simplicity. No elaborate menu, no artful appetisers, just good-quality, fresh food at reasonable prices. Start with home-made soup of the day, then choose from 12 colourful salads displayed on the counter. Two hot dishes are offered daily. Examples include chick pea and aubergine savoury and brown rice with fennel and peas. Follow with fruit salad, or try the home-made yoghurt. Fresh fruit juices and herb teas are healthy thirst quenchers.

LONDON

Quick Bite

**Royal Festival Hall,
Riverside Café**

South Bank, SE1
01-928 3246

Map 12 D4

Open 10–8 (Fri–Sun till 10)
Closed December 25 & Lunch
December 26

Typical prices: Black-eyed bean
soup 85p
Vegetable lasagne £2.75
Luncheon Vouchers accepted

Watch the traffic on the Thames while enjoying a lunch or supper at this stylish establishment much patronised by concert-goers and artists. Keep it simple, with soup and a sandwich or, for a more substantial meal, try a mushroom salad followed by poached halibut or grilled chicken breast. Cold platters and a large choice of side salads are displayed on the self-service counter and there are hot specials like vegetable lasagne and lentil stew. Fresh fruit salad or yoghurt to follow.

LONDON

LONDON *Quick Bite* Sabras

263 High Road,
  Willesden Green,
  NW10
01-459 0340

Map 9 A3

Open 12.30–9.15
Closed Mon, 2 weeks August &
  2 weeks Christmas
Indian vegetarian cooking

Typical prices: Deluxe thali £7
  Mini thali £5
Credit: Access, Amex, Diners, Visa
Luncheon Vouchers accepted

It is satisfying to find yet another restaurant devoting itself to the vegetarian cuisine of one continent. Most of the dishes at Sabras are from southern India and the only difficulty may be in deciding what to try first. Don't miss dhokala—a steamed square of light-textured gram flour, lentils and yoghurt, served with mustard seeds, coconut and fresh coriander. There are superb curries and spiced dishes aplenty, with refreshing lassi (home-made yoghurt blended with ice) to drink. Fresh juices, too, including carrot and cucumber, and lemon tea to follow.

LONDON *Restaurant* Saga

43 South Molton
  Street, W1
01-408 2236

Map 11 B3

Lunch 12.30–2.30 Dinner 6.30–10
Closed Sun, Bank Holidays,
  1 week August & 10 days
  Christmas
Japanese cooking

Average price £30
Set D from £20
Credit: Access, Amex, Diners, Visa

Booking is vital at this smart and stylish Japanese restaurant. Diners have a number of choices—they can feast on raw fish at the sushi bar, go for the hotplate grills at the teppan-yaki counter, or choose from the main menu. Both presentation and preparation are to a high standard, and there are plenty of options for healthy eaters. Su-no-mono—marinated octopus, mackerel and seaweed—makes a tasty appetiser, while a main course could be grilled sea bass or salmon or beef teriyaki. Fruit and sorbet to follow.

LONDON *Quick Bite* Sagarmatha

339 Euston Road,
  NW1
01-387 6531

Map 11 C2

Open 12–2.45 & 6–11.45
Closed December 25 & 26
Indian cooking

Typical prices: Chaola £2.75
  Chicken tikka £2.95
Credit: Visa
Luncheon Vouchers accepted

Sagarmatha is the Nepali for Mount Everest, which is on the border of Nepal and Tibet—hence the strong Tibetan influence on the largely Hindu menu at this modest but very fine restaurant. The tandoori specialities are well recommended, and chicken tikka would make a good choice for those for whom healthy eating is important. There are excellent thalis, unbeatable biryanis, fragrant pilaus and a good variety of vegetable dishes, salads and sambals like raita. Delicious lychees, mangoes and guavas for dessert.

LONDON *Restaurant* Shaheen of Knightsbridge

225 Brompton Road,
  SW3
01-581 5329

Map 12 B5

Meals noon–midnight
Indian cooking

Average price £15
Credit: Access, Amex, Diners, Visa

First-class raw materials are prepared and cooked with quiet competence at this smart Indian restaurant. The tandoori provides a number of dishes that are ideal for healthy eaters, such as mildly spiced king prawns or chicken tikka. Vegetables range from a simple dhal to a full-flavoured vegetable curry and the Basmati rice is cooked to perfection. Two simple salads are also on the menu and there are six different Indian breads. Desserts include a choice of mango, lychees, guava or pineapple.

16 Cheval Place, SW7
01-589 7918

Map 12 B4

Lunch 12–2.30 Dinner 7–11.30
Closed Sun & Bank Holidays
Pakistani cooking

Average price £20
Set L £9.75
Credit: Access, Amex, Diners, Visa

The menu at this long-established Pakistani restaurant is wonderfully explicit, making the choice of a healthy dish simplicity itself. Starters include shorba—a herbed consommé—or you can break with Indian tradition and choose melon or grapefruit. Tandoori specialities like seekh kebab or grilled king prawns are simple and tasty. The rice dishes and breads are excellent and vegetarians are well catered for with dishes like Basmati rice cooked with browned onions and spices, or the popular vegetable kebab. Fresh fruit to follow.

41 Cathedral Place,
  Paternoster Square,
  EC4
01-236 5974

Map 11 D3

Open 7.30–6.15
Closed Sat, Sun, Bank Holidays &
  3–4 days Christmas

Typical prices: Bean chilli &
  brown rice £2.40
  Apricot & walnut cake 65p
(Minimum lunchtime charge
  £1.50)
Luncheon Vouchers accepted

The choice is anything but slender at this little gem of a vegetarian restaurant, surrounded by office blocks. The self-service counter positively groans with generously-filled wholemeal baps and rolls, and there are up to seven super salads, including cabbage and cauliflower. Pulses are put to good use in dishes like bean moussaka and chick pea cutlets, and the vegetable and nut combinations are equally successful. Fresh fruit salad and a good choice of healthy cakes to follow.

18 Theberton Street,
  N1
01-359 8033

Map 11 D1

Lunch 12–3 Dinner 6–11
Closed December 25 & 26
Indian vegetarian cooking

Average price £9
Credit: Amex, Visa

Within weeks of opening, this coolly contemporary restaurant had attracted a lively local clientele. The vegetarian
menu is comprised largely of dishes from southern India
and includes several items ideal for the health-conscious
diner. Begin, perhaps, with khati—a vegetable kebab
served with salad—and then sample one of the five
delicious dosas, all served with the pale green coconut
chutney that owes its colour to fresh coriander. Accompany
your meal with sweet or salted lassi.

LONDON *Restaurant* **Swiss Centre**

Leicester Square, W1
01-734 1291

Map 11 C3

Lunch 12–2.30 Dinner 6–12 (Sun
  till 11)
Closed December 25 & 26
Swiss cooking

Average price £20
Set L & Set D £19.50 (Chesa)
Credit: Access, Amex, Diners, Visa

The Swiss Centre restaurants have plenty to offer the
health-conscious. At the elegant Chesa on New Coventry
Street you can dine in style on air-dried beef and ham from
the Engadine, followed by perch fillets with onion, tomato
and avocado. The Locanda fondue restaurant (with a
vegetarian fondue) has an outstanding salad bar. All four
restaurants, including the Taverne (Swiss regional cooking) and the Rendezvous (snacks and grills) have a
vegetarian menu offering a selection of inexpensive dishes.

25 Marylebone High
  Street, W1
01-486 1872

Map 11 B2

Open noon–midnight
Closed December 25 & 26
Turkish cooking

Typical prices: Imam biyaldi £1.80
  Grilled lambs' kidneys £4.85
Credit: Access, Amex, Diners, Visa

Colourful murals and large ornamental brass trays provide an authentic background for traditional Turkish food at this popular restaurant. Good-quality raw materials and judicious use of herbs and spices create dishes that are full of flavour. The karisik meze, a platter of mixed hors d'oeuvre, makes a good starter, or you could try their home-made lentil soup. A recent addition is a large self-service salad bar. There are plenty of grilled dishes to suit the slimmer or healthy eater, including marinated chicken breast cooked over charcoal. Vegetarian dishes too.

19 Exhibition Road,
  SW7
01-584 8359

Map 12 A5

Open 12–2.30 & 6.30–11 (Sun
  12.30–3 & 6.30–11)
Closed Bank Holiday weekends &
  2 days Christmas
Thai cooking

Typical prices: Egg noodles &
  chicken £3.75
  Vegetarian noodles £3.75
Credit Access, Amex, Diners, Visa

Just a short walk from South Kensington tube station is this stylish Thai restaurant. Customers are given a friendly welcome, whether they be shoppers in search of a quick bite, or dedicated diners with time to spare. The former will appreciate the quick noodle menu, with dishes such as angel's hair noodles with slivered beef. The main menu is extensive and interesting. Try the crab claw and prawn hot pot with a spicy salad and rice, and finish on a healthy note with fresh tropical fruits or sorbet.

113

LONDON
Restaurant
Twenty Trinity Gardens

20 Trinity Gardens,
  SW9
01-733 8838

Map 10 C6

Lunch 12.30–2.30 Dinner 7–10.30
Closed Lunch Sat, all Sun, Bank
  Holidays & 1 week Christmas

Average price £14
Set L & Set D £7.50 & £10.50
Credit: Visa

This modish, tiled restaurant is a particularly popular meeting place for the smart young set. In summer there's a special lunchtime salad menu, served al fresco on fine days, which includes sole and salmon trout terrine, smoked mackerel and spring chicken salad. Set meals are the general pattern (you can choose a single dish at lunchtime) and a typical two-course meal might be avocado, grapefruit and prawn salad followed by kingfish steak with coconut sauce. There's always a vegetarian dish such as cashew nut and mushroom cutlets.

LONDON
Quick Bite
Victoria & Albert Museum, New Restaurant

Cromwell Road, SW7
01-581 2159

Map 12 A5

Open 10–5 (Sun 2.30–5.30)
Closed Fri, January 1, May Bank
  Holiday, December 25 & 26

Typical prices: Split pea & lentil
  soup 85p Three bean salad 55p

Museums are easy on the eye but hard on the feet. Take a welcome break at this light and airy restaurant and enjoy a healthy snack at the same time. You don't have to be a museum visitor to eat here as the access in Exhibition Road bypasses the entrance desk. Four separate self-service counters make for speed and efficiency. Breakfast (with muesli) is served till 11.30; from midday enjoy cold meats, mackerel and very good salads. Hot dishes are also available and there's always something for vegetarians.

LONDON   *Quick Bite*   Village Delicatessen & Coffee Shop

61 Blythe Road, W14
01-602 1954

Map 10 B5

Open 9.30–4 (Sun 10–2)
Closed Bank Holidays

Typical prices: Butter bean bake
  £1.95 Spring vegetable risotto
  £2.25
Luncheon Vouchers accepted

Generous portions of good wholesome food make for satisfied customers at this cheerful little coffee shop beneath a busy delicatessen. Starters run to smoked mackerel pâté, houmus and home-made soup, and light lunches include baked potatoes with a large choice of fillings. Vegetarians are well served with dishes like wholewheat pasta with walnut and parsley sauce, or spring vegetable risotto. There is usually at least one simple chicken dish and pulses are given new zest in creations like mixed bean moussaka and butter bean bake.

LONDON   *Quick Bite*   Wholemeal Vegetarian Café

1 Shrubbery Road,
  SW16
01-769 2423

Map 10 C6

Open 12–10.30
Closed December 25 & 26
Vegetarian cooking

Typical prices: Sweet & sour
  vegetable casserole £2.30
  Broccoli & mushroom crumble
  with rice £2.70

This hospitable restaurant attracts a stream of customers throughout the day and is positively packed at lunchtime when it often becomes necessary to share one of the polished pine tables. Flavoursome soups like sunflower and onion or country vegetable serve as preludes to main courses like vegetable goulash or courgette quiche. Salads are excellent—varied and well dressed—and vegetables are lightly cooked so that natural flavours are retained. Herbs and spices are used to good effect.

LONDON *Quick Bite* Wilkins Natural Foods

61 Marsham Street,
  SW1
01-222 4038

Map 12 C5

Open 8–5
Closed Sat, Sun & Bank Holidays
Vegetarian cooking

Typical prices: Macaroni & mixed
  vegetables £1.38
  Fruit crumble 72p
Luncheon Vouchers accepted

On sunny days this little establishment becomes a popular pavement café. The attractions are obvious: tasty wholesome vegetarian and vegan snacks at low prices to eat on the spot or take away. Soups, salads, filled wholemeal baps and flans are always available with a hot soup such as barley broth and a savoury of the day which might be macaroni with mixed vegetables or vegetable pie. Finish with fruit salad and yoghurt. Cakes and bakes are served with fresh fruit juices, decaffeinated and dandelion coffee, tisanes and sparkling mineral water.

LONDON *Quick Bite* Windmill Wholefood Restaurant

486 Fulham Road,
  SW6
01-385 1570

Map 12 A6

Open 11–10.45 (Sun from 7pm)
Closed Bank Holidays & 1 week
  Christmas
Wholefood cooking

Typical prices: Mixed vegetables
  in cashew nut sauce £2.60
  Vegan orange cake £1.10

Despite crowded conditions the atmosphere at this wholefood restaurant is very relaxed. Food is ordered from a counter display or a list chalked on the blackboard. There is always a soup (choose a large or small helping), a selection of eight freshly made salads, and a main course like pasta and mushrooms in spinach sauce. Vegans are catered for with dishes like Tahitian vegetable curry. Puddings also include vegan specialities such as fruit or orange cake together with fresh fruit salad.

77 Marylebone Lane, W1 01-486 3862 Map 11 B3	77 Marylebone Lane Lunch 12–3 Dinner 6–11 **Closed** December 25
37 Panton Street, SW1 01-839 7258 Map 11 C3	37 Panton Street Lunch 12–3 Dinner 6–11 **Closed** December 25 & 26

Indian vegetarian cooking

Average price £10
Set L & Set D from £6
(Minimum charge £4)
Credit: Access, Amex, Diners, Visa

Ask for a limbupani while you mull over the menu at either of these popular vegetarian restaurants. Sounds exotic, but it is in fact fresh lemon juice in water—a perfect start to a healthy repast. To continue, try chapatis with paneer (cottage cheese) or settle for a South Indian speciality in the shape of a lentil pizza, the famous uthappam, with cabbage, tomato or onion topping. An intriguing eggless 'omelette' and a range of rice dishes and dosas extend the choice. Choose a variety of dishes or a fixed price meal which offers good value. Fruit salad to follow.

19 Canonbury Lane, N1
01-226 9791

Map 11 D1

154 Upper Street, N1
01-226 8463

Map 12 D1

19 Canonbury Lane Dinner only
5–12.30
Closed Bank Holidays & 2–3 days
Christmas

154 Upper Street meals noon–
midnight
Closed December 25

Chinese cooking

Average price £15
Set D from £6.50 (Canonbury
Lane)
Set L & Set D from £8.20 for two
(Upper Street)
Credit: Access, Amex, Diners, Visa

These are sister restaurants, one specialising in Szechuan and Peking dishes, the other (in Upper Street) favouring somewhat more conventional, largely Cantonese, cuisine. Both offer outstanding service by dedicated personnel and consistently excellent cooking. At Canonbury Lane you might dine on clear fish soup, braised prawns, stir-fried mushrooms and bamboo shoots with noodles. An Upper Street healthy meal might be abalone and asparagus soup, steamed sea bass with lo-hon vegetables and rice. At both establishments the choice is vast, and the Upper Street menu includes a vegetarian set dinner for two.

We welcome complaints and bona fide recommendations on the tear-out pages for readers' comments. They are followed up by our professional team. Please also complain to the management instantly.

LONDON   *Restaurant*   **Yumi**

110 George Street, W1
01-935 8320

Map 11 B3

Lunch 12–2.30 Dinner 6–10.45
Closed Lunch Sat, all Sun, Bank
  Holidays, 1 week August &
  1 week Christmas
Japanese cooking

Average price £20
Credit: Access, Amex, Diners, Visa

Caring, courteous service, coupled with delicious Japanese cooking, makes this a delightful restaurant. Sit shoeless and cross-legged before low tables in the sushi bar and choose from 30 different types of sushi or try a set menu such as 'Tokujyo', which offers 8 different fish, 1 nori roll and 1 egg roll. The selection of fish might include cuttlefish, tuna, sea bass, sole and mackerel with salmon and salmon roe. If preferred, there are conventional tables in the restaurant, or private rooms (with low tables) where an extensive range of Japanese specialities is served.

LONDON   *Quick Bite*   **Zen W3**

83 Hampstead High
  Street, NW3
01-794 7863

Map 9 B2

Open 12–11.30
Closed December 25, 26 & 27

Typical prices: Avocado & sesame
  oil salad £2
  Charcoal-grilled fish steaks £7
Credit: Access, Amex, Diners, Visa

Lawrence Leung has declared his Chinese restaurant an additive-free zone (monosodium glutamate is banned). Oil and cornflour are kept to a minimum and the menu is designed around the best and freshest natural ingredients available. Start, perhaps, with yin yang seaweed, advance to king prawns steamed with fennel, and conclude with passion fruit sorbet. Vegetarians are well provided for with dishes such as jade salad—fresh green noodles with bean curd—and sea-spice aubergine.

HEALTHY EATING OUT
—IN—
ENGLAND

ENGLAND

ENGLAND

ENGLAND

ENGLAND

ENGLAND

ENGLAND

ENGLAND

ENGLAND

GUIDE TO ESTABLISHMENTS

ALFOLD CROSSWAYS

 Pub

Napoleon Arms

Near Cranleigh
Loxwood
(0403) 752357

Map 6 D3 Surrey

Last order 10 pm
Free House

Typical prices: Lemon sole £3.20
    Sardine sandwich £1.25
Credit: Access, Amex, Diners, Visa

Set back from the road, this white-painted inn with its pretty front patio offers traditional pub snacks plus a few more substantial specials like grilled sole or sirloin steak. Filled baked potatoes are a favourite choice and there is a wide range of open sandwiches on wholemeal bread. Composite salads such as smoked mackerel or sardine are always on offer and omelettes are cooked to perfection, fluffy on the outside, moist in the middle. Vegetarians will find regular dishes on the menu, including a vegetable curry on brown rice. Green figs to follow.

ALSAGER

Pub

Manor House

Audley Road, Near
  Stoke-on-Trent
Alsager (093 63)
  78013

Map 3 C4 Cheshire

Last order 10 pm
Free House

Typical prices: Chicken curry
  £2.05 Lentil soup 70p
Credit: Access, Amex, Diners, Visa

Seafood is a speciality at this handsome red-brick inn on the border between North Staffordshire and South Cheshire. A healthy meal might consist of grilled lemon sole or plaice, served with a jacket potato and salad, with lentil soup as a starter and a freshly prepared fruit salad for dessert. Wholemeal bread is served (with polyunsaturated margarine if preferred) and both natural yoghurt and skimmed milk are used in cooking wherever possible. At lunchtime there is an attractive buffet.

ALTRINCHAM *Quick Bite*

Nutcracker
Vegetarian Restaurant

43 Oxford Road
061-928 4399

Map 3 C4
Greater Manchester

Open 10–4.45 (Wed till 2)
Closed Sun & Bank Holidays
Vegetarian cooking

Typical prices: Vegetable risotto
£2.05 Apricot & date slice 42p

Vegetarians are not the only visitors to this popular and long-established restaurant. Drop in for lunch and enjoy a bowl of lentil soup with wholemeal bread (with polyunsaturated margarine if preferred), a bumper salad or the dish of the day. This might be a vegetable risotto with brown rice or perhaps a cottage cheese and mixed nut bake. Fresh fruit salad is always on the menu as is natural yoghurt served plain or Greek-style, with honey. Lots of scones and healthy bakes like apricot and date slice or muesli bars for tea or coffee time.

AMBLESIDE *Quick Bite*

Harvest

Compston Road
Ambleside
(0966) 33151

Map 3 C3
Cumbria

Open 10.30–2.30 & 5–8.30
Closed Thurs September–June,
Mon–Wed January–Easter & all
November–December 27
Vegetarian cooking

Typical prices: Lentil, tomato &
tarragon soup 80p
Russian-style macaroni £3.45

Hikers in need of extra energy call at the Harvest for one of their special whisked egg drinks like orange and apple with honey. Other pick-me-ups you'll find hard to put down include wholesome bakes like carob cake or banana loaf. Lunch might be fresh pineapple with yoghurt followed by Mexicali bean casserole and a raw salad of chopped organically grown vegetables. To finish, a fresh fruit salad, perhaps, or a dried fruit snow topped with coconut. Children will enjoy the tasty millet burgers.

123

AMBLESIDE	*Quick Bite*	Zeffirellis

Compston Road
Ambleside
(0966) 33845

Map 3 C3
Cumbria

Garden Room Café open 10–5.30;
   Pizzeria open 12–3 & 5–9.45
Closed Tues & Wed November–
   March except Christmas–Jan 1
Vegetarian wholefood cooking

Typical prices: Wheatmeal &
   sesame pizza funghi £2.50
   Wheatmeal lasagne £3.85
Credit: Access, Visa

This cleverly designed centre comprises cinema, restaurants and shopping arcade. Cappuccino and espresso coffee, tea and sustaining yoghurt drinks are served with home-made bakes at the leafy garden café on the ground floor, while the upper deck is the location for a smart wholefood pizzeria. Wheatmeal and sesame pizzas are the main attraction but there is also a supporting cast of lovely starters, salads, pasta dishes and meatless main courses like ratatouille. Yummy fruit salads and sorbets.

ASCOT	*Pub*	Stag

63 High Street
Ascot
(0990) 21622

Map 6 D3
Berkshire

Last Order 10 pm (limited menu
   Sun)
Closed December 25 eve
Brewery Friary Meux

Typical prices: Chicken salad
   £2.30 Vegetable lasagne £2

Ann McCarthy makes her own wholewheat pasta at this cheerful high-street inn, where traditional pub food is served together with healthy dishes like vegetable chilli on brown rice, and fresh salmon and prawn lasagne. Organically grown vegetables are used where possible and light snacks such as filled jacket potatoes and poached eggs on smoked haddock are enthusiastically received. Fresh fruit salad is a summer speciality; in winter there's always a fruit crumble, made with just a sprinkling of sugar.

ASHBURTON

Quick Bite

Ashburton Coffee House

27 West Street
Ashburton
(0364) 52539

Map 8 C2
Devon

Open 10–6 (Sun from 12.30)
Closed Mon–Sat October–Easter

Typical prices: Lentil loaf £1.60
Home-made soup 90p

Brenda Hale's healthy attitude to good food is everywhere apparent at this delightful and well-patronised coffee house. The morning array of bakes and sandwiches is supplemented at midday by tempting savoury dishes like aubergine moussaka, Neapolitan pasta or black-eyed bean casserole. Prawn salad is a popular light meal and soups include the unusual hot Moroccan harrira and chilled gazpacho. Wholemeal bread is served, and fresh fruit is always available. Drinks include fruit juice, barley cup and nettle or herb tea.

ASHFORD-IN-THE-WATER

Quick Bite

Cottage Tea Room

Fennel Street
Bakewell
(062 981) 2488

Map 4 D4
Derbyshire

Open 10.30–12 & 2.30–5.30
Closed Tues, January 1, Good
Friday, December 25 & 1 week
October

Typical prices: Hovis tea £1.75
Home-made oat biscuit 25p
(Minimum lunchtime charge
£1.50)

This tea room in the picturesque Derbyshire Peak District is run by Bill and Betty Watkins. Their home-baked bread is excellent and their cakes are a cut above the average. Call in for a cup of morning coffee or herbal tea. In the afternoon, traditional teas are served, including the popular Hovis or savoury tea. Bill and Betty bake the bread themselves under licence and serve it with home-made preserves and date and walnut or cherry cake. Low-fat spreads are always available.

ASHTEAD   *Quick Bite*   Bart's

34 The Street
Ashtead
(037 22) 75491

Map 6 D3
Surrey

Open 10–2 (Thurs–Sat also 6–10)
Closed Sun, Mon, Good Friday &
    December 25 & 26
Vegetarian cooking

Typical prices: Lentil & buckwheat
    slice £2
    Chilli bean casserole £3.95

Carefully cooked and enjoyable food at affordable prices—
that's the simple prescription at this smart vegetarian
restaurant in Ashtead's main shopping street. The short
lunch menu offers a soup such as tomato or lentil, with a
light wholemeal roll, also flans, filled jacket potatoes,
salads and hot savouries such as almond risotto (with
brown rice) or chilli bean casserole. A slightly more
substantial but still reasonably priced menu operates in the
evening. Everything—even the ices—is home-made, and
drinks include tisanes, barley cup and fresh fruit juices.

ASHWELL   *Pub*   Bushel & Strike Inn

Mill Street, Near
  Baldock
Ashwell
(046 274) 2394

Map 6 D2
Hertfordshire

Last order 10 pm
Brewery Wells

Typical prices: Poached wild
    salmon £5.50
    Stir-fry chicken £3.25
Set meals £6.95 (Sun & Bank
    Holidays)
Credit: Access, Amex, Diners, Visa

The salads are simply marvellous at this delightful village
pub. Sandy Lynch has a repertoire of over 50 combinations
at her fingertips and at least a dozen are available every
day, ranging from Chinese leaves with tangerine, to
celeriac with toasted almonds or cauliflower with green
pepper and spring onions. In addition, the cold buffet
offers well-seasoned roast beef, poached salmon and
smoked mackerel. Hot dishes include kebabs, casseroles,
stir-fries and simple fish dishes like grilled brill.

ATHERSTONE *Quick Bite* **Cloisters Wine Bar & Bistro**

ENGLAND

66 Long Street
Atherstone
(082 77) 67293

Map 5 B1
Warwickshire

Open 10–2 & 7–11
Closed December 25

Typical prices: Lamb & courgette
bake £4.65 Mexican chicken &
brown rice £4.95
Credit: Access, Visa

Movie stars like Dietrich look down on diners at this newly-extended and decorated wine bar and bistro. The menu now has a strong Mexican influence with dishes like kidney beans and meatballs in a chilli and wine sauce served on brown rice. Another bean dish, butter beans with broccoli and smoked cheese, will find favour with vegetarians. Locally-produced goats' yoghurt is used in starters and simple grilled fish dishes are always available with a selection of salads and wholemeal bread. Desserts are limited but fresh fruit salad is always on the menu.

AVEBURY *Quick Bite* **Stones**

High Street
Avebury
(067 23) 514

Map 5 B3
Wiltshire

Open 10–6
Closed end October–mid March

Typical prices: Sweet & sour
cashew crumble £2.30
'Tiger Pie' £2.30

Right next door to the Wiltshire Archaeological Museum is this interesting restaurant, the preserve of Dr Hilary Howard. During the season she serves scones, sandwiches and cakes all day, as well as speciality teas and juices. Only pure unadulterated ingredients are used, salt is kept to a minimum and jams are low in sugar. At lunchtime there are hearty soups, cheese platters and savoury dishes like spinach and flageolet croustade, Mexican chilli bake and sweet and sour cashew crumble (vegan).

127

AYLESBURY   *Restaurant*   Pebbles

Pebble Lane
Aylesbury
(0296) 86622

Map 5 C2
Buckinghamshire

Lunch 12–2 (Sun 12.30–2.30)
   Dinner 7–10 (Fri & Sat till 10.30)
Closed Lunch Sat, Dinner Sun, all
   Mon, 3 weeks August & 1 week
   Christmas

Average price £20
Set L £12.50
Set D £15 & £22.50
Credit: Access, Amex, Diners, Visa

A cobbled lane in the town centre leads to this informal family-run restaurant. David Cavalier is a dedicated and inspired cook whose artistry owes much to the influence of chefs like Mosimann and the Roux brothers. Top-quality raw materials are carefully prepared and presented and several 'cuisine naturelle' dishes appear on the menu. Try, for instance, veal kidney and woodland mushrooms with yoghurt and chive sauce and, for dessert, a selection of sorbets and fresh fruits.

AYLESBURY   *Quick Bite*   Wild Oats

38 Buckingham Street
Aylesbury
(0296) 433055

Map 5 C2
Buckinghamshire

Open 9–3
Closed Sat, Sun, Bank Holidays &
   1 week Christmas

Typical prices: Vegetable dhal
   £1.35 Peppers stuffed with
   cottage cheese 85p
Luncheon Vouchers accepted

Although primarily a takeaway restaurant, specialising in healthy home cooking, Wild Oats does have a small seating area for on-the-spot eating. Stop for a wholemeal, sesame or granary bread sandwich—or heap high a salad platter from the vast selection of raw materials available. Hot savouries range from liver and bacon pot or pork and prawn casserole to vegetarian and vegan dishes like chick pea and pepper casserole. For afters there's live yoghurt and honey or fresh fruit.

BAKEWELL   *Quick Bite*   Aitch's Wine Bar & Bistro

4 Buxton Road
Bakewell
(062 981) 3895

Map 4 D4
Derbyshire

Open 11.30–2.30 & 7–11 (Sun till 10.30)

Closed Sun October–May, January 1 & December 25

Typical prices: Mediterranean vegetable soup 80p
Slimmer's salad £2.25

Don't drop Aitch's—it's a wine bar healthy eaters in Bakewell have come to value for skilfully cooked fresh fish. Try the swordfish with broccoli, or fresh tuna steaks, or choose a simple slimmer's salad for a quick bite that won't damage the diet. Other options include tandoori lamb or chicken, light quiches and coleslaw salad. Good wholemeal bread is served, and there is fresh fruit salad for those who are sufficiently strong-willed to pass up the more calorific concoctions. Vegetarians get a bit of a raw deal—only salads and baked potatoes.

BAKEWELL   *Quick Bite*   Green Apple

Diamond Court,
Water Street
Bakewell
(062 981) 4404

Map 4 D4
Derbyshire

Open 12–2 & 7–10

Closed Dinner Mon, all Tues & Sun & December 25 & 26

Typical prices: Spinach & mushroom wholewheat lasagne £2.95 Middle Eastern carrot purée £1.95
Credit: Access, Diners, Visa

Roger Green's extensive repertoire makes a menu full of interest at this contemporary restaurant in a side street off Bakewell's main square. His dishes display an evident sympathy towards health-conscious eaters. You'll find mackerel and cider mousse alongside aubergine pâté as a starter, and main courses such as spinach and mushroom lasagne keeping company with beef Miroton with salad. Puds include thick Greek yoghurt, fresh fruit salad and berry fruits in season.

ENGLAND

BAKEWELL *Quick Bite* Marguerite & Stephanie

1 Rutland Square
Bakewell
(062 981) 4164

Map 4 D4
Derbyshire

Open 9–4.45 (Sun 2–5)
Closed Sun, October–April & 3
  days Christmas

Typical prices: Lentil soup 80p
  Pasta bake £2.40
Credit: Access, Visa

Running a coffee shop in a place called Bakewell must impose certain obligations. Fortunately Marguerite and Stephanie rise to the challenge and bake extremely well. Their moist iced banana cake is renowned. However, they do also produce healthier food—dishes like cottage pie with lentils, wholemeal lasagne and pasta bake. Sandwiches are freshly made to order and there is a selection of composite salads including a slimmer's platter. Desserts are limited for the healthy eater, alas, so round off your meal with a cup of Earl Grey or herb tea.

BARNARD CASTLE *Quick Bite* Priors Restaurant

7 The Bank
Teesdale
(0833) 38141

Map 4 D2
Co Durham

Open 10–5 (June–August till 7)
Closed Sun January–April,
  January 1 & December 25
Vegetarian wholefood cooking

Typical prices: Lentil shepherd's
  pie £1.35
  Brazil nut pasta bake £1.35
Credit: Access, Amex, Diners, Visa

You'll find the Prior family's restaurant at the back of an arts and crafts shop in the town centre. Drop in for a cup of African mint tea or an apricot health drink, and mull over a menu that includes imaginative wholefood dishes made from organically grown vegetables. Try stuffed vine leaves, courgette kofta curry or aubergine lasagne. There are always three or four wholemeal quiches, filled rolls and sandwiches, plus two hot soups and a selection of salads. Desserts include fresh fruit salad and fruit crumble.

BARTLOW — *Pub* — Three Hills

Near Linton
Cambridge
(0223) 891259

Map 6 E2
Cambridgeshire

Last order 9.30 pm
Brewery Greene King

Typical prices: Vegetarian lasagne
£2.90 Grilled trout £4.95

Whatever the weather, the welcome is warm at this delightful village pub and Steve and Sue Dixon put on a wholesome and hearty spread. The menu always includes a satisfying soup served with wholemeal bread. In addition there are pizzas as well as simple grilled fish, salads, steak and chicken. At least four dishes a day are made specially for vegetarians, including a popular Italian pepper pie and a cashew nut risotto. Desserts include simple sorbets. On fine Sundays there's a barbecue in the delightful walled garden.

BASINGSTOKE — *Restaurant* — Franco's

22 Hampstead House
Basingstoke
(0256) 50754

Map 5 C3
Hampshire

Lunch 12–2.30 Dinner 7–10.30
(Sat till 11)
Closed Lunch Sat, all Sun,
January 1, Good Friday &
December 25 & 26
Italian cooking

Average price £15
Credit: Access, Amex, Diners, Visa

Pasta has become a great favourite with healthy eaters and it is certainly a speciality of this jolly but very simple town-centre restaurant. Enjoy the Taliani family's really tasty Italian home cooking. If you must pass up the pasta—which would be a pity—plump for the delicious minestrone followed by a dish such as grilled Dover sole or brill cooked in white wine. Other favourite dishes are fegato di vitello alla salvia—fresh calf's liver with sage—or for the non-meat eater tonno e fagioli—tuna and beans.

3 Queen Street
Bath
(0225) 24846

Town plan Bath
Avon

Open 10–5.30 (Sat 9.30–6, Sun
   11–6)
Closed December 25 & 26

Typical prices: Vegetarian lasagne
   £2.50 Open sandwich £1.35
   (Minimum lunchtime charge
   £1.50)
Luncheon Vouchers accepted

It is worth waiting for a table at this elegant, graciously-furnished Georgian tea shop-cum-restaurant, where excellent leaf teas, freshly-cooked savouries and delectable cakes continue to earn accolades from both local customers and visitors to the town. Simple snacks include generous open wholemeal sandwiches, and there are daily specials like haricot bean casserole or vegetarian lasagne made with fresh wholewheat pasta. Try the chilli con carne or spinach quiche with one of their super salads and, in conclusion, sample the fruit sorbets.

BATH *Quick Bite* Moon & Sixpence

6a Broad Street
Bath
(0225) 60962

Town plan Bath
Avon

Open 12–2.30 & 5.30–10.30.(Sat
   till 11, Sun 12–2 & 7–10.30)
Closed December 25 & 26

Typical prices: Smoked mackerel
   & salad £4.75
   Sea bass cooked with julienne of
   ginger & vegetables £8.50
Credit: Access, Amex, Visa

Poached pink lake trout, smoked mackerel, barbecued chicken, tomatoes stuffed with cottage cheese, nuts and celery—these are just a few of the healthy options on offer at this welcoming wine bar. The lunchtime buffet includes an array of salads, marinated mushrooms and succulent cold meats, with granary bread. More ambitious dishes are available on the evening menu. Order a sophisticated starter such as chicken quenelles, followed by sea bass with a julienne of fresh ginger and root vegetables.

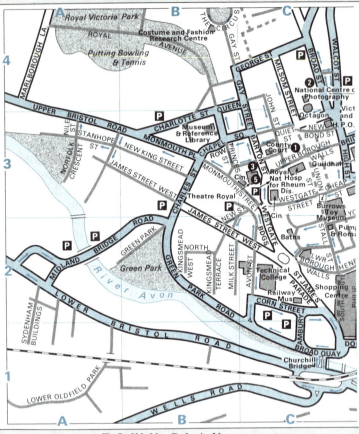

BATH

T O W N   P L A N

ENQUIRIES

(tel code: 0225)

Tourist Information 62831
Railway 63075
Bus 64446
Coach 64446

BATH

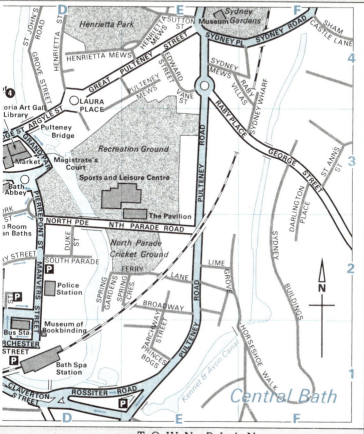

T O W N   P L A N

ESTABLISHMENTS LISTED

1. **Canary**
   3 Queen Street

2. **Moon & Sixpence**
   6a Broad Street

3. **Popjoy's**
   Sawclose

4. **Rossiter's**
   38 Broad Street

5. **Theatre Vaults**
   Sawclose

BATH   *Restaurant*   Popjoy's

Sawclose
Bath
(0225) 60494

Town plan Bath
Avon

Dinner only 6–10.30
Closed Sun, Mon, Bank Holidays
    & 4 weeks Christmas

Average price £18
Set D £16.50
Credit: Access, Visa

This exquisitely restored Georgian house, once the home of Beau Nash and his mistress Juliana Popjoy, is now under new ownership. As before the fixed-price menu changes six times a year and offers imaginative food which retains all the natural flavour of the ingredients used. All the sauces are made without fat or flour and with only the occasional addition of cream. Polyunsaturated margarine, natural yoghurt and skimmed milk play minor roles in an ambitious menu. Side salads are included in every meal.

BATH   *Quick Bite*   Rossiter's

38 Broad Street
Bath
(0225) 62227

Town plan Bath
Avon

Open 10–5
Closed Sun & Bank Holidays

Typical prices: Ratatouille terrine
    £2.95 Fish provençale & fresh
    pasta £3.25
Credit: Access, Visa

Mornings begin with a breakfast of yoghurt and muesli or croissant and citron pressé at this stylish restaurant within a busy store. Scones and cakes are on display throughout the day while from midday to 3 pm there's a small selection of light and generally healthy hot savouries, all made on the premises. Soups like celery and walnut or carrot and orange lead to main dishes like fresh vegetable terrine, courgettes provençale with home-made pasta or cauliflower and courgettes au gratin.

Sawclose
Bath
(0225) 65074

Town plan Bath
Avon

Open 12–2.30, 6–7.30 & 9–11
Closed Sun, Mon eve if no show &
December 25

Typical prices: Cheesy stuffed
courgettes £2.80 Grilled
mackerel with orange £3.95
Credit: Access, Diners, Visa

The dramatic stone vaults of the Theatre Royal provide a super setting in which to enjoy simple tasty food before and after the show, and at lunchtime. The midday and pre-theatre menus are appropriately light, with options like home-made soup, spinach and bacon crêpes, chicken with tarragon and grilled mackerel with orange. Both side salads and fresh vegetables are offered. Late-night dinners invariably include a fish dish, perhaps poached brill or salmon trout, and grilled sirloin served plain or with sauce, as preferred. There is always a vegetarian dish.

BEAULIEU   *Restaurant*   **Montagu Arms Hotel,**
Restaurant

Palace Lane
Beaulieu
(0590) 612324

Map 5 C4
Hampshire

Lunch 12.30–2 Dinner 7.30–10

Average price £20
Set L from £7.95
Set D from £14.95
Credit: Access, Amex, Diners, Visa

Good cooking and good health go hand in hand at this luxurious restaurant in the New Forest, where you can dine traditionally on roasts or grills or select a lighter, more modern meal. Whatever your choice, it will be accompanied by wholemeal bread and lightly cooked fresh vegetables (where possible, organically grown) or a crisp side salad. Brown rice and wholewheat pasta are frequently used. A vegetarian dish such as courgette charlotte is always on the menu.

BEAULIEU Montagu Arms Hotel, Wine Press

Palace Lane
Beaulieu
(0590) 612324

Map 5 C4
Hampshire

Last order 8 pm
Free House

Typical prices: Hot cauliflower &
  broccoli casserole £1.75
  Wholemeal pizza £2
Credit: Access, Amex, Diners, Visa

This comfortable and attractively refurbished bar (formerly called Spats) continues to provide a good range of wholesome food. The salad bar is especially noteworthy and offers a wide selection, served solo or with up to six dressings including a yoghurt and aniseed blend. Augment the salad platter with herring and egg or low fat cottage cheese and you have a healthy meal. Hot dishes such as chicken breast with bean sprouts are advertised on a blackboard menu—and there are filled baked potatoes for a satisfying snack.

BELBROUGHTON *Quick Bite* Coffee Pot

High Street, Near
  Stourbridge
Belbroughton
(0562) 730929

Map 5 B2
Hereford & Worcester

Open 10–5 (Sun 12.30–5.30)
Closed Mon, Bank Holidays
  except Good Friday, December
  24–31 & Tues & Wed after all
  Bank Holiday Mondays except
  Easter

Typical prices: Bean & vegetable
  hot pot £1.85
  Wholemeal quiche £2.10

Despite the name, this restaurant's fame stems from the amazing selection of teas on offer. There were over 40 varieties at the last count, served with milk, lemon or honey. Hot toddies are also served along with tangy fresh fruit drinks and mineral water. At lunchtime there are delicious dishes like bean and vegetable hot pot, vegetable bake or seafood pasta. Wholemeal flour is used for breads and pastries and salads are splendid. Puddings are described as 'old-fashioned and tempting'. Be warned!

BERKHAMSTED *Quick Bite* Cook's Delight ★

360 High Street
Berkhamsted
(044 27) 3584

Map 6 D2
Hertfordshire

Open Thurs & Fri 10–9, Sat 10–3,
 Sun 12–5
Closed Mon–Wed, Bank Holidays
 except Good Friday, 1 week
 August & December 24–30

Typical prices: Vegetable claypot
 £4 Banana cake 95p
Credit: Access, Visa
Luncheon Vouchers accepted

The Tylers care passionately about the quality of their food and serve vegetarian, vegan and macrobiotic meals of very high quality in their tiny restaurant at the back of a health-food shop. Organically-produced wholefoods are used when possible and fats and sugars are kept to a minimum. Very good soups, claypots, buckwheat quiches and salads are always available with a range of healthy desserts. On Saturday evenings the fundamentally vegetarian menu is expanded to include fish and white meat.

BERWICK-UPON-TWEED *Quick Bite* Wine Bar

1 Sidley Court, off
 Marygate
Berwick-upon-Tweed
(0289) 302621

Map 2 D5
Northumberland

Open 10–3 & 6.30–10.30
Closed Mon eve, all Sun,
 January 1 & December 25 & 26

Typical prices: Smoked trout
 £1.80 Bean casserole £2.15

Top marks to Sue and David Nisbet for making their excellent wine bar a haven for healthy eaters. Sue does much of the cooking herself. Try her vegetable broth or a filled wholemeal roll for a light snack, or take time to enjoy a local rainbow trout baked in lemon juice and served with new potatoes and salad. Smoked trout is also a speciality and composite salads include ham, tongue and Northumberland gammon. Plenty of choice for the vegetarian too with dishes like bean casserole or lentil moussaka.

BIRMINGHAM *Restaurant* Dynasty

93 Hurst Street
Birmingham
021-622 1410

Map 5 B2
West Midlands

Meals 12–11.30 (Thurs–Sat
  12 till midnight)
Closed December 25 & 26
Chinese cooking

Average price £16
Set L & Set D from £7
Credit: Access, Amex, Diners, Visa

This smart restaurant in the heart of Birmingham's Chinatown specialises in Peking and Cantonese cooking. The attractively presented menu gives plenty of information about the various dishes, including the interesting aside that shark's fin soup is traditionally believed to bestow virility. Lovers of seafood will be spoilt for choice. Varieties depend upon the season but you might be offered steamed sea bass, yellow croaker or Dover sole. The steamer is also used for chicken with lotus leaf and mushrooms. Good-quality raw materials and competent cooking.

BIRMINGHAM *QuickBite* La Galleria Wine Bar

Paradise Place
021-236 1006

Map 5 B2
West Midlands

Open 12–2.30 & 5.30–10.30 (Fri &
  Sat till 11)
Closed Sun & Bank Holidays

Typical prices: Lasagne £2.80
  Tuna fagioli £2.50
Credit: Access, Amex, Diners, Visa
Luncheon Vouchers accepted

A visit to the new library complex in Paradise Place could take a lot longer than anticipated, such is the lure of this popular Italian-style restaurant and wine bar. Fish is a speciality and thanks to an excellent local market, is always extremely fresh. There's a wide choice: on just one day you might find halibut, salmon, sardines, sole, red mullet and even calamari—any one of which will be cooked simply if preferred. Vegetarians will find an interesting range of pasta dishes and salads.

BIRMINGHAM   *Quick Bite*   Gingers

7a High Street, Kings
   Heath
021-444 0906

Map 5 B2
West Midlands

Open 6.30pm–9pm
Closed Sun & Bank Holidays
   except Good Friday
Vegetarian cooking

Typical prices: Vegetable & chick
   pea curry £4.60
   Mushroom layer bake £4.70

Herbs and spices are shrewdly used at this attractive little vegetarian restaurant about 2 miles from Birmingham city centre. Ably prepared and flavoursome dishes include Spanish cashew paella, which is a tasty combination of brown rice, lightly cooked vegetables and cashews that retain their crispness. Try it with a selection of fresh crunchy salads or sample the Basque ratatouille—a variation with pulses. Soups are served with wholemeal bread and low-fat spread is available on request. Desserts include fresh fruit salad or Swiss carrot cake.

BIRMINGHAM   *Restaurant*   Michelle

182 High Street,
   Harborne
021-426 4133

Map 5 B2
West Midlands

Lunch 12–2 Dinner 7–10 (Fri & Sat
   till 10.30)
Closed Sun & some Bank Holidays
French cooking

Average price £14
Set D from £8
Credit: Access, Visa

A poached fresh fish dish is always on the menu at this cheerful and unpretentious bistro-style restaurant. Chef Christian Vale, son of the eponymous Michelle, also offers a separate vegetarian menu with simple starters like avocado vinaigrette, melon or crudités, plus four or five main dishes including nut cutlets with a choice of sauces, baked avocado or omelettes. Wholemeal bread and salads are available, and vegetables may be ordered without butter or sauce if preferred.

ENGLAND

BIRMINGHAM · *Restaurant* · Rajdoot

12 Albert Street
021-643 8805

Map 5 B2
West Midlands

Lunch 12–2.30 Dinner 6.30–11.30
Closed Lunch Sun & Bank
 Holidays, & December 25 & 26
Indian cooking

Average price £16
Set L from £5.60
Set D from £11
Credit: Access, Amex, Diners, Visa

Ever since the first Rajdoot opened in Chelsea more than 20 years ago, these restaurants have been delighting customers with authentic Indian dishes and pleasant service. Tandoori dishes barbecued in a traditional clay oven include a chicken or fish tikka and selection of kebabs. Curries range from a delicately spiced prawn masala with a hint of garlic and ginger to that perennial favourite — roghan josh. There are dishes based on pulses, some really delicious vegetables and an excellent chicken pilau served with vegetable curry.

BIRMINGHAM · *Restaurant* · La Santé

182 High Street,
 Harborne
021-426 4133

Map 5 B2
West Midlands

Dinner only 7–10
Closed Sun, Mon & Bank Holidays
Vegetarian cooking

Average price £10
Credit: Access, Visa

This elegant French restaurant above Michelle seeks to elevate vegetarian cookery to haute cuisine. The elaborate menu has some interesting choices for the healthy eater. Start perhaps with crudités, or fresh grapefruit with walnuts and peppers, enlivened by a touch of ginger and drop of kirsch. Continue with a tasty pilaff with aubergines, mushrooms, tomato and chick peas. Desserts include fruit salad and pear and ginger crumble and there are teas and tisanes to follow. Service is helpful and quietly courteous.

BIRMINGHAM *Quick Bite* Time for a Break

16 New Street
021-643 7582

Map 5 B2
West Midlands

Open 9–5 (Thurs till 7, Fri & Sat till 5.30)

Closed Sun, Easter Monday & December 25 & 26

Typical prices: Jacket potatoes £1.10 Vegetable lasagne £1.70
Credit: Access, Visa
Luncheon Vouchers accepted

The name of this self-service coffee shop situated on the first floor of Boots will strike a chord with shoppers everywhere. It is a perfect place to stop and take a break and enjoy a healthy snack. Help yourself to tasty open sandwiches such as prawn salad on wholemeal bread, or choose a wholemeal quiche. There's hot soup midday, plus a selection of tasty savouries like vegetable lasagne and stuffed peppers. Jacket potatoes are always popular and there are regular vegetarian dishes – all served in a pleasant and spanking clean setting.

BIRMINGHAM *Quick Bite* Wild Oats

5 Raddlebarn Road,
  Selly Oak
Birmingham
021-471 2459

Map 5 B2
West Midlands

Open 12–2 & 6–9
Closed Sun, Mon, Bank Holidays
  & 1 week Christmas
Vegetarian cooking

Typical prices: Mexican bean pot £2.95 Cashew nut roast £2.95

This modestly furnished vegetarian restaurant about 2 miles from Birmingham city centre serves well-prepared and carefully cooked food. The interesting menu has plenty to offer the healthy eater. Lunch might be watercress soup with wholemeal bread (plus polyunsaturated margarine), followed by one of the hot savouries from their extensive list of takeaway items. Lentil lasagne, perhaps, or bean, marrow and corn casserole. With your meal you'll be served two salads from a splendid selection.

BISHOP'S CASTLE　*Quick Bite*　No 7

7 High Street
Bishop's Castle
(0588) 638152

Map 5 A2
Shropshire

Open 10–4 (Wed till 2, Fri 9.30–3.30) & 7.30–12
Closed Sun & Mon

Typical prices: Lentil & tomato soup 70p
　　Chicken casserole £1.60

Kay Townsend, No 7's friendly owner, has a keen interest in healthy cooking. This is reflected in a daily changing menu that includes home-made soups, houmus-filled jacket potatoes, simple chicken casseroles and brown rice risotto. The special dish might be chick peas with smoked sausage, or leek and mushroom hot pot. Salads are always served and polyunsaturated margarine is provided for the wholemeal bread. Both natural yoghurt and skimmed milk are used and there are plenty of choices for vegetarians. Dinners (booking only) are more elaborate.

BISHOPS LYDEARD　*Quick Bite*　Rose Cottage

Near Taunton
Bishops Lydeard
(0823) 432394

Map 5 A3
Somerset

Open 12–2 & 7–10
Closed Sun, Mon, Lunch Good Friday, first 2 weeks November & 2 weeks Christmas

Typical prices: Local trout £3.95
　　Vegetarian moussaka £2.65

For good healthy food, freshly cooked and with plenty of flavour, pop into this pleasant cottage restaurant. Start with home-made vegetable soup or try the tasty tortellini. Local trout is a speciality, grilled or poached and served plain or with a low-fat or fat-free sauce. There's always a vegetarian selection, including a meatless moussaka and a vegetable platter. Extras such as rack of lamb appear on the evening menu. Wholemeal bread is served with every meal and fresh fruit is always there for the asking.

BISHOP'S WALTHAM *Quick Bite* Casey's

Corner of Bank &
  Brook Streets
Bishop's Waltham
(048 93) 6352

Map 5 C4
Hampshire

Open 10–5 & 7–10.30
Closed some Bank Holidays

Typical prices: Spicy bean &
  vegetable casserole £2.25
  Vegetarian quiche £1.35
Set D from £9.75
Credit: Access, Visa

Friendly service is the hallmark of this characterful restaurant, where a genuine interest in healthy cooking is displayed by Stephen and Janine Casey. Wholefood products are used where possible and bread, biscuits and cakes are baked on the premises. By day there's a balanced selection of dishes including pizzas, omelettes, baked potatoes and salads. The evening menu is equally kind to customers concerned about health and includes simple starters and main courses like poached salmon with cucumber sauce. Sorbet is a delicious alternative to 'sinful' sweets.

BOOT *Quick Bite* Brook House Restaurant

Holmrook, Eskdale
Eskdale
(094 03) 288

Map 3 B3
Cumbria

Open 8.30am–8.30pm
Closed November–Easter

Typical prices: Spiced lentil cakes
  £2.35 Houmus £1.80

Brook House is a welcome haven for walkers in the Lakeland's Eskdale area. Dawn travellers can stop for breakfast in the cosy dining room while later arrivals (after 10.30 am) have the choice of a simple snack, a light meal, a traditional tea, or a more substantial reviver like grilled sirloin steak with jacket potato and peas. There are several vegetarian dishes such as spiced lentil cakes and savoury nut loaf, and fish lovers will find oven-baked trout on the bar menu. Brown bread sandwiches are also available.

145

BOTLEY   *Restaurant*   Cobbett's

13 The Square
Botley
(048 92) 2068

Map 5 C4
Hampshire

Lunch 12–2 Dinner 7.30–9.45 (Sat
  7–10)
Closed Lunch Sat & Mon, all Sun,
  Bank Holidays & 2 weeks
  summer
French cooking

Average price £20
Set L £8.50
Credit: Access, Amex, Visa

Health and good living are constant companions at this lovely old beamed restaurant. Lucie Skipwith's expertise in the kitchen and her enthusiasm for healthy eating are immediately apparent. The exciting menu includes simple fish and chicken dishes, superb salads and wholesome vegetarian dishes. Vegetables will be served without sauces on request and where sauces are an integral part of a dish, they are prepared without flour. Wholemeal bread is always available. Desserts include water ices and fresh fruit salads.

BOURNEMOUTH   *Quick Bite*   Flossies

73 Seamoor Road,
  Westbourne
Bournemouth
(0202) 764459

Map 5 B4
Dorset

Open 8–5 (Fri & Sat & all July–
  September till 10)
Closed Sun
Vegetarian cooking

Typical prices: Pasta shells in
  tomato sauce £1.50
  Lentil, carrot & dill bake £1.50
Luncheon Vouchers accepted

Are you a healthy eater or vegetarian and your partner a dedicated carnivore? If so, then Flossies & Bossies may suit you both. At ground level there's an informal vegetarian restaurant with lots of healthy dishes, while the basement bistro boasts casserole-style food like boeuf bourguignonne. Stay on top and you'll encounter dishes like cheese and millet risotto, pizza and onion quiche, plus lots of salads. You'll also find pulse-based dishes such as black-eyed beans in parsley sauce and lentil, carrot and dill bake.

BOURNEMOUTH — *Quick Bite* — Salad Centre

22 Post Office Road
Bournemouth
(0202) 21720

Map 5 B4
Dorset

Open 9–6 (July–September till 8)
Closed Sun & December 25 & 26
Vegetarian wholefood cooking

Typical prices: Mixed bean bake
£1.72 Wholewheat pasta salad
78p
Luncheon Vouchers accepted

Only pure natural ingredients are used at this vegetarian wholefood restaurant and, as the name suggests, the salads are pretty special—made with raw fresh fruit, vegetables, pasta, rice and pulses. There are also soups and savoury dishes like broccoli and red bean casserole, ratatouille with brown rice, cheese and spinach rissoles or vegetable pie. Jacket spuds are available with lots of different fillings and desserts include dried fruit salad and home-made yoghurt. Decaffeinated coffee and a selection of teas and infusions are served throughout the day.

BOURTON-ON-THE-WATER — *Restaurant* — Rose Tree

Riverside
Bourton-on-the-Water
(0451) 20635

Map 5 B2
Gloucestershire

Lunch (Sun only) 12.30–2 Dinner
7.30–10
Closed Dinner Sun & Mon, Bank
Holidays & 5 weeks from mid
January

Average price £17.50
Set D £8.95 (Tues–Fri) & £14.95
Credit: Access, Amex, Diners, Visa

Chris and Val Grundy host this picturesque beamed restaurant on the river Windrush. Their two fixed-price menus offer a small but well chosen selection of dishes with the emphasis on freshness and good-quality ingredients. Local vegetables are used in the home-made soup and other starters include mushrooms baked in red wine and herbs and delicately smoked seafood salad. Vegetarians are best catered for on the cheaper (£8.95) menu.

147

ENGLAND

BOWNESS-ON-WINDERMERE

Quick Bite

Hedgerow

Greenbank,
Lake Road
Windermere
(096 62) 5002

Map 3 C3
Cumbria

Open 11–9
Closed Tues & Wed October–April
& 2 weeks November
Vegetarian cooking

Typical prices: Avocado pâté &
salad £1.50
Red dragon casserole £3.40
Credit: Access, Diners, Visa

Hard work, imagination and attention to detail continue to make this a successful vegetarian restaurant. Ingredients are carefully selected and combined to make tasty wholesome dishes. Start with home-made soup, natural fruit juice, nut or chick pea pâté, or simply fresh fruit. Savouries change daily and include unusual dishes like red dragon casserole (adzuki beans, vegetables, garlic and ginger) and Peruvian pots – a hot potato bake with pepper and chilli sauce. Don't miss the fruit snow – dried fruit and coconut (with no added sugar), served with yoghurt.

BOX

Pub

·Chequers Inn

Market Place
Box
(0225) 742383

Map 5 B3
Wiltshire

Last order 9.30 pm
Brewery Usher

Typical prices: Chicken curry
£3.95 Aubergine & red bean
bake £2.50

Charming and hospitable landlords Kenneth and Jackie Martin soon set guests at their ease at this attractive inn at the foot of Box Hill. On a largely traditional pub menu there are several items of interest to healthy eaters, including grilled trout with salad and baked or new potatoes, grilled steak and chicken casserole. Daily specials, chalked on the blackboard, include vegetarian dishes like courgette and hazelnut bake or ratatouille with rice. Hot soup is served in winter.

BRADFORD — *Quick Bite* — Pizza Margherita

Argus Chambers,
  Hall Ings
Bradford
(0274) 724333

Map 4 D3
West Yorkshire

Open 10.30–11 (Fri & Sat till
  11.30)
Closed January 1 & December 25
  & 26

Typical prices: Pescatore pizza
  £2.60 Tomato salad 75p
Credit: Access, Visa
Luncheon Vouchers accepted

Watch the pizza chef at work while you wait for your meal at this modern and spacious restaurant in Bradford's city centre. Thin well-cooked bases (wholemeal also available) and generous toppings make tasty nutritious treats. Simple salads are always on offer, and starters like marinated mushrooms, tonno e fagioli and smoked mackerel pâté with pitta bread may be doubled as main courses. An unusual addition to the menu is the pizza Idaho—a potato base topped with tomatoes, cheese and herbs.

BRADFORD-ON-AVON — *Quick Bite* — Corner Stones

32 Silver Street
Bradford-on-Avon
(022 16) 5673

Map 5 B3
Wiltshire

Open 9–5
Closed Sun & December 25 & 26

Typical prices: Vegetarian soup
  75p Cauliflower, lentil &
  mushroom casserole £1.40

The aroma of new-baked bread from Barbara Gibson's bakery next door brings a stream of customers into her teashop. She caters for all tastes with a variety of wholesome and enjoyable dishes. At lunchtime there's always a vegetarian soup, plus a selection of salads, sandwiches, baked potatoes and ploughman's platters. The blackboard special might be macaroni cheese, cauliflower, lentil and mushroom casserole or hot smoked mackerel served with salad and wholemeal bread.

ENGLAND

BRAMPTON   *Restaurant*   Tarn End

Talkin Tarn
Brampton
(069 77) 2340

Map 3 C2
Cumbria

Lunch 12.30–1.45 Dinner 7.30–9
Closed Dinner Sun in winter & all
  mid January–mid February
French cooking

Average price £20
Set L £8.50
Set D £14.50
Credit: Access, Amex, Diners, Visa

Despite a relatively remote location, this lakeside restaurant offers an interesting selection of dishes with sometimes surprising ingredients such as fresh wild mushrooms and wild duck. The small but select à la carte menu includes several dishes served without rich sauces, such as medallion of monkfish with herbs or roast maize-fed chicken. For vegetarians there is an interesting selection that includes a salad with cottage cheese and egg white dressing. Food in the restaurant is French but several Italian dishes are available at the bar.

BRANSCOMBE   *Pub*   Masons Arms

Near Seaton
Branscombe
(029 780) 300

Map 8 C2
Devon

Last order 9.45pm
Free House

Typical prices: Seafood salad
  £3.90 Lentil & nut rissoles plus
  two courses £10
Credit: Access, Visa

Hospitality and healthy eating go hand in hand at this 14th-century smugglers' inn on Devon's south-east coast. The village bakery provides all the bread and fresh fruit and vegetables are supplied by local farms. With such an abundance of first-class ingredients, the chef has wisely kept the menu simple. Bar snacks include home-made soup, granary rolls, salads, and hot dishes like lamb kebabs with pitta bread. In the restaurant salmon and leek soup and dressed crab are among the dishes on offer.

BRIDGNORTH

Quick Bite

Sophie's Tea Rooms

Bank Street
Bridgnorth
(074 62) 4085

Map 5 A2
Shropshire

Open 10–5.30 (Sun 2–6)
Closed Sun & Thurs in low season
& 4 days Christmas

Typical prices: Home-made soup
60p Chick pea & walnut
casserole £2.25

Whatever the weather, the welcome is warm at this charming Victorian tea parlour. In winter, coal fires burn in both the upstairs non-smoking area and the downstairs room, and the home-made soup with freshly-baked crusty bread provides instant sustenance. There are snacks in the form of scrumptious salads, sandwiches, baps and toasts. Daily specials include savoury pancakes and chicken and vegetable casserole and there are several vegetarian dishes, all served with brown rice. Beverages include tea, tisanes and juices.

BRIDGWATER

Quick Bite

Bridge Restaurant

Binford Place
Bridgwater
(0278) 451277

Map 5 A3
Somerset

Open 9.30–5.30
Closed Sun , Bank Holidays &
1 week Christmas

Typical prices: Quiche & large
salad £3
Fresh fruit salad £1

This modest restaurant bridges the gap between breakfast and bedtime by serving a selection of at least a dozen healthy salads, together with a range of very good cakes and bakes. Generously filled granary rolls are available all day and at lunchtime there is also a hearty soup, a savoury special such as cauliflower cheese, and snacks like filled jacket potatoes. The salads include pasta, pulses and rare treats like sweet and sour bean sprouts and Chinese mushrooms. For dessert there is fresh fruit salad.

BRIDPORT *QuickBite* Moniques Wine Bar

East Street
Bridport
(0308) 25877

Map 8 C2
Dorset

Open 12–2 & 7–9.30 (Fri & Sat till
  10)
Closed Sun, January 1 &
  December 25 & 26

Typical prices: Mixed bean soup
  90p Ratatouille £1.85

Moniques is a mine of information about what's on in
Bridport—posters advertising local events deck the walls,
sparking many a conversation. Monique's daily-changing
menus are equally interesting. Lunchtimes offer most
choice to healthy eaters; a typical menu might include
vegetable soup, corn-on-the-cob, a selection of salads and
several specials, ranging from stuffed peppers with beef
and brown rice to wholefood cottage pie with lentils and
split peas. Evenings offer slightly more sophisticated
menus, with starters like artichoke vinaigrette or smoked
prawns (go easy on the garlic dip). Main courses always
include an exotic casserole and a vegetarian dish.

Oxley Green, Near
  Robertsbridge
Brightling
(042 482) 212

Map 6 E3
East Sussex

Last order 10 pm
Closed Mon except Bank Holidays
Free House

Typical prices: Curried vegetables
  £2.50 Vegetarian lasagne £2.50

This inn has a fascinating history. It was built in 1811 as a result of a pact between the rector of Brightling and John Fuller, eccentric local character and MP for Sussex. John Fuller, planning ahead, wanted to have a pyramid-shaped tomb erected in the churchyard; the rector wished to see a pub opposite the church moved to a more seemly location. An accommodation was reached and the Fullers Arms was built on the Robertsbridge road, ¾ mile from Brightling. It is a warm and friendly establishment, serving wholesome food of high calibre. The extensive bar menu has over 20 main courses, many of them traditional pub favourites like steak and kidney pie, but with a concern for healthy cooking evident in light wholemeal pastry and fillings composed only of prime ingredients with the minimum of fat. Vegetarians are well catered for with dishes like vegetarian lasagne, leek and potato bake and ratatouille. A popular dish is a medley of six lightly-cooked vegetables with freshly-ground spices, served with cheesy spinach and brown rice. Chips are taboo—no deep-fried foods are served. Salads are a summer speciality, along with fresh berry fruits and summer puddings. Winter sweets include wholesome low-sugar crumbles and a very special banana and walnut pudding.

Our inspectors never book in the name of
Egon Ronay's Guides; they disclose their
identity only after paying their bills.

BRIGHTON (HOVE)   *Quick Bite*   Blossoms

81 George Street
Brighton
(0273) 776776

Town plan Brighton
East Sussex

Open 8.30–4.30 (Sun 12–2.15)
Closed Bank Holidays except
 Good Friday

Typical prices: Blossoms' mixed
 health salad £1.20
 Poached salmon salad (Lunch
 Sun) plus two courses £5.95

The largely vegetarian menu at this busy self-service coffee shop provides plenty of healthy options for shoppers. The home-made soup is served with a wholemeal roll (and polyunsaturated margarine if liked) and there is a good selection of composite salads together with wholemeal quiche or lentil roast. Pasta and pulses are widely used in the hot vegetarian dishes and fresh fruit salad adds a finishing touch. Meat and fish dishes are also on offer, often as pies and therefore not particularly healthy.

BRIGHTON   *Quick Bite*   Food for Friends

17a Prince Albert
 Street
Brighton
(0273) 202310

Town plan Brighton
East Sussex

Open 9am–10pm (Sun from
 11.30)
Closed Christmas–New Year
Vegetarian cooking

Typical prices: Rice & cashew nut
 burgers £1.30
 Tagliatelle florentine £1.30
Luncheon Vouchers accepted

Simon Hope does more than simply serve vegetarian food—he works tirelessly to relate traditional culinary techniques to wholefood ingredients. He produces wholemeal pastry and cakes that are beautifully light—and wholemeal croissants that succeed spectacularly. These are served, along with muesli and granola, at breakfast (9–11). Soups and snacks follow and by noon the menu has expanded to include dishes like red bean casserole, cauliflower bake, and rice and cashew nut burgers.

BRIGHTON *Restaurant* French Connection

11 Little East Street
Brighton
(0273) 24454

Town plan Brighton
East Sussex

Lunch 12–2 Dinner 7–10
Closed Sun, 2 weeks January &
   first week July

Average price £20
Set L £8.50
Set D £10.65
Credit: Access, Amex, Diners, Visa

Walls crammed with photographs of the notable and newsworthy attest to the popularity of this ground-to-basement restaurant where fixed-price and à la carte menus satisfy special-occasion diners and celebrities alike. There is no overt emphasis on healthy cooking beyond the home-made wholemeal bread, but the menu offers plenty of dishes suitable for diners conscious of diet. You could, for instance, choose jellied consommé with sherry followed by baked lettuce-wrapped trout filled with prawns. The lunch menu always includes a vegetarian dish.

BRIGHTON *Restaurant* Gar's

19 Prince Albert Street
Brighton
(0273) 21321

Town plan Brighton
East Sussex

Lunch 12–2 Dinner 5.30–11.30
Closed December 25 & 26 & first
   week January
Chinese cooking

Average price £15
Set L & Set D from £7.50
Credit: Access, Amex, Diners, Visa

Simplicity is the key to this unassuming little restaurant run by the Cheung brothers. Excellent raw materials, carefully prepared and sympathetically treated, give good results. There are many dishes that healthy eaters can choose with confidence, including lemon chicken, Cantonese-style, steamed fresh prawns and Peking braised fish. From the grill come barbecued skewered chicken, fillet steak and king prawns, and there is a choice of rice and noodle accompaniments. Lychees and fresh fruit salad to follow.

BRIGHTON

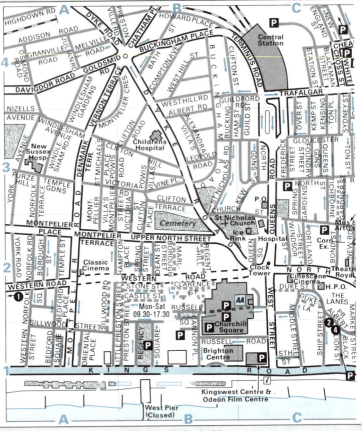

TOWN PLAN

ENQUIRIES

(tel code: 0273)

Tourist Information	23755
Railway	25476
Bus	206666
Coach	206666

BRIGHTON

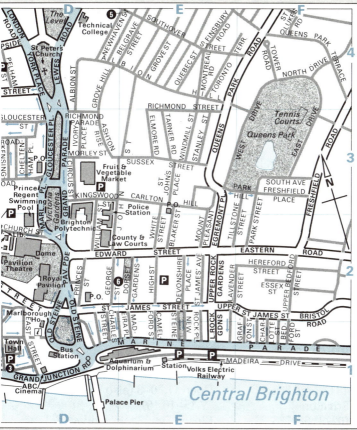

Central Brighton

TOWN PLAN

ESTABLISHMENTS LISTED

1. **Blossoms**
   81 George Street (Hove)

2. **Food for Friends**
   17a Prince Albert Street

3. **French Connection**
   11 Little East Street

4. **Gar's**
   19 Prince Albert Street

5. **The Greys**
   105 Southover Street

6. **Saxons**
   48 George Street

ENGLAND

BRIGHTON · *Pub* · The Greys

105 Southover Street,
  off Lewes Road
Brighton
(0273) 680734

Town plan Brighton
East Sussex

Last order 9 pm
No bar food Sat–Tues except Sat
  eve
Brewery Whitbread

Typical prices: Fish kebab & salad
  £3.25 Chicken with fresh ginger,
  honey & rosemary £3.25
Credit: Visa

Jackie Fitzgerald is a self-taught cook of considerable expertise who produces a varied and always interesting menu. Good home-made soup is available daily, with wholemeal or Jackie's own soda bread, and main courses make use of market-fresh fish and vegetables. Typical meals could be poached trout, grilled plaice on the bone and rump steak. Vegetarians are enthusiastically catered for with dishes like baked fennel with Parmesan and houmus with pitta bread. Jacket potatoes with various toppings such as chilli go down well with a simple salad.

BRIGHTON · *Quick Bite* · Saxons

48 George Street
Brighton
(0273) 680733

Town plan Brighton
East Sussex

Open 11.30–3 (also Wed–Sat
  7.15–10.15)
Closed Sun, Bank Holidays & 1
  week Christmas
Vegetarian cooking

Typical prices: Wholemeal cheese
  flan £1.70 Red kidney bean
  ragout & brown rice £1.50

Saxons wears two faces; by day it is a counter-service café and by night a candlelit restaurant where friendly waitresses take orders for simple but superior vegetarian food. A typical and highly recommended soup of the day might be a delicately flavoured tofu with summer vegetables. The wholemeal pastry is commendably light, making the hot cheese and vegetable flans a favourite choice. Rice, pasta and pulse dishes are well represented and there's a first-rate salad bar.

1a Avon Crescent,
  Hotwells
Bristol
(0272) 22921

Town plan Bristol
Avon

Dinner only 7–11 (Fri & Sat till
  11.30)
Closed Sun, Mon, Bank Holidays
  except Good Friday & 2 weeks
  Christmas

Average price £14

The crowds come early and stay late so it is best to book at this friendly informal bistro where the food is consistently well cooked and there is much to interest healthy eaters. Start perhaps with whole smoked trout or gazpacho, and make your main course grilled lemon sole, turbot or brill. Crisp, lightly cooked vegetables are something of a speciality and salads are always on offer. Gillian Howard does use butter and cream in much of her cooking, but is always glad to provide simple dishes, low fat spreads and natural yoghurt instead of cream.

BRISTOL   *Quick Bite*   Rainbow Café

10 Waterloo Street,
  Clifton
Bristol
(0272) 738937

Town plan Bristol
Avon

Open 10–5.30
Closed Sun, Bank Holidays &
  1 week Christmas

Typical prices: Lentil & tomato
  soup 80p
  Cashew nut loaf £1.20
  Luncheon Vouchers accepted

Alison Moore and Tim Ansell serve up delicious soups in this delightful little craft shop-cum-café. Try the butter bean and lemon, or the celery and dill, with a satisfying slice of wholemeal bread for a simple nourishing snack. At lunchtime there is a selection of pasta dishes and hot pots, while excellent fresh salads are daily features. Regular vegetarian specialities include aubergine and kidney bean stew and gratin of fennel and tomato with green salad. Simple fish dishes are an occasional extra.

BRISTOL

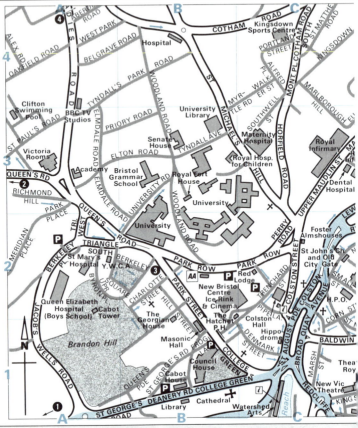

TOWN PLAN

ENQUIRIES

(tel code: 0272)

Tourist Information	293891
Railway	294255
Bus	553231
Coach	541022
Airport .... Lulsgate (027 587)	4441

BRISTOL

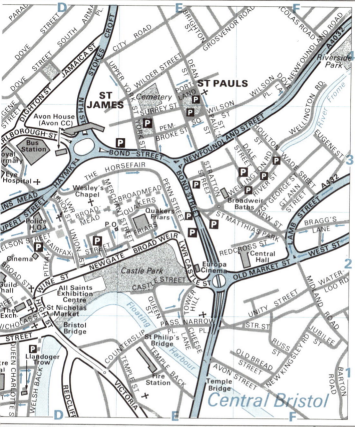

TOWN PLAN

ESTABLISHMENTS LISTED

1. **Howards**
   1a Avon Crescent, Hotwells

2. **Rainbow Café**
   10 Waterloo Street, Clifton

3. **Rajdoot**
   83 Park Street

4. **Wild Oats II**
   85 Whiteladies Road

BRISTOL   *Restaurant*   Rajdoot

83 Park Street
Bristol
(0272) 28033

Town plan Bristol
Avon

Lunch 12–2.15 Dinner 6.30–11.30
Closed Lunch Sun & Bank
 Holidays
Indian cooking

Average price £14
Set L from £5
Set D from £9.50
Credit: Access, Amex, Diners, Visa

This long-established restaurant, one of a chain, has clearly got the recipe for success. Authentic Punjabi dishes are prepared from fresh ingredients and served in attractive surroundings. The vegetables are highly praised. Try sag paneer—spinach with home-made spiced cottage cheese and herbs—or aloo jeera—dry cooked potatoes with cumin seeds. Gently spiced curries and tandoori dishes barbecued in a traditional clay oven form the foundation of an extensive menu and the obliging staff are happy to suggest suitable dishes for anyone on a special diet.

BRISTOL   *Quick Bite*   Wild Oats II

85 Whiteladies Road,
 Clifton
Bristol
(0272) 734482

Town plan Bristol
Avon

Open 10 am–10 pm (Mon & Tues
 till 6, Fri & Sat till 10.30)
Closed December 25 & 26
Vegetarian wholefood cooking

Typical prices: Wok-fried tofu
 £5.50 Seitan Stroganoff £6.75
Luncheon Vouchers accepted

This spacious split-level restaurant caters for a variety of healthy diets, such as vegan, diabetic or macrobiotic. No chemicals, preservatives, additives, or artificial foods are permitted. A point is made of using only organic vegetables and natural sweeteners, and dairy produce is kept to a minimum. Some of the delights to be tried are tofu cocktail or miso soup as starters, and stir-fried vegetables or pizza as main courses. Desserts include sorbets, soya ice cream and strawberry tofu whip.

BROADWAY *Restaurant* Collin House Hotel Restaurant

Collin Lane
Broadway
(0386) 858354

Map 5 B2
Hereford & Worcester

Lunch (Sun only) 12–1.30 Dinner 7–9
Closed Dinner Sun to non-residents & December 25 & 26
English cooking

Average price £15
Set L £12.50 Set D from £11
Credit: Access, Visa

A set menu usually signifies limited choice—not so at Collin House Hotel, where the selection of dishes on offer is so tantalising that you need to allow extra time for happy contemplation. What you pay depends on which main course you select. Choose chicken breast baked with yoghurt, garden herbs and lemon, for instance, and you can add any starter and pudding of your choice for an inclusive price of £11. You may find it hard to say no to the delicious home-made ice creams like guava or tamarillo but you can always choose cheese instead.

BROADWAY *Quick Bite* Goblets Wine Bar

High Street
Broadway
(0386) 852255

Map 5 B2
Hereford & Worcester

Open 12–2, 3–5 & 6–9.30 (Sun from 7)
Closed 2 weeks Christmas

Typical prices: Vegetable lasagne £3.90 Chicken drumsticks with watercress sauce £2.25
Credit: Access, Amex, Diners, Visa

It is worth waiting for a table at this popular wine bar next to the Lygon Arms (see overleaf), for the menu has lots to offer the healthy eater. The choice is simple but varied—four each of starters, main courses and desserts, plus blackboard specials. Start, perhaps, with grapefruit and melon in mint vinaigrette; choose grilled trout or chicken and broccoli to follow; and finish with fresh fruit salad or biscuits and cheese. Vegetable lasagne and cauliflower cheese are favoured by vegetarians.

ENGLAND

BROADWAY  *Restaurant* Lygon Arms Restaurant

High Street
Broadway
(0386) 852255

Map 5 B2
Hereford & Worcester

Lunch 12.30–2 (Sun till 2.30)
Dinner 7.30–9.15 (Sat till 9.30)

Average price £24
Set L £12.25
Set D £19.50
Credit: Access, Amex, Diners, Visa

A healthy concern for good food pervades the atmosphere at this imposing restaurant. There's always a lowfat dish on the menu such as poached halibut in a natural yoghurt sauce with black pepper. Both meat-lovers and vegetarians are generously catered for. Chef Alain Dubois invites customers who prefer their food cooked simply to make their wishes known as all dishes are prepared to order. Vegetables are served lightly cooked and a green or mixed salad is always available, with or without a dressing. Savouries such as Welsh rarebit are also on offer.

BROME *Pub* Oaksmere

Near Eye
Diss
(0379) 870326

Map 6 F2
Suffolk

Last order 10pm
Free House

Typical prices: Whole baked
  whiting with lemon £2.95
  Bean & vegetable casserole
  £2.25
Credit: Access, Amex, Diners, Visa

Off the main road in attractive gardens, this hotel bar has a wonderful old-world atmosphere. The well-prepared bar snacks include favourites like home-made soup, sandwiches and ploughman's with imaginative extras like fresh wholewheat pasta with lumpfish caviar, and stir-fried vegetable salad. On the more substantial side there are chargrilled steaks, but remember to check the daily specials. Home-made raspberry yoghurt ice cream to follow. Full meals are available in the restaurant.

BURGHFIELD *Restaurant* Knights Farm

Near Reading
(0734) 52366

Map 5 C3
Berkshire

Lunch 12.30–1.30 Dinner 7.30–9
Closed Lunch Sat, all Sun, 1 week
   Christmas & 3 weeks August–
September

Average price £20
Set L £9.95 & £15
Set D £20.50
Credit: Access, Amex, Diners, Visa

Check directions when booking at this charming converted farmhouse, where new owners continue to produce stylish fixed-price menus with a wide choice of dishes. The healthy eater might lunch on a pear with cheese and herb pâté followed by poached halibut with spinach from the 'quick' menu, or settle down to French bean and grapefruit salad and poached chicken breast with ginger and lime. A fine range of English and French cheeses appears on both menus. Vegetarian alternatives are imaginative and a vegan menu can be constructed at 24 hours' notice.

BURNHAM-ON-CROUCH *Restaurant* Contented Sole

80 High Street
Maldon
(0621) 782139

Map 6 E3
Essex

Lunch 12–2 Dinner 7–9.30
Closed Sun, Mon, last 2 weeks July
   & 4 weeks Christmas

Average price £16
Set L £6.50

The success of this long-established family-run restaurant is to a large extent attributable to scrupulously fresh raw materials. These are carefully selected and expertly cooked, as in the fine grilled halibut steak. All fish dishes can be served without sauce on request. Meat dishes are equally dependable and range from fillet and entrecôte steak to venison. A vegetarian menu is also available and includes dishes like wholewheat pasta with tomato and vegetables and lentil and peanut croquettes.

BURY ST EDMUNDS   *Quick Bite*   Beaumonts

6 Brentgovel Street
Bury St Edmunds
(0284) 706677

Map 6 E2
Suffolk

Coffee shop open 9.30–5;
   Restaurant open 11–4
Closed Sun & Bank Holidays
Vegetarian wholefood cooking

Typical prices: Celery & hazelnut
   roast £1.90
   Mushroom Stroganoff £1.75
Credit: Access, Visa
Luncheon Vouchers accepted

This strictly vegetarian establishment is a boon to the health-conscious inhabitants of Bury. It offers a very good range of thoughtfully cooked and reasonably priced light meals in pleasant surroundings. The complex comprises health-food store, coffee shop and restaurant, the last mentioned serving starters like celery and apple soup and main courses such as vegetable goulash or haricot bean casserole. Organically grown vegetables are used wherever possible and desserts include sugar-free sorbets. Vegan dishes are always on the menu.

CAMBRIDGE   *Quick Bite*   Nettles

6 St Edward's Passage,
   King's Parade

Map 6 D2
Cambridgeshire

Open 9–8 (Sat 9 till 3)
Closed Sun & Bank Holidays
Vegetarian wholefood cooking

Typical prices: Chilli bean bake
   £1.20 Lentil hot pot & winter
   vegetables £1.20

This tiny restaurant has a brisk takeaway trade, which is probably just as well as there are only three small tables. Built as part of the Arts Theatre Complex, it offers cheerful vegetarian food. Join the queue for hearty soups, wholemeal bread, simple snacks and hot savouries. Lunchtime specials make good use of pasta and pulses in dishes like wholewheat noodles in spicy tomato sauce, and lentil hot pot. There are always two salads, one green, one grain-based, plus quiches and pizzas.

CANTERBURY

Quick Bite

Il Vaticano
Pasta Parlour

35 St Margaret's Street
Canterbury
(0227) 65333

Map 6 F3
Kent

Open 11am–11pm (Sun 12–10)
Closed December 25 & 26

Typical prices: Fettuccine al pesto
£2.60 Ravioli al Vaticano £2.95
Credit: Access, Amex, Diners, Visa
Luncheon Vouchers accepted

Home-made, fresh pasta is the chief attraction at this informal city-centre restaurant where the menu proudly proclaims it to be nourishing, low in calories and high in protein. Accompanying sauces vary from rich mushroom or bolognese to simple pesto or carbonara. There is also lasagne. Really healthy eaters can play it safe and have a starter like melon and Parma ham or gazpacho, followed by a substantial salad. Sorbets are always available and beverages include natural apple juice. Another branch in Ashford called Il Cardinale Pasta Parlour.

CANTERBURY

Quick Bite

Sweet Heart
Patisserie

Old Weavers House,
  St Peter's Street
Canterbury
(0227) 458626

Map 6 F3
Kent

Open 9–6 (summer till 10.30)
Closed 2 weeks in winter

Typical prices: Mexican bean
  soup £1.20
  Wholewheat pasta salad £1.50

Wear blinkers when visiting this outstanding pâtisserie or the temptation offered by the excellent cakes may be impossible to resist. For the strong there are healthy alternatives such as the German wholegrain bread or jacket potatoes, offered with a range of toppings including cottage cheese and prawns. There's a health bar serving muesli, fresh fruit and yoghurt-based desserts and the salads are composed of organically grown vegetables. Savoury specialities include vegetarian dishes.

CARTMEL FELL *Pub* Mason's Arms

Strawberry Bank, Near
  Grange-over-Sands
Crosthwaite
(044 88) 486

Map 3 C3
Cumbria

Last order 8.45pm
Closed December 25
Free House

Typical prices: Russian vegetable
  pie & salad £3.25
  Indian snack platter £3.75

This splendid converted farmhouse, perched high on Strawberry Bank, has fine views of the surrounding countryside. Inside, the bar has much character, the welcome is genuine and the food is very good indeed. Vegetarians are particularly well catered for with at least six daily dishes (some suitable for vegans) identified by colour coding on the blackboard menu. These include courgette lasagne, red bean moussaka and stuffed vine leaves with pitta. Excellent soup is made daily and there's a range of composite salads and sandwiches. Fruit salad to follow.

CASTLE CARY *Quick Bite* Old Bakehouse

High Street
Castle Cary
(0963) 50067

Map 5 A3
Somerset

Open 9–5.30 (Mon till 1.30)
Closed Sun
Wholefood cooking

Typical prices: Vegetable pie
  £1.50 Raisin & bran loaf 85p

Organically grown produce is used to good effect at this pretty little wholefood restaurant and shop. In summer you may sit in the vine-canopied courtyard to savour the slimmer's cottage cheese and fruit salad. Come indoors for carrot and orange soup with a home-made granary roll, or plump for pizza or prawn and mushroom quiche. Pasta appears in spinach and tomato lasagne and pulses in such dishes as green lentil rissoles. Spiced fruit compote makes a fitting finale.

CASTLE CARY — *Quick Bite* — Tramps Wine Bar

Woodcock Street
Castle Cary
(0963) 51129

Map 5 A3
Somerset

Open 11.30–3.30
Closed Sun, Mon, January 1 &
 December 25 & 26

Typical prices: Lentil soup £1.50
 Grilled sardines £2.10

Curry and rice and all things nice—that's the recurrent theme at this village wine bar and delicatessen, where scones, flapjacks and bakes happily share the bill with chicken tikka, lamb kofta and other spicy delights. Those who like their lunches light will enjoy the healthy salads, perhaps with a plate of smoked prawns or assorted cold meats. There's always soup and a vegetarian dish such as curry with pilau rice and meat-lovers will find sirloin steak grilled to their taste. Watch the blackboard for daily fish specials like poached haddock or grilled sardines.

CAULDON LOWE — *Quick Bite* — Staffordshire Peak Arts Centre

Near Waterhouses
Waterhouses
(053 86) 431

Map 4 D4
Staffordshire

Open 10.30–5.30 (Fri till 9 May–
 September)
Closed Mon–Thurs November–
 March
Vegetarian cooking

Typical prices: Lentil hot pot £2.75
 Mushroom burgers £2.20
Credit: Access, Amex, Diners, Visa

Good wholesome vegetarian food rewards the traveller at this former schoolhouse high in the Staffordshire Peak District. Early visitors will find simple cakes and bakes on display. From noon, hot food is available. The day's choice might be vegetable soup with wholemeal bread, lentil hot pot or vegetarian lasagne, while lighter bites include delicious Staffordshire oatcakes with courgettes, filled jacket potatoes and mushroom burgers. Healthy salads include tabbouleh and coleslaw.

CHAGFORD

Restaurant

Teignworthy Restaurant

Frenchbeer
Chagford
(064 73) 3355

Map 8 B2
Devon

Lunch by arrangement only
Dinner 7.30–9.30

Average price £23
Set D £19.50
Credit: Access, Visa

John and Gillian Newell serve beautifully prepared prime produce at their hotel on the edge of Dartmoor. Their food is much sought-after, with dishes like local guinea fowl in watercress sauce with stuffed tomatoes proving irresistible. The fixed-price menus are beautifully balanced and healthy. Crisply cooked vegetables are organically grown, there are good salads, dishes based upon rice, pasta and pulses and at least one vegetarian item on every menu. Natural yoghurt and polyunsaturated margarine are used where appropriate and fresh fruit salads are always available.

CHEAM

Restaurant

Al San Vincenzo

52 Upper Mulgrave
  Road
01-661 9763

Map 6 D3
Surrey

Lunch 12–2 Dinner 6.30–9.30 (Sat
  till 10)
Closed Sun except Mothering
  Sunday & Bank Holidays except
  Good Friday
Italian cooking

Average price £17
Set L & Set D £14.50
Credit: Access, Amex, Diners, Visa

Here, at last, in this delightful restaurant, is Italian food that not only tastes delicious, but is also good for you. Everything is cooked to order (allow time for this) from top-quality raw materials, including organic vegetables and hormone-free meats. Natural flavours predominate in dishes like seafood casserole with fresh tomato sauce, fresh tuna steak, wild rabbit stew and grilled meats with mango sauce. Imaginative fresh fruit desserts include figs with grapes, and mango with dolcelatte.

CHELTENHAM

Quick Bite

Forrest
(Wine Bar)

Imperial Lane
Cheltenham
(0242) 38001

Map 5 B2
Gloucestershire

Open 12.30–2.15 & 6.30–10.30
Closed Sun & Bank Holidays
  (except Mon eve)

Typical prices: Spiced chick peas
  with ginger £1.95
  Grilled chicken leg £3.50
Credit: Access, Visa

Food is consistently well cooked at this informal basement wine bar in the town centre. Healthy eaters can choose from a list of vegetarian dishes and regular snacks that includes soups, fresh spinach and cheese quiche, or spiced potatoes and aubergines with pitta bread, yoghurt and salad. Hot dishes of the day listed on a blackboard include grilled chicken or rump steak, courgette moussaka or vegetable lasagne. There's also an impressive cold table, with low and medium fat cheeses, crudités, houmus, pâté and a fine array of salads.

CHELTENHAM

Quick Bite

Retreat
(Wine Bar)

10 Suffolk Parade
Cheltenham
(0242) 35436

Map 5 B2
Gloucestershire

Open 12–2.15 & 6–9
Closed Sun & Bank Holidays

Typical prices: Smoked mackerel
  salad £1.75 Chilli with yoghurt &
  cucumber dressing £2.45
Credit: Access, Amex, Diners, Visa
Luncheon Vouchers accepted

Advance to the Retreat and sample a good selection of salads with rare roast beef, baked ham, rollmops, smoked mackerel, paprika chicken or cheese. Add a brown pitta bread or a granary slice and you have the makings of a healthy meal. This hugely popular wine bar is always packed, so come early and avoid having to wait for hot dishes like wholewheat spaghetti bolognese, barbecued chicken with jacket potato or ratatouille on brown rice. Vegetables can be served without butter or sauce.

171

CHENIES *Restaurant* Bedford Arms Thistle Hotel Restaurant

Near Rickmansworth
Chorleywood
(092 78) 3301

Map 6 D3
Buckinghamshire

Lunch 12.30–2.30 Dinner 7–10

Average price £22
Credit: Access, Amex, Diners, Visa

The menu at this formal restaurant boasts classical dishes like lobster bisque and Chateaubriand. It is therefore surprising to find a varied and extensive vegetarian menu with a choice, subject to availability, of over 40 starters and 20 entrées. There's also a wide selection of vegetables. Starters include grilled mushrooms with herbs and garlic, and whole date and almond salad, and to follow you might have pancakes stuffed with spicy red beans or a sauté of vegetables with garlic, ginger and bean curd. If the vegetarian menu is preferred, advise when booking.

CHESTER *Quick Bite* Abbey Green

2 Abbey Green, off
  Northgate Street
Chester
(0244) 313251

Map 3 C4
Cheshire

Open 10–3.30 & 6.30–10.30
Closed Sun, Mon & Bank Holidays
  except Good Friday
Vegetarian cooking

Typical prices: Mushroom burger
  £1.95 Cheese, leek & potato pie
  with salad £1.80
Credit: Access
Luncheon Vouchers accepted

Chester can be proud of this fine vegetarian restaurant close to the cathedral. The establishment has its own bakery and by day offers home-made granary bread with soups and baked jacket potatoes. Open salad sandwiches include cashew nut and soft cheese, and there's houmus for vegans. By night the menu is more extensive and half the dishes are vegan. Starters include minted avocado and orange salad while main courses run to very good curries, crêpes and dolmas. The fresh fruit salad is terrific.

CHESTER   *Restaurant*   Chester Grosvenor Restaurant

Eastgate Street
Chester
(0244) 24024

Map 3 C4
Cheshire

Lunch 12–2.30 Dinner 7–10
Closed December 24–26
French cooking

Average price £25
Set L £9.75
Set D £16
Credit: Access, Amex, Diners, Visa

Whether one chooses the luncheon buffet, the du jour menu or the seasonal à la carte, there is plenty for the health-conscious diner at this luxurious restaurant, where the emphasis is on fresh ingredients. Starters include chilled vegetable soup with sorrel, and marinated Dee salmon but, if something even simpler is preferred, Ogen melon and asparagus are usually available. Chargrilled Scottish beef and Welsh lamb are offered as alternatives to the more elaborate entrées, and delicately sauced fish dishes will be served plain if preferred.

CHESTER   *Quick Bite*   Farmhouse

Millett's Store,
 9 Northgate Street
Chester
(0244) 311332

Map 3 C4
Cheshire

Open 9.30–5.30
Closed Sun, January 1,
December 25 & some other Bank
 Holidays

Typical prices: Barley &
 mushroom casserole £1.20
 Wholemeal scone 40p
Luncheon Vouchers accepted

Cut through the camping department on the first floor of Millett's Store and discover a pleasant self-service restaurant. The best bet in terms of healthy eating is the cold table, which offers at least five freshly prepared salads, together with cold meats, spicy chicken and particularly good wholemeal flans. Hot dishes are also available from around 11 until mid-afternoon. Consult the hanging blackboards for daily specialities like beef and lentil casserole. Efficient staff keep the place spotless.

CHESTER   *QuickBite*   Pierre Griffe Wine Bar

4 Mercia Square
Chester
(0244) 312635

Map 3 C4
Cheshire

Open 11.30–3 & 5.30–10.30 (Fri &
    Sat till 11)
Closed Sun & December 25 & 26

Typical prices: Vegetarian pâté
    £1.30 Potato & onion soup 85p

Select a salad at this simple wine bar on the upper level of
a shopping precinct. Sit on the terrace in summer or come
indoors for a warming bowl of home-made soup in winter.
The cooking is done by two local women who know their
customers and produce straightforward unsophisticated
dishes like home-baked ham, flans and casseroles. Wholewheat lasagne is sometimes on offer and vegetarians are
catered for with pizzas and pâtés. Natural yoghurt is used
where appropriate and vegetables are available without
butter or sauce.

CHICHESTER   *QuickBite*   Chats Brasserie

Unit 5, Sharp Garland
    House, Eastgate
Chichester
(0243) 783223

Map 5 C4
West Sussex

Open 9.30–4 (Sat till 5.30)
Closed Sun & Bank Holidays

Typical prices: Home-made
    quiche 95p
    Open sandwiches £1.95
Luncheon Vouchers accepted

Soups, salads and sandwiches are prime favourites at this
bright little restaurant. A sandwich may be an open or shut
case. In the first category try the rare roast beef and
horseradish or the cottage cheese and walnut, generously
piled on brown bread and served with a choice of side
salads that includes coleslaw, Waldorf and pasta.
Wholemeal quiches are good value—consult the blackboards for daily specials. Sweets include fruit sorbets and
fresh fruit salad.

CHICHESTER *QuickBite* Clinch's Salad ★ House

14 Southgate
Chichester
(0243) 788822

Map 5 C4
West Sussex

Open 8–5.30
Closed Sun & Bank Holidays

Typical prices: Lentil rissoles
£1.55 Butter bean bake £1.55
Luncheon Vouchers accepted

Getting into this particular Clinch is a most pleasurable experience thanks to excellent cooking and attention to detail in an environment enhanced by fresh flowers. The fare is primarily vegetarian, with some simple fish dishes such as fresh salmon or mackerel with mushroom and celery stuffing. Hearty cakes and bakes are served morning and afternoon, while from about noon the choice widens to include lovely light wholemeal flans, a selection of first-class salads and savouries such as lentil rissoles with yoghurt sauce and butter bean bake.

CHICHESTER *Pub* Nags

3 St Pancras
Chichester
(0243) 785823

Map 5 C4
West Sussex

Last order 9.30pm
No bar food Sun eve
Free House

Typical prices: Carvery lunch £6
 Vegetarian lasagne £2
Credit: Access, Amex, Diners, Visa

Customers are assured of a healthy meal at this handsome town-centre pub. Chef's specialities include breast of chicken with fresh fruits, grilled trout and cassoulet. Daytime visitors go for ploughman's lunches and salads (at least five) or hot dishes like chilli con carne or vegetarian lasagne. The carvery offers excellent value with a selection of meat and game that includes rare roast beef and succulent guinea fowl, served with a variety of carefully cooked vegetables or with a salad from the buffet.

CHICHESTER — *QuickBite* — St Martin's Tea Rooms

St Martin's Street
Chichester
(0243) 786715

Map 5 C4
West Sussex

Open 10–6
Closed Sun, Mon, Bank Holidays
& 2 weeks Christmas

Typical prices: Cottage cheese
open sandwich £1.75
Vegan cake 60p

A pretty little garden frames this charming terraced-house tea room, where nostalgia is evoked by cucumber sandwiches and traditional afternoon teas. The lunchtime menu owes much to organically grown produce and caters extremely well for vegetarian and vegan customers. Tasty vegetable soups are served with wholemeal bread, and there are daily specials like nut roast or vegetable lasagne. The Welsh rarebit is a model of its kind, scones are made with honey instead of butter and there is a special vegan cake studded with cashew nuts.

CHICHESTER — *QuickBite* — Savourie

38 Little London
Chichester
(0243) 784899

Map 5 C4
West Sussex

Open 12–2 & 7–10
Closed Sun, Mon & December 25
& 26

Typical prices: Cod & prawn au
gratin £2.95
Jacket potato from 85p
Credit: Access, Amex, Diners, Visa

This spacious restaurant makes a civilised setting for an enjoyable meal. The small but interesting menu changes every fortnight, but always includes several dishes to suit the healthy eater. There's invariably a hot home-made soup and often a chilled alternative, such as tomato and orange. Cold main courses (hot ones are on offer too) might be roast beef, smoked mackerel or crab and prawn quiche, served with a selection of salads and jacket potatoes. Vegetarian dishes available on request.

CHIPPING NORTON — *Quick Bite* — Nutters

10 New Street
Chipping Norton
(0608) 41995

Map 5 B2
Oxfordshire

Open 10–4.30
Closed Sun, Mon & 3 days
 Christmas

Typical prices: Lentil soup £1
 Vegetarian curry £1.75

Elizabeth Arnold is a former health education lecturer who puts her experience to excellent use in this attractive self-service restaurant. Eat indoors at tables decked with pretty pastel cloths, or sit in the delightful walled garden. Wholesome bakes include fat-free scones, made with honey and wholemeal flour, non-dairy cakes and lovely fruit slices. Principles of healthy eating are obviously adhered to in dishes like chicken in white wine with mushrooms, or vegetarian curry and brown rice. Salads are crisp and colourful. Don't miss the raspberry and apple crumble.

CHRISTCHURCH — *Quick Bite* — Salads

8 High Street
Christchurch
(0202) 476273

Map 5 B4
Dorset

Open 10–3
Closed Sat, Sun, Bank Holidays,
 2 weeks February & 2 weeks
 Christmas
Wholefood cooking

Typical prices: Cheese flan 70p
 Lentil bake 80p
Luncheon Vouchers accepted

Excellent salads make a tempting display on the self-service counter of this summery little restaurant, sprucely decorated in green and white. The Misses Cameron and Simmons take great pride in their establishment and everything is carefully prepared and of a very high standard. A typical lunchtime spread might include freshly-made lentil soup , delicious wholemeal artichoke flan and a hot special such as spicy kidney beans or pasta and mushrooms in tomato sauce.

CIRENCESTER

Quick Bite

Brewery
Coffee Shop

Brewery Court
Cirencester
(0285) 4791

Map 5 B3
Gloucestershire

Open 10–5.30
Closed Sun, Good Friday &
  Christmas–New Year

Typical prices: Leek & pasta bake
  £2.15 Smoked mackerel £1
  (Minimum lunchtime charge £1.50)

Although the name of this attractive establishment sounds like a contradiction in terms, all is harmony within its walls. Owned by the Cirencester Workshops Trust and associated with its crafts complex, the coffee shop is a focal point for local artists, whose paintings make ever-changing murals. Cakes and bakes are served throughout the day, and at lunchtime there are simple soups and salads, plus daily specialities like Russian fish pie, chilli con carne or haddock lasagne. There's always a vegetarian dish or two. The herby nut roast is particularly popular.

COCKERMOUTH

Restaurant

Quince ★
& Medlar

13 Castlegate
Cockermouth
(0900) 823579

Map 3 B2
Cumbria

Dinner only 7–9.30 (Fri & Sat
  till 10)
Closed Sun, Mon & Bank Holidays
Vegetarian cooking

Average price £12
Credit: Access, Visa

This establishment calls itself a 'fine food vegetarian restaurant' and so it is. Fresh flowers, panelled walls and candlelight create an intimate setting for beautifully balanced and carefully cooked meals. Start, perhaps, with baked courgettes with rosemary, topped with Parmesan crumble—the vegetables still crisp and the topping extremely tasty. Main courses include a seed and nut bake which teams four types of nut with three sorts of seed to make a medley of complementary textures and flavours.

Embleton
Bassenthwaite Lake
(059 681) 394

Map 3 B2
Cumbria

Open 10.30–5.30, also 7–9 Thurs,
  Nov–Jan Sat & Sun 10.30–4.30
  also 7–9 Fri & Sat
Closed end October–Easter
  except weekends Nov–Jan

Typical prices: Home-made soup
  95p Baked potato & salad £2.40
  (Minimum lunchtime charge £2)

Half a mile from the A66 is Wythop Mill where vintage woodworking machinery can be seen powered by a waterwheel. It is well worth a visit, particularly if combined with a call at the proudly maintained tea room-cum-restaurant. Everything is freshly made here and healthy choices range from simple bakes to light meals such as home-made lentil soup with herb scones, or filled baked potatoes with a choice of four or five salads. The suppers (now bookable) offer similar wholesome fare and vegetarians can be catered for with advance notice.

COCKWOOD *Pub* Ship Inn

Near Exeter
Starcross
(0626) 890373

Map 8 C2
Devon

Last order 10pm
Brewery Courage

Typical prices: Grilled fresh
  salmon £6.75
  Fisherman's lunch £1.75
Credit: Amex

This inn was originally a victualler's house readying sailing ships for sea. It still provides visitors with a tempting selection of provisions. The seafood is superb and ranges from a simple plate of fresh cockles to an impressive platter on which crab, salmon, prawns, cockles and other seafoods are arranged on a generous salad. Starters include fresh mussels, smoked mackerel and local oysters and there's always a tasty fish soup. Steaks and sandwiches too, and vegetarian dishes available on request.

ENGLAND

COGGESHALL  *Restaurant* White Hart Hotel Restaurant

Market End
Coggeshall
(0376) 61654

Map 6 E2
Essex

Lunch 12.30–2 Dinner 7.30–9.30
Closed Lunch Mon & Sat, Dinner
Sun to non-residents, all Fri,
August & 1 week Christmas

Average price £22
Set L £11.75 (Sun only)
Credit: Access, Amex, Diners, Visa

First-class ingredients are competently cooked at this roomy and rather grand hotel restaurant. Grills served with tomato, mushrooms and a jacket potato offer good value to the diner who prefers to avoid sauced dishes—although it would be a shame not to try one of the specialities such as loin of Dutch veal served with a sauce of shallots, rosemary and white wine. The Mersea oysters and fresh whole lobster are commended. Vegetables are crisp and lightly seasoned. Some vegetarian dishes—fairly costly—are included on the menu.

COGGESHALL *Pub* Woolpack Inn

91 Church Street
Coggeshall
(0376) 61235

Map 6 E2
Essex

Last order 9.30pm
No bar food Sun–Tues eves
Brewery Ind Coope

Typical prices: Lentil soup £1.15
Chicken tikka £2.50

Local legend claims there's a resident ghost at this creeper-clad 15th-century inn—certainly it is the favourite haunt of many local residents! Visitors are drawn in by the sheer charm of the building and stay to sample Judith Hutchinson's tasty cooking. This includes simple snacks like houmus with pitta bread, wholemeal sandwiches and home-made soup with garlic bread, plus healthy light meals such as grilled Dover sole with salad or chicken tikka with rice. Prior warning for vegetarian food, please.

COLCHESTER *Quick Bite* **Bistro Nine**

9 North Hill
Colchester
(0206) 576466

Map 6 E2
Essex

Open 12–2 & 7–10.45
Closed Sun, Mon & 1 week
  Christmas

Typical prices: Vegetarian dish of
  the day £1.50
  Poached salmon cutlet £5.95
Credit: Access, Visa

Vegetarian dishes are dear to the heart of the chef at this pleasant city bistro and, in addition to preparing a wide range of meat-based dishes, he delights in devising daily specialities like spinach and nut lasagne—layers of pasta with spinach and nutty tomato sauce, topped with cheese. Snacks, served downstairs, include simple soups and filled jacket potatoes. Upstairs a wider and more expensive menu caters for healthy appetites with starters like marinated herring and main courses that include poached salmon cutlet.

CONGLETON *Quick Bite* **Odd Fellows ★ Wine Bar & Bistro**

20 Rood Hill
Congleton
(0260) 270243

Map 3 C4
Cheshire

Open 12–2 & 6.45–11 (Fri & Sat
from 6.30, Sun 7–10.30)
Closed Lunch Sun, Bank Holiday
Mon & December 25–27

Typical prices: Prawn & salmon
salad £4.85 Leek quiche £2
Credit: Amex

Highly polished dark wood forms a beautiful background for the fine display of salads including roast beef, baked ham, tuna, prawn and smoked salmon. Hot dishes are served too, starting with very good home-made soup. Main courses include vegetarian or vegan lasagne, a ratatouille cheese bowl and tandoori pork kebabs. Also excellent grilled steaks served with jacket potatoes or a root vege-table purée. No wholemeal bread, but polyunsaturated margarine is served with the French bread.

CORSE LAWN *Restaurant* Corse Lawn ★ House

Near Tirley
Tirley
(045 278) 479

Map 5 B2
Gloucestershire

Lunch 12–2 Dinner 7–10
Closed Dinner Sun & all second
 week January

Average price £18
Set L £10.50 (Sun £12.50)
Set D £14.50
Credit: Access, Amex, Diners, Visa

This lovely old coaching inn, built in 1745, is a fabulous find. Baba Hines is a dedicated cook who seeks out top-quality ingredients and combines them with masterful skill. A typical dinner chosen from the à la carte menu might begin with sorrel soup, progress to baked sea bass with white wine and mussels, and conclude with a fresh sorbet. There's also an inspired vegetarian menu. Lunches are light and lovely, with shellfish a speciality. Oysters, langoustine and lobster are featured alongside the salads, terrines and simple cheese platters.

CORTON *Pub* Dove at Corton

Near Warminster
Warminster
(0985) 50378

Map 5 B3
Wiltshire

Last order 9.30pm
No bar food Sun eve or all Mon
Closed 2 weeks mid January &
 December 25
Free House

Typical prices: Savoury walnut
 loaf £5 Salad platter £3.50
Credit: Access, Visa

In the heart of the Wiltshire countryside, this charming little pub has plenty to offer customers in search of a healthy snack or meal. Starters include gazpacho, smoked trout or chilled melon. Salad platters based upon roast beef or peeled prawns make more substantial main courses and there's an interesting vegetarian menu. Try walnut loaf with spinach soufflé or savoury pancakes on a bed of vegetable purée. Throughout the summer fresh salmon mayonnaise is a daily speciality.

COVENTRY *Restaurant* Trinity House Hotel ★
Herbs Restaurant

28 Lower Holyhead
Road
Coventry
(0203) 555654

Map 5 B2
West Midlands

Dinner only 6.30–9.30
Closed Sun, Bank Holidays &
December 24–January 5
Vegetarian cooking

Average price £10

Taking vegetarian cooking into the gourmet class is chef and co-owner of this excellent restaurant, Robert Jackson. Situated in a small privately-owned hotel, Herbs has rapidly acquired an enviable reputation and regular customers number many non-vegetarians unable to resist the imaginative dishes. The only drawback, for the healthy eater, is that wine and cream are used in some sauces—although dishes will be served without sauce if preferred. Start perhaps with the curried vegetable pâté, followed by aubergine, pepper and mushroom lasagne.

CROYDON *Quick Bite* Hockneys

98 High Street
01-688 2899

Map 6 D3
Surrey

Open 12–10.30
Closed Sun, Mon, Bank Holidays,
  2 weeks August & 2 weeks
  Christmas
Vegetarian cooking

Typical prices: Vegetable
  Stroganoff £3 Dhal soup £1
Credit: Access, Amex, Diners, Visa
Luncheon Vouchers accepted

Situated in the Arts Centre complex, this is a friendly and well-run establishment. Contemporary decor (Hockney etchings, naturally) gives a light and airy feel and food is enticing and thoroughly enjoyable. By day you choose your meal from the ground floor counter and eat upstairs; after dark, candlelit dinners are served at the tables. Starters include gazpacho and houmus, whilst main lines are savoury pulse and pasta bakes, quiches, falafel or vegeburgers. Booking required in the evenings.

ENGLAND

CROYDON · *Quick Bite* · **Munbhave**

305 London Road,
  West Croydon
01-689 6331

Map 6 D3
Surrey

Open 6–11 (Sat till 12)
Closed Mon, January 1,
  December 25 & 26 & 2 weeks
  summer
Indian vegetarian cooking

Typical prices: Stuffed aubergine
  £3.85 Masala Dhosa £3.95
Credit: Access, Visa

Kesh Tank and his family run this simple Indian vegetarian restaurant with great enthusiasm. A member of the family is always on hand to advise the adventurous who prefer not to take the easy option of ordering a set meal. Some of the dishes you might like to try are black pea and yoghurt fritters, vegetable cutlets with onion salad, whole stuffed aubergine and a bhindi (okra) special. Rice and pulse dishes, breads and special vegetables make interesting accompaniments and there is fresh fruit to follow. Beverages include lassi (salted or sweet), fruit juices and teas.

CUCKFIELD · *Restaurant* · **Ockenden Manor Hotel Restaurant**

Ockenden Lane, Near
  Haywards Heath
(0444) 416111

Map 6 D3
West Sussex

Lunch 12.30–2 Dinner 7.15–9.15
  (Sun till 8.30)
Closed Dinner December 25

Average price £25
Set L £12
Set D £16.50
Credit: Access, Amex, Diners, Visa

Healthy eaters can dine out in style at this elegant oak-panelled restaurant. Garry Leaf is the skilful chef whose aim is to produce essentially English food with an element of French flair, using only fresh produce of good quality. Start, perhaps, with smoked salmon with cucumber yoghurt, continue with fillet steak poached in consommé with wild mushrooms and chives, and finally surrender to a simple yoghurt and orange mousse. There is also an excellent vegetarian menu.

No stowaways aboard.

Birds Eye Cod Fillet Fish Fingers have only
100% natural ingredients. No artificial colours or flavourings.

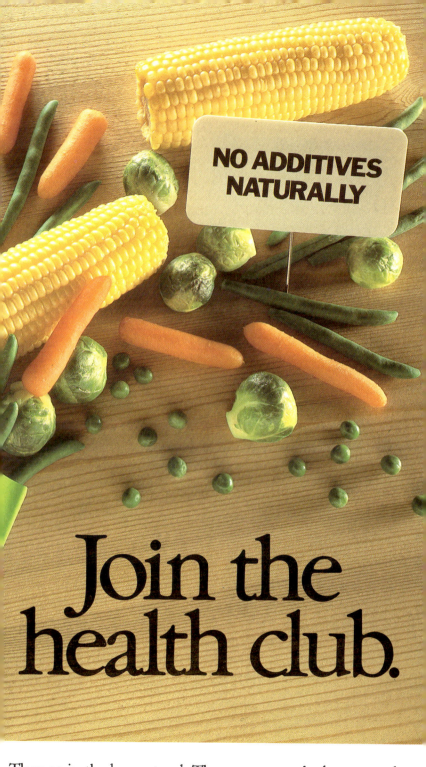

NO ADDITIVES NATURALLY

Join the health club.

They go in the bag natural. They come out the bag natural.
We've nothing more to add.

ENGLAND

DARTINGTON Cranks Health ★ Food Restaurant

Shinners Bridge, Near
  Totnes
Totnes
(0803) 862388

Map 8 C2
Devon

Open 10–5
Closed Sun in winter, January 1,
  Good Friday & 2–3 days
  Christmas
Vegetarian cooking

Typical prices: Vegetable crumble
  £2.75 Apricot slice 60p
Luncheon Vouchers accepted

The name of Cranks needs no introduction to healthy eaters. The first of these restaurants, in London's Marshall Street, was a trailblazer that introduced a new and healthier way of eating out to the British public. This West Country offshoot maintains the same high standards. Food is light and tasty and includes home-made soup, pizzas and simple savoury dishes like vegetable crumble and chilli bean casserole. Salads based on lentils and brown rice and heaped in earthenware bowls taste as good as they look. Desserts do justice to fresh and dried fruit.

DEDHAM  Dedham Vale Hotel, Terrace Restaurant

Stratford Road
Colchester
(0206) 322273

Map 6 E2
Essex

Lunch 12–2 Dinner 7–10 (Sun till
  9.30)
Closed Lunch Sat

Average price £18
Set L £7.50 (Sun £11.25)
Credit: Access, Amex, Diners, Visa

Many of the dishes on offer at this delightful restaurant are fresh and light. Start, perhaps, with Ogen melon filled with a refreshing grape sorbet or tomatoes stuffed with salmon trout mousse, and proceed to foil-baked halibut steak. Alternatively browse at the admirable buffet (available Monday to Friday). Steaks, chops and kebabs are served from the grill and there is a small selection of vegetarian dishes such as vegetable terrine in pastry or vegetable lasagne. Desserts include fresh fruit salads.

190

DERBY

Lettuce Leaf

21 Friar Gate
Derby
(0332) 40307

Map 4 D4
Derbyshire

Open 10–7.30
Closed Sun & Bank Holidays
Vegetarian wholefood cooking

Typical prices: Vegetables
  provençale £1.80
  Lettuce leaf muesli 95p
Luncheon Vouchers accepted

Cathy Shepherd aims to offer an antidote to prepacked push-button food at her pleasantly unpretentious wholefood restaurant. Eggs are farm-fresh, wholemeal flour is used and ingredients are free of artificial additives and preservatives as far as possible. A different vegetable soup is made each day and there are specials like marrow provençale and celery hot pot. Also flans, omelettes and lots of splendid salads assembled to order. One or two vegan dishes are always on offer and desserts include fresh fruit salad and yoghurt with honey or blackcurrants.

DEVIZES

Pub

Bear Hotel

Market Place
Devizes
(0380) 2444

Map 5 B3
Wiltshire

Last order 11pm
Brewery Wadworth

Typical prices: Slimmer's salad
  £2.75
  Vegetarian nut cutlet £3.95
Credit: Access, Amex, Visa

Healthy eaters are admirably catered for at this handsome and historic inn. The choice ranges from slimmers' sandwiches at the bar to selections from the buffet in the Lawrence Room. Salads vary from shredded cabbage with peppers, courgettes and yoghurt dressing to chick peas with tahina dressing. There's also an à la carte menu specifically aimed at those who prefer plainly cooked food without rich sauces and an equally well-conceived vegetarian menu.

191

DEVIZES   *Quick Bite*   Wiltshire Kitchen

11 St John's Street
Devizes
(0380) 4840

Map 5 B3
Wiltshire

Open 9.30–5.30
Closed Sun, Bank Holidays &
   1 week Christmas

Typical prices: Tomato, celery &
   apple soup 75p
   Haddock & mushroom lasagne
   £2.85

Ann Blunden cooks superbly at this simple largely self-service restaurant. There is a marvellous array of cakes and bakes available all day, and around noon a variety of tasty savoury dishes is ready. Everything is home-made and of a very high quality. Make a start with a well-flavoured soup such as lentil and cumin, or tomato, celery and apple. The main dish might be spinach and mushroom lasagne or one of Ann's melt-in-the-mouth seafood roulades. Salads or crisp, carefully cooked vegetables will be served with your meal and jacket potatoes are always on offer.

DORCHESTER   *Quick Bite*   Potter In

19 Durngate Street
Dorchester
(0305) 68649

Map 5 B4
Dorset

Open 10–5
Closed Sun & Bank Holidays

Typical prices: Lentil bake 80p
   Banana cake 40p
Credit: Access, Visa

A score of salads sets the scene at this friendly self-service restaurant. Interesting combinations include pickled cabbage with ginger, mushrooms with coriander, and cauliflower with peppers and tomato. Heap your plate high or forsake the salad bar in favour of savouries like lentil bake or chick pea roast. There are hearty chicken or beef casseroles too, and filled jacket potatoes. Wholemeal bread is served with polyunsaturated margarine, and there's a not-too-sweet apple and blueberry crumble.

EASINGWOLD

 Quick Bite

Truffles

Snowdon House,
 Spring Street
Easingwold
(0347) 22342

Map 4 D3
 North Yorkshire

Open 9–5.30 (Sat till 5)
Closed Sun & Mon (except some
 Bank Holiday weekends),
 January 1 & December 25 & 26

Typical prices: Vegetarian
 pancake £1.75
 Cottage cheese & apple
 sandwich 75p

Regular customers praise the friendliness of the staff and the fresh and tasty snacks and light bites at this attractively designed coffee shop. An all-day choice includes soup, fresh wholemeal sandwiches and salads with cottage cheese and apple, roast ham or prawns. Lunchtime brings a specials selection that includes vegetarian pancakes, stir-fry vegetables with brown rice and a variety of omelettes. There is a small, rather traditional children's menu and set afternoon teas are available from 3pm. Decaffeinated coffee and herbal teas are served all day.

EASTBOURNE

Quick Bite

Ceres Health
Food Restaurant

38a Ashford Road
Eastbourne
(0323) 28482

Map 6 E4
East Sussex

Open 9.30–5
Closed Sun & Bank Holidays

Typical prices: Butter bean soup
 75p Spaghetti napoletana £1.68
Luncheon Vouchers accepted

Conveniently situated behind a shopping centre, this restaurant has a long-standing reputation for serving healthy food. The original vegetarian menu has now been extended to include simple white meat and fish dishes but the emphasis is still on food like ratatouille, cauliflower cheese, tuna-filled jacket potatoes and nut roast. Nourishing soups are made daily, and there is a selection of composite salads. Fresh fruit in yoghurt is an appealing afterthought and fresh fruit salad is always on offer too.

EASTBOURNE *Quick Bite* Nature's Way ★

196 Terminus Road
Eastbourne
(0323) 643211

Map 6 E4
East Sussex

Open 9.30–5
Closed Sun, Mon & Bank Holidays
  (except Good Friday), 1 week
  March–April, 1 week November
  & 1 week Christmas
Vegetarian cooking

Typical prices: Lentil casserole
  £1.60 Vegetable curry £1.60
Luncheon Vouchers accepted

As its name suggests, this vegetarian restaurant takes a natural view of healthy eating. Dishes are detailed on a blackboard and dispensed from a self-service counter. Specials, some of which are suitable for vegans, vary with the season, but vegetable hotpot, nut loaf, cashew nut and rice bake, and vegetable and bean curry are typical. Filled jacket potatoes are also served, as are salads, and there is a range of cakes like the popular nutty log, plus fresh fruit salad to follow. Wholemeal bread is served, with polyunsaturated margarine.

EASTON *Pub* White Horse

Near Woodbridge
Wickham Market
(0728) 746456

Map 6 F2
Suffolk

Last order 9pm
Brewery Tollemache Cobbold

Typical prices: Wholemeal
  spaghetti £2.75
  Fisherman's pie £2.95
Credit: Access

Plenty of birds at this village pub—all feathered and housed in enclosures in the garden and on the picturesque pond. Admire them before popping indoors for one of David Grimwood's delicious bar snacks. Local ingredients are used to impressive effect in dishes like dressed Cromer crab, baked soles and fresh sardines. In winter there's always a traditional hearty soup, while in summer there is taramasalata with wholemeal toast. Rice and pasta appear in a variety of dishes.

EFFINGHAM Plough

Orestan Lane
Bookham
(0372) 58121

Map 6 D3
Surrey

Last order 8.30pm
No bar food Sun
Brewery Courage

Typical prices: Stuffed courgettes
£1.95 Seafood pasta £2

Everything is freshly prepared at this friendly pub. Careful preparation and capable cooking is evident on a black-board menu that includes plenty of healthy dishes. Home-made soup is always on offer, with wholemeal bread, and at least two different salads. One of the most popular is egg and prawn, served simply with a separate dressing. Sand-wiches run to roast beef, prawn and crab and there are delicious savoury dishes, some suitable for vegetarians. These might include mushrooms provençale or chicken risotto with brown rice. Fresh fruit is always available.

ELLAND *Quick Bite* Berties Bistro ★

7 Town Hall Buildings
Halifax
(0422) 71724

Map 4 D4
West Yorkshire

Open 7–11 (Sun 5–9.30)
Closed Mon, January 1 &
December 25 & 26

Typical prices: Poached salmon &
watercress sauce £5.95
Brown bean stew £3.85

Victorian in character, contemporary in cuisine—that's Berties, a bistro whose imaginative evening meals are always well patronised. Starters include grilled red mullet provençale and spinach and chicken terrine. The main course might be grilled trout with almonds, lime and ginger, or a poached lemon sole, served sauced or plain. There is always at least one vegetarian main course. The sweets trolley is best waved aside—Berties bombe could sabotage the best of healthy intentions.

195

ELSLACK — *Pub* — Tempest Arms

Near Skipton
Earby
(0282) 842450

Map 3 C3
North Yorkshire

Last order 10 pm
Closed December 25 eve
Free House

Typical prices: French onion soup
£1.25 Poached Salmon £4.50

Close enough to the junction of the A59 and A56 for convenience, yet sufficiently far removed to avoid dense traffic, this is a well-run and most acceptable inn. The landlord, Frenchman Francis Pierre Boulongne provides a wide range of bar meals suitable for healthy eaters, from his low-calorie platter, a combination of raw vegetables, prawns, salmon, fruit and natural yoghurt, to simple fish dishes. Poached salmon, grilled halibut, baked bonito are all regularly on offer. Grilled steaks please the meat-lovers and vegetarian lasagne is always available.

EMPINGHAM — *Pub* — White Horse

2 Main Street, Near
   Oakham
Empingham
(078 086) 221

Map 6 D1
Leicestershire

Last order 9.45pm
Brewery John Smith

Typical prices: Fresh grilled
   sardines £1.95
   Vegetarian burger £3.25
Credit: Access, Amex, Diners, Visa

Cooking is consistently good at this popular and well run pub close to Rutland Water. Raw materials are undeniably fresh—many of them, come from the family farm. The cheeses are particularly well chosen, with ten varieties on offer including many low and medium-fat varieties. There's a good range of salads, and fish dishes like baked trout or grilled swordfish are ideal for healthy eaters. A carefully prepared vegetarian special, such as nut burgers, is always on the menu. Staff are friendly and helpful.

40 North Street
Emsworth
(0242) 373390

Map 5 C4
Hampshire

Open 10–5

Closed Sun & December 25 & 26

Typical prices: Baked potato &
  chilli £1.30
  Rice & vegetable bake £1.95

Anna Warburton is the moving force behind this informal restaurant, with its charming conservatory and peaceful garden. Everything is home-made and available throughout the opening hours. Scones, cakes and bakes are always on offer, together with a delicious selection of savoury items. Good nourishing soups, pizzas and filled jacket potatoes are the order of the day, with vegetable cutlets and tasty brown bread sandwiches or simple snacks like fishcakes with home-made tomato sauce. Fresh fruit to follow—or a light citrus sorbet.

ESHER *Restaurant* Good Earth

14 High Street
Esher
(78) 62489

Map 6 D3
Surrey

Lunch 12–2.30 (Sun 12.30–3)
  Dinner 6–11.30 (Sun 6–11)
Closed December 24–27
Chinese cooking

Average price £16.50
Set L £12
Set D £14
Credit: Access, Amex, Diners, Visa

This successful and well-run establishment is an offshoot of a popular chain of stylish Chinese restaurants in London (see page 78). With over a hundred dishes on the menu, making a healthy choice is not difficult, just time consuming. Get off to a good start with the romantically named green jade soup, which owes its colour to spinach and its texture to finely chopped chicken. Seafood is a speciality and grilled prawns with piquant sauce are perennially popular. Interesting vegetable and bean curd dishes.

197

EXETER *Quick Bite* Cooling's Wine Bar

11 Gandy Street
Exeter
(0392) 34183

Map 8 C2
Devon

Open 11–2.15 & 5.30–10.15
 (summer evenings until 10.45)
Closed Sun, Bank Holiday
 lunches, Jan 1 & Dec 25 & 26

Typical prices: Four dip main
 course salad selection £2
 Chicken Waldorf £1.95
 Luncheon Vouchers accepted

An extensive and imaginative selection of salads is available at this hugely popular wine bar, where those in the know slip in before the mealtime melée. Try the egg, vegetable and cheese platter, the curried eggs with salad or the combination of four main course salads attractively presented on one plate which is a great favourite with lunchtime patrons. Traditional English dishes like cottage pie are always available and vegetarians are catered for. Fresh fruit salad is available only in summer—otherwise puds are on the lavish side.

FARNHAM *Pub* Spotted Cow

3 Bourne Grove
Farnham
(0252) 726541

Map 5 C3
Surrey

Last order 10 pm
No bar food Mon eve
Brewery Courage

Typical prices: Chicken & chick
 pea stew £2.60
 Whole plaice £3.50
Credit: Access, Visa

In a sylvan setting south of Farnham you'll find the Spotted Cow. Plates decorate the white painted walls and good honest home cooked dishes are advertised on a blackboard menu. Enjoy a bowl of wholesome soup, a salad with baked mackerel or cottage cheese or one of the daily specials. A vegetarian dish such as bean casserole or vegetable lasagne, maybe, or a simple grilled plaice. Pulses appear in dishes like chicken and chick pea stew, and there is fresh fruit salad to round off your repast.

FAVERSHAM

Quick Bite

Recreation★ Tavern

16 East Street
Faversham
(0795) 536033

Map 6 E3
Kent

Open 12–2 & 7–10
Closed December 25 eve–
January 3

Typical prices: Tuna fish &
wholemeal pasta salad £1.20
Smoked chicken £2.50
(Minimum lunchtime charge £4)
Credit: Access, Visa

The standard of cooking and presentation at this pleasant self-service restaurant is consistently high. Healthy vegetable dishes include lentil and onion croquettes, home-made houmus and a range of fine tasty and imaginative salads, like fennel and feta cheese or squid, lemon and coriander. Soups are skilfully flavoured and yoghurt is used to moderate spicy dishes, as in the curried turkey casserole. Magnificent puddings weaken the will power, but luckily there's an excellent grapefruit sorbet or cheese and biscuits and decaffeinated coffee as an antidote.

FAWKHAM

Restaurant

Brandshatch Place Restaurant

Ash Green
(0474) 872239

Map 6 E3
Kent

Lunch 12–2.30 Dinner 7–9.30
Closed Lunch Sat, all Sun &
December 25–January 4

Average price £20
Credit: Access, Amex, Diners, Visa

Chef Colin Liddy is a skilled professional who presents a rather special vegetarian menu with a choice of starters and a soup such as cider and onion with strips of apple. Main dishes are not always particularly healthy but include a fresh vegetable risotto. Wholemeal pasta and brown rice are used often and guests who scorn sauces will enjoy simple dishes like suprême of chicken with limes. Fresh wholemeal bread is available, and natural yoghurt and skimmed milk are used. Vegan dishes on request.

199

FAWLEY — *Pub* — Walnut Tree

Near Henley-on-
  Thames
Turville Heath
(049 163) 360

Map 5 C3
Buckinghamshire

Last order 10pm
Brewery Brakspear

Typical prices: Mushroom burger
  £3.95 Grilled Dover sole £6.95
Credit: Access, Visa

What distinguishes this modern red brick pub is the diversity of dishes on its daily menu. With over 60 to choose from the healthy eater should find plenty to please. You can make a very good meal from starters like fresh vegetable timbale with watercress sauce, or home-made soup. To follow, there is grilled trout or steak with salads and new potatoes, mushroom burgers or vegetarian pancakes, and plenty of salads ranging from ham to tuna fish. Desserts include a delicious tropical fruit salad.

FLETCHING — *Pub* — Griffin Inn

Newick
(082 572) 2890

Map 6 D3
East Sussex

Last order 9pm
Free House

Typical prices: Spaghetti alla
  carbonara £2.95
  Salade niçoise £2.50
Credit: Access, Amex, Visa

Lunch in the bar of this warm and friendly pub may be a simple snack like a filled jacket potato or French bread sandwich, or a more substantial dish such as spaghetti carbonara or braised oxtail. Crêpes are a speciality—try the vegetarian variety with apple, celery, walnuts and grapes. On quiet evenings customers may choose dishes from the restaurant menu and might build a healthy meal around salade niçoise and grilled steak or vegetable Stroganoff with yoghurt sauce. Excellent, often organic, vegetables.

FLITWICK

Restaurant

Flitwick Manor Restaurant

Church Road
Flitwick
(0525) 712242

Map 6 D2
Bedfordshire

Lunch 12–2 Dinner 7–9.30,
Sat 7–10
Closed Dinner Sun & all
December 25 & 26

Average price £23
Set L & Set D from £10.80
  (Vegetarian menu)
Credit: Access, Amex, Diners, Visa

The extensive menu at this elegant 17th-century manor house has a definite fishy bias and includes Helford oysters and lobster from the manor's own tanks. 'Spa cuisine' dishes highlighted on the à la carte menu are for guests who prefer low calorie healthy eating. The choice includes grilled salmon on a bed of spinach, and for vegetarians, marmande tomatoes stuffed with cheese and wild mushrooms and served with pilaff. Three fixed-price menus, featuring shellfish, vegetarian and Chinese cuisine, extend the range. Desserts include fresh fruits and citrus ices.

FROGHALL

Quick Bite

Wharf Eating House

Foxt Road, Near
  Cheadle
Ipstones
(053 871) 486

Map 4 D4
Staffordshire

Open 11–6 Spring Bank Holiday–
  end September also from Easter
  11–5 Thurs–Sun
Closed Mon & end Oct–mid
  March

Typical prices: Home-made soup
  90p Vegetarian lasagne £1.25
Credit: Access, Diners

The Froghall Wharf passenger service offers trips by horse-drawn narrow boat along the picturesque Caldon Canal. Enjoy the scenery while sampling wholesome home cooking: pizzas, filled jacket potatoes and vegetarian pâté, cream teas, too, for those who throw caution to the winds. Landlubbers can enjoy the same selection and more at the Wharf Eating House. The owners are vegetarians, so it is not surprising that their special talent is for preparing meatless dishes like feuilleté of vegetables.

ENGLAND

FROME — *Quick Bite* — Settle

15 Cheap Street
Frome
(0373) 65975

Map 5 B3
Somerset

Open 9–5.30 (Thurs till 2 & 4 in
    summer), Sun & Bank Holidays
    2.30–6.30
Closed Sun (October–April) &
    January 1 & December 25 & 26

Typical prices: 'Settle Bobbin'
    £2.20
    Filled jacket potato £1.75
Credit: Access, Visa

Mob-capped waitresses serve some delectable dishes at this 17th-century tea shop. In answer to a plea from vegetarian visitors for more imaginative dishes, Margaret Vaughan has invented 'Settle Bobbins'—light wholemeal pastry whirls filled with crisp fresh vegetables and sunflower seeds and topped with a little local Cheddar cheese. Also on the menu are jacket potatoes and omelettes. More substantial dishes include chicken casserole with brown rice, and grilled trout, and there is always a selection of salads, and tempting cakes.

FYFIELD — *Pub* — White Hart

Near Abingdon
Frilford Heath
(0865) 390 585

Map 5 C3
Oxfordshire

Last order 10pm
Closed December 25 & 26 eves
Free House

Typical prices: Lentil pâté £1.50
    Vegetarian pie £2.45
Credit: Access, Amex, Diners, Visa

The garden of this fine 15th-century pub is lovely. Fine days find it filled with customers who enjoy a variety of interesting bar snacks. There are several healthy choices including lentil pâté, vegetable lasagne and wholemeal quiches. The home-baked granary bread is delicious and could easily become addictive. Salads are crisp and fresh and vegetables without sauces are available. Vegetarians are catered for with dishes like bean and lentil pie and meat lovers will find simple grilled steak.

202

GITTISHAM

Restaurant

Combe House
Hotel Restaurant

Near Honiton
Honiton
(0404) 2756

Map 8 C2
Devon

Lunch (Sun only) at 1pm Dinner
7.30–9.30
Closed early January–end
February

Average price £18
Set L from £11.50
Set D from £16.50
Credit: Access, Amex, Diners, Visa

A stately Elizabethan mansion, Combe House has two elegant dining rooms where seasonally changing set menus include healthy starters like ceviche of sole with scallops, or smoked trout with quail's eggs. The main course might be chargrilled steak or poached salmon. In the evening there's also a rather conventional vegetarian menu, including dishes such as pipérade and stuffed peppers. Pasta and rice dishes are also available and baked potatoes are served as an accompaniment. Fresh fruit salad to follow.

GLASTONBURY

Quick Bite

Rainbow's End
Café

17a High Street
Glastonbury
(0458) 33896

Map 5 A3
Somerset

Open 10–4.30 (Tues 9.30–4.30)
Closed Sun, Wed, Bank Holidays
& 2 weeks Christmas
Vegetarian wholefood cooking

Typical prices: Chick pea &
vegetable crumble £1.40
Yoghurt & banana flan £1

Mornings start with muesli, home-made yoghurt and wholemeal scones at this vegetarian café. At lunchtime the choice widens to include soups like carrot and orange or lentil and spinach. The daily special might be chick pea and vegetable crumble or stuffed aubergines. Snackers might prefer slices of well topped pizza with salads. Finish with fresh fruit salad (with no added sugar) or try the prune whip. Throughout the day specialist teas are served and the home-made lemonade is a great favourite.

ENGLAND

GOSFORTH *Quick Bite* Girl on a Swing

1 Lansdowne Place
Tyneside
(091) 2859672

Map 4 D2
Tyne & Wear

Open 6.30pm–11.30pm
Closed Sun & Bank Holidays
Vegetarian wholefood cooking

Typical prices: Stuffed vine leaves
£1.50 Spicy stewed okra with
tabbouleh £3.50

Vegetarian dishes from all over the world make a trip to this popular restaurant a convivial and interesting outing. Start in the Ukraine, perhaps, with a perfectly seasoned borsch with sourdough bread. Then travel to Turkey for imam biyaldi—savoury stuffed aubergines—or journey to Peru for papas arequipena, which combines potatoes, peanuts and onions with cheese and chilli. Finally come back to earth and England with a simple gooseberry fool or fresh fruit salad. Capable cooking and helpful staff make this a popular spot, so booking is advised.

GRANGE-IN BORROWDALE *Quick Bite* Grange Bridge Cottage

Near Keswick
Keswick
(0596) 84201

Map 3 B2
Cumbria

Open 10–5.30
Closed Mon (except Bank
Holidays & July–September) &
all November–Easter except
occasional weekends

Typical prices: Pasta bake & salad
£1.50 Houmus & salad £1.35

Relax in a sturdy cottage chair in this comforting little tea room and tuck in to simple, well cooked snacks or light meals. Scones, made from wholemeal flour, are a firm favourite with the holidaymakers who return year after year. For a simple healthy meal try the home-made soup with wholemeal bread (plus polyunsaturated margarine if preferred) and add a salad bowl with cheese or a slice of vegetarian flan. Houmus and piping hot pizzas are always available and there are daily specials like pasta bake.

GRANTHAM — *Quick Bite* — Knightingales

Guildhall Court,
  Guildhall Street
Grantham
(0476) 79243

Map 4 E4
Lincolnshire

Open 9.30–4.30
Closed Sun & Bank Holidays
  except Good Friday
Vegetarian wholefood cooking

Typical prices: Mushroom
  Stroganoff £1.95
  Celery & cashew nut soup 65p

Decor is attractive at this charming little side-street restaurant. A counter displays some of the day's offerings while details of the specials are chalked on a blackboard. The selection varies daily, and everything is prepared to a high standard. Quick bites include pâtés and savoury bakes such as lentil and cider roast and red bean chilli. There are usually at least four carefully assembled salads, which will be based upon brown rice, wholemeal pasta or red and white cabbage. Wholesome treats include excellent carrot cake, carob slices and flapjacks.

GRASMERE — *Restaurant* — Wordsworth Hotel, Prelude Restaurant

Near Ambleside
Grasmere
(096 65) 592

Map 3 B2
Cumbria

Lunch 12.30–2 Dinner 7–9 (Fri &
  Sat 7–9.30)

Average price £20
Set L £7.95 (Sun only)
Set D £15
Credit: Access, Amex, Diners, Visa

Cuisine nouvelle is the inspiration for several dishes at this lovely old lakeland hotel. Main courses like breast of wild duck with glazed apple slices display the talent of the chef. On the basis of healthy eating, the restaurant scores highly with rice, pasta and pulses appearing regularly. Wholemeal bread is served, with polyunsaturated margarine if preferred and both natural yoghurt and skimmed milk are used where appropriate. Sweets such as fresh fruit on a mango purée with almond butterflies are a delight.

ENGLAND

205

ENGLAND

GREAT DUNMOW   *Restaurant*   Starr

Market Place
Great Dunmow
(0371) 4321

Map 6 E2
Essex

Lunch 12–1.30 Dinner 7–10
Closed Lunch Sat & Mon, Dinner
  Sun, 3 weeks August & 1 week
  Christmas–New Year

Average price £20
Set L £12.95
Credit: Access, Amex, Diners, Visa

At first glance the menu at this welcoming restaurant would appear to have little to offer the health-conscious customer, but it is worth investigating further. The pasta is home-made and you are welcome to have a main course portion if neither the whole roast poussin with garlic and limes nor the spicy duck appeal to your culinary conscience. You could, of course, choose market-fresh Dover sole or poached salmon. Both vegetables and salads will be supplied without dressings or sauces, if preferred. Afters include plum crumble, fresh fruits and light sorbets.

GREAT MILTON *Restaurant*   Le Manoir Aux★ Quat' Saisons Restaurant

Church Road
Great Milton
(084 46) 8881

Map 5 C3
Oxfordshire

Lunch 12.15–2.30 Dinner 7.15–
  10.30
Closed Lunch Tues, Dinner Sun,
  all Mon & Dec 24–Jan 21
French cooking

Average price £40
Set L £19.50 & £37 Set D £37
Credit: Access, Amex, Diners, Visa

Superlatives are quite rightly applied to the cooking of Raymond Blanc. When cooking is of such calibre it seems pedantic to analyse it from the point of view of healthy eating alone yet on this score as on others, Raymond Blanc is sympathetic to public concern. His supremely light touch means sauces only enhance, never mask flavours, but if you prefer food unsauced you could select fresh lobster braised in a basil scented juice and served with fresh garden vegetables.

GREAT TORRINGTON

Quick Bite

Rebecca's

8 Potacre Street
Torrington
(0805) 22113

Map 8 D1
Devon

Open 9am–10pm
Closed Sun & 3 days Christmas

Typical prices: Fresh vegetable
curry £1.50
A proper beanfeast £4
Luncheon Vouchers accepted
Credit: Access, Amex, Visa

Traditional British food with family appeal is the formula at this highly successful West Country restaurant. Paul and Jill Lilly serve anything from a teacake to a three-course meal throughout opening hours. Everything is home-made and service is warm and friendly. Light snacks include cheese scones with cress, herb omelettes and soup with wholemeal bread. There's always a selection of steaks, chops, sole and seafood, sauced or plain. Vegetarian dishes run from a simple beanfeast to an elaborate pasta, nut and mixed vegetable medley.

GREAT YARMOUTH

Quick Bite

Friends Bistro

55 Deneside
Great Yarmouth
(0493) 852538

Map 6 F1
Norfolk

Open 10–4 & 7–10
Closed Mon evening, all Sun &
Bank Holidays

Typical prices: Chilli bean
casserole £2.95 Nut roast &
brown rice salad £2.95
Credit: Access, Visa
Luncheon Vouchers accepted

Just off one of Great Yarmouth's main shopping streets is this friendly little restaurant where visitors can find plenty of healthy dishes. At lunch time there's a short but interesting menu comprising hot dishes like chilli bean casserole or chicken risotto, together with at least three salads and vegetarian specialities such as leek croustade. The evening menu is more extensive, with starters such as salmon slice (layered with gherkins, hard-boiled egg and tomatoes), and main courses including lamb cutlets.

ENGLAND

207

GRIMSTHORPE *Restaurant* Black Horse Inn Restaurant

Near Bourne
Edenham
(077 832) 247

Map 6 D1
Lincolnshire

Lunch 12–1.45 Dinner 7–9.45 (Sat 7–10.30)
Closed Sun, Bank Holidays except Easter weekend, & December 24–30

Average price £14
Set L & Set D from £10.95
Credit: Access, Amex, Visa

The Black Horse has gained a good reputation for its above-average English cooking, but this is not its only claim to fame. It also exhibits a concern for healthy food and slimmers are shown particular consideration. Low-calorie dishes marked with an 's' include a variety of interesting salads and main courses like grilled trout and plaice, rack of lamb, and fillet of sole. Desserts include fresh blackcurrant sorbet and fresh fruit. Vegetarians are catered for on the Buttery menu.

HALSTEAD *Restaurant* Halstead Tandoori

73 Head Street
Halstead
(0787) 476271

Map 6 E2
Essex

Lunch 12–2 Dinner 6–11
Closed December 25 & 26
Indian cooking

Average price £12
Credit: Access, Amex, Diners, Visa

This popular Indian restaurant has plenty to offer in terms of healthy eating. Tandoori dishes owe their flavour to spices and yoghurt and are surprisingly low in fat and calories. An average portion of tandoori chicken has only about 300 to 400 calories. So make a sensible selection from the comprehensive menu and add variety to your diet. There are plenty of curries, including choices for vegetarians. Fresh fruit includes mangoes, lychees, papayas and pineapples and fruit salad is always on the menu.

1 Parliament Street
Harrogate
(0423) 64659

Map 4 D3

York
6 St Helen's Square
York
(0904) 59142

Map 4 E3

Ilkley
32 The Grove
Ilkley
(0943) 608029

Map 4 D3

Northallerton
118 High Street
Northallerton
(0609) 5154

Map 4 D3
North Yorkshire

Harrogate open 9–5.30 (Sun 10–6)
Closed January 1 & December 25 & 26

York open 9am–9pm
Closed January 1 & December 25 & 26

Ilkley open 9.30–5.30 (Sat from 9 & Sun till 7)
Closed December 25

Northallerton open 9–6 (Sun from 10)
Closed January 1, Easter Sunday & December 25 & 26

Typical prices: Swiss health breakfast £2.75
Tuna fish & cucumber sandwich £1.20

Every town needs a Bettys—a café and tearoom serving good tea, wholesome cakes and bakes and appetising (and additive free) light meals. Everything is done for the customer's comfort. There's a changing area for babies, a children's menu and plenty of high chairs. Adults can relax while quaffing one of a variety of delicious drinks and enjoy a quick bite of scrambled egg with salmon, Welsh rarebit, omelette, salad, sandwiches or a savoury slice of something like pepper and mushroom flan. Sorbets, fresh fruit in season and a delicious yoghurt parfait with orange, apple, grapes and an almond topping are available for dessert.

HASLEMERE   *Pub*   Crowns

Weyhill
Haslemere
(0428) 3112

Map 6 D3
Surrey

Last order 10.30pm
Brewery Friary Meux

Typical prices: Prawn haddock &
    courgette pie £3.45
    Cauliflower cheese £2.85
Credit: Access, Amex, Diners, Visa

One of the blackboards at this fashionable pub is devoted solely to fish and seafood, so there is ample choice for healthy eaters. Try the poached salmon steak or smoked haddock, or a simple grilled trout, brill or lemon sole. Alternatively, settle for a mammoth bowl of chicken chowder with wholemeal bread, or a hot spinach and ham bake or a filled jacket potato. Daily vegetarian specials include a tasty vegetable and bean curry and a flavoursome cauliflower cheese. Portions are generous—with luck you'll be able to resist late temptations like treacle tart.

HASTINGS   *Quick Bite*   Brant's

45 High Street, Old
    Town
Hastings
(0424) 431896

Map 6 E4
East Sussex

Open 10–5 in summer (Wed till
    2), 10–4 in winter
Closed Wed in winter, Sun all
    year, Bank Holidays, 2 weeks
    April & 2 weeks autumn

Typical prices: Vegetable
    macaroni £1.35
    Nut savoury 95p
Luncheon Vouchers accepted

Pictures by local artists (for sale) brighten up the walls of this pleasant little vegetarian restaurant. The menu is not extensive, but what there is is cooked with care. Early callers will find cakes like apricot, walnut and coconut slices side by side with savoury flans and salads. Between noon and 2pm there are always several hot specials including an excellent nut savoury and a tasty chick pea curry. Natural yoghurt is used in sauces and dressings and there are fresh fruit salads and flans to follow.

HAWK GREEN — *Pub* — Crown Inn

Marple, Near
  Stockport
061-427 2678

Map 4 D4
Greater Manchester

Last order 9.45pm
Brewery Robinsons

Typical prices: Smoked salmon &
  prawn pizza £2.90
  Grilled plaice £5.75
Credit: Access, Amex, Diners, Visa

Open sandwiches are just one of the specialities at this pleasant old coaching inn. Prawns make a nutritious topping, especially if the mayonnaise is omitted or served separately. You could also enjoy the prawns as a salad, with rye crispbread and plenty of crisp fresh vegetables. There are starters like tandoori chicken wings or home-made soup followed by chargrilled steak or plaice or a seafood platter. Jacket potatoes are always available and vegetables will be served without butter or sauce if preferred. Freshly-squeezed orange juice is always on offer.

HELMSLEY — *Restaurant* — Black Swan Hotel Restaurant

Market Place
Helmsley
(0439) 70466

Map 4 E3
North Yorkshire

Lunch 12.30–2 Dinner 7.30–9.30
Closed Dinner December 25

Average price £22
Set L £8.50
Set D £11.50
Credit: Access, Diners, Visa

The standard of cooking is high at this elegant restaurant, where an interesting menu has been assembled with evident thought. A good selection of starters includes gravlax of Loch Fyne salmon with endive salad, and a beautifully presented melon with orange and rose-petal sorbets. Main dishes include salmon coulibiac with buck-wheat, and breast of chicken with raspberry sauce and vinaigrette. Vegetarian starters and salads. Wholemeal bread is served with polyunsaturated margarine if preferred.

HEREFORD — *Quick Bite* — Fodder

2 Capucin Yard,
  Church Street
Hereford
(0432) 58171

Map 5 A2
Hereford & Worcester

Open 10–4.30
Closed Sun & Bank Holidays
Vegetarian wholefood cooking

Typical prices: Tofuburger 85p
  Vegetable nut bake £1.20

Just off Church Street's pedestrian walkway you'll find Capucin Yard, where on fine days wrought-iron tables are set outside this small, friendly vegetarian restaurant. The place is good news for healthy eaters, as additive-free ingredients, organic vegetables and minimum salt are used where possible. Lunches include nut loaf, crunchy vegetable bake, savoury slices and salads from half a dozen regularly replenished bowls. These might include crudités, burghul wheat, fresh red cabbage, bean salad and bean sprouts with corn. Take-away service offered.

HEREFORD — *Quick Bite* — Marches

24 Union Street
Hereford
(0432) 55712

Map 5 A2
Hereford & Worcester

Open 8.30–5.30
Closed Sun, Bank Holidays & 2–3
  days Christmas
Wholefood cooking

Typical prices: Nut roast 65p
  Wholewheat pasta salad 40p
Credit: Access, Amex, Visa

Billed as Britain's largest health food complex, Marches consists of a two-floor restaurant, a health food shop and a gift gallery. Two self-service counters display a fine array of wholesome items, including at least a dozen salads. There is always a choice of wholemeal flans including mushroom and onion and courgette and leek and although the menu is predominantly vegetarian a quick service bar does serve attractive plated salads with chicken or ham. Conclude with a crunchy apple or fresh fruit salad.

HIGH LORTON · *Quick Bite* · White Ash Barn

Near Cockermouth
Lorton
(090 085) 236

Map 3 B2
Cumbria

Open 10.30–5
Closed end October–1 week
 before Easter

Typical prices: Quiche & assorted
 side salads £2.50
 Wholemeal scone 40p

Stella George's pressed flower pictures are a feature of this gift shop-cum-tea room and her artistry is equally evident on the salad bar. The range of snacks is limited but the Swedish salad comes highly commended—try it with a slice of quiche or home-baked gammon, or select a less substantial snack such as freshly cut sandwiches made with home-baked wheatmeal bread and polyunsaturated margarine. Pasta and pulses are used in salads and there are regular vegetarian dishes. Beverages include tea and fresh fruit juices.

HOLT · *Pub* · Old Ham Tree

Near Trowbridge
North Trowbridge
(0225) 782581

Map 5 B3
Wiltshire

Last order 10pm
Free House

Typical prices: Seafood pasta
 £2.30 Cornish plaice £2.75
Credit: Access, Diners, Visa

The food is straightforward and satisfying at this unpretentious pub close to the village green. The bar is comfortably furnished and the menu has familiar favourites like toasted sandwiches and simple salads. Daily specials introduce healthy hot dishes such as wholemeal pasta with seafood, and brown rice, ham and mushroom risotto. On Thursdays fresh fish is delivered from Cornwall and those in the know settle down to enjoy mackerel, lemon sole or fresh crab. Vegetarian dishes on request.

HONLEY · *Pub* · Coach & Horses

Eastgate
Huddersfield
(0484) 666135

Map 4 D4
West Yorkshire

Last order 9.30pm
No bar food eves
Closed December 25
Brewery Bass Yorkshire

Typical prices: Waldorf salad
&2.80
Fresh baked trout &3.50

Stop for lunch at this busy pub and be sure of a nutritious meal. Up to a dozen salads are served every day, including a slimmer's special with cottage cheese, lean ham and pineapple, served with crispbreads. Sandwiches are freshly made on wholemeal bread and there is also a good range of simply cooked meat and fish dishes. Starters include clear chicken and vegetable soup and there is usually a vegetarian dish. More elaborate vegetarian meals will be provided on request. Bistro-style dinners are available on Monday evenings only.

HOPE · *Quick Bite* · Hopechest

Near Sheffield
Hope Valley
(0433) 20072

Map 4 D4
Derbyshire

Open 9.15–5
Closed Sun, also Mon (except
August & December) &
December 25

Typical prices: Home-made soup
& roll 85p
Yoghurt & honey 55p
Credit: Access, Diners, Visa

Senior citizens pay less for a hot or cold drink at this tiny tea room in the heart of the Hope Valley. The Hopechest is actually a shop selling crafts, dresses, accessories, books, haberdashery and health foods. It is run by three retired schoolteachers who take it in turns to cook the splendid savoury and sweet treats. The choice is limited but includes soup, cheese scones and wholemeal vegetable flans, with yoghurt and honey or fresh fruit sorbets to finish. The tea is very good and fresh fruit juices are also on offer.

HORLEY *Pub* Ye Olde Six Bells

Church Road
Horley
(0293) 782209

Map 6 D3
Surrey

Last order 9.30pm
Brewery Vintage Inns

Typical prices: Pasta tricolor £2.40
    Vegetable risotto £2.40
Credit: Access, Amex, Diners, Visa

You can almost hear the wind in the willows at this marvellous old pub on the River Mole. In the Monks Pantry upstairs there is a fine cold buffet of good looking salads with rare roast beef, smoked mackerel, wholemeal quiches or cottage cheese. Natural yoghurt is used in cooking and salad dressings and wholemeal bread is always available. There are vegetarian dishes like celery, caraway and walnut soup and vegetable risotto. Veal korma and lamb creole are among more adventurous dishes available in the evenings.

HUNGERFORD *Restaurant* Bear at Hungerford Restaurant

Charnham Street
Hungerford
(0488) 82512

Map 5 C3
Berkshire

Lunch 12.30–2 Dinner 7.30–9.30
    (Fri & Sat till 10)
Closed December 26

Average price £20
Set L from £10.45
Set D from £13.45
Credit: Access, Amex, Diners, Visa

Hunger is enjoyably assuaged at this charming 13th-century inn restaurant. The chef makes imaginative use of garden and hedgerow ingredients—the summer and autumn menu includes such dishes as chilled nettle soup with peppers, and breast of duck with elderflower vinegar. Vegetarian specialities, like avocado mousse with iced herbs and vegetable strudel with mustard noodles are attractively presented. Desserts include a delightful terrine of summer fruits with raspberry coulis.

215

ENGLAND

HYTHE — *Quick Bite* — **Natural Break**

115 High Street
Hythe
(0303) 67573

Map 6 F3
Kent

Open 9–5
Closed Sun & Bank Holidays
Vegetarian cooking

Typical prices: Bean & burghul
  wheat casserole £1.60
  Vegetable curry & rice £1.60

Small and simply furnished, this vegetarian restaurant attached to a wholefood store does a brisk trade. The morning selection of scones and slices gives way at about 11.30 to a range of savouries such as lentil lasagne, bean and burghul wheat casserole, and vegetable curry with brown rice. Filled jacket potatoes are also popular, and home-made soups are served with very good wholemeal bread and polyunsaturated margarine, if preferred. Both skimmed milk and natural yoghurt are used and there is fresh fruit salad to follow.

IDE — *Restaurant* — **Old Mill**

20 High Street
Exeter
(0392) 59480

Map 8 C2
Devon

Lunch 12–2 Dinner 7–9.45
Closed Sun, December 25 & 26 &
  January 1

Average price £20
Set L £5.65
Set D £10.95 (Mon–Fri)
Credit: Access, Amex, Visa

Once an old flour mill and bakery, this black and white painted building has simple old-world charm. The standard of cooking is good and service friendly. In addition to fixed-price menus there's a separate selection of fish dishes such as red mullet with rosemary plus an attractive vegetarian menu including pot pourri of fruit with cinnamon and lemon sauce. Tempting desserts include a featherweight trio of fruit mousses (pear, kiwi and raspberry), served on a purée of the appropriate fruit.

IPSWICH — *Quick Bite* — Marno's

14 St Nicholas Street
Ipswich
(0473) 53106

Map 6 F2
Suffolk

Open 10.30–2.15 & Thurs–Sat
  7–10
Closed Sun & Bank Holidays
Vegetarian cooking

Typical prices: Nut roast £1.50
  Vegetable compote £1.50

In an area where there are few good vegetarian restaurants, Marno's is a real find. Teas, tisanes and coffees (dandelion and decaffeinated amongst others) are served throughout the day, with wholesome bakes and cakes. From noon more substantial items move into the spotlight. Soup of the day, served with wholemeal bread, might be lentil or carrot and orange, and there's a daily choice of four hot dishes such as mushroom and pasta bake or lentil and vegetable roast. Five or six interesting salads complete the spread, and afters include fresh fruit in natural juice with yoghurt.

JEVINGTON — *Restaurant* — Hungry Monk

Near Polegate
Polegate
(032 12) 2178

Map 6 E4
East Sussex

Lunch (Sun only) 12–2.30 Dinner
  7–10.30
Closed December 24–26

Average price £17.50
Set L £11.20
Set D £12.10

Make sure you book at this charming beamed restaurant, where Nigel and Susan Mackenzie and their treasured chef, Ian Dowding, go to great lengths to please their patrons. They enjoy developing special dishes such as aubergine and lentil pancakes or hot vegetable roulade for vegetarians and will treat requests from other diners with equal consideration. The fine balanced menu has plenty for the health conscious and concludes with superb sweets. Try their famous banoffi pie.

ENGLAND

3 Stramongate Kendal (0539) 20341	Kendal open 9–5 **Closed** Sun & Bank Holidays
Map 3 C3 Cumbria	
Preston 20 Friargate Preston (0772) 555855	Preston open 9–5 **Closed** Sun & Bank Holidays Wholefood cooking
Map 3 C3 Lancashire	Typical prices: Crunchy nut tagliatelle £1.40 Lentil bake £1.25

As the name suggests, a healthier style of eating is the aim of these two new self-service restaurants. The wholefood menu is largely vegetarian but there is often a single chicken dish or a fish speciality. All the cooking is done on the premises using high quality additive free ingredients. Cakes, breads and bakes (using wholemeal flour and no animal fats) include an irresistible gingerbread and the scones are light and well flavoured. Hot dishes include crunchy nut tagliatelle (with wholemeal pasta), mushroom Stroganoff and lentil bake.

---- ¶⬓¶ ----

Changes in data may occur in establishments after the Guide goes to press. Prices should be taken as indications rather than firm quotes.

---- ¶⬓¶ ----

129 Highgate
Kendal
(0539) 29254

Map 3 C3
Cumbria

Open 6–10 (Fri & Sat till 11) & Sun
  7–10
Closed 3 days Christmas

Typical prices: Mediterranean
  bean & vegetable casserole
  £3.45 Plaice stuffed with
  mushrooms £3.60
Credit: Access, Visa

The Moon waxes but its popularity never seems to wane. Evenings only (which seems apt), it offers a constantly changing menu of considerable interest to both vegetarians and meat-lovers. For the former there are tasty dishes based on pasta and pulses, such as vegetable and cashew nut curry, and Mediterranean bean and vegetable casserole. Fish dishes include trout stuffed with watercress, almond and lemon, and there's also a tasty haddock lasagne (wholemeal pasta is always used). Chicken and bean-sprout crumble is another hot favourite, and salads are super. Best to pass up the puddings.

ENGLAND

KENDAL *Quick Bite* Waterside Wholefoods

Kent View
Kendal
(0539) 29743

Map 3 C3
Cumbria

Open 9–4
Closed Sun & January 1 &
 December 25 & 26
Vegetarian wholefood cooking

Typical prices: Pea & almond
 soup 95p
 Vegetable pilaff £1.60

This small wholefood shop-cum-restaurant serves lots of simple snacks and light meals. Morning callers find bakes like sticky fig cake or carrot slice on the menu and at about 11am a blackboard lists daily specials like pea and almond soup, bean pilaff or avocado, cottage cheese and walnut salad. Everything is freshly prepared in a small kitchen visible from the dining area, and organic vegetables are mostly used. On sunny days you can move into the fresh air and sit at tables beside the River Kent.

KESWICK *Quick Bite* Mayson's

33 Lake Road
Keswick
(0596) 74104

Map 3 B2
Cumbria

Open 9.30–5 & 6.30–10
Closed Monday evening

Typical prices: Mixed bean
 casserole £1.75
 Chicken tikka £5
Credit: Access, Amex, Visa

Another establishment with a split personality: during the day it operates on a self-service basis, with wholesome dishes like home-made soup with a herb roll or baked jacket potatoes with assorted fillings. Also pasta, pizzas and a daily chicken dish. After 6.30 the menu takes on an exotic air and offers unusual starters like marinated prawns with popcorn or North African chick pea soup. Main courses include chicken tikka and Javanese grilled fillet steak and a variety of vegetarian and vegan dishes.

KESWICK *Quick Bite* Underscar Hotel

Applethwaite
Keswick
(07687) 72469

Map 3 B2
Cumbria

Open 10–6
Closed mid December–mid
February

Typical prices: Selection of open
sandwiches £2.25
Seafood pancake £4
Credit: Access, Amex, Diners

The setting of this elegant hotel with its splendid views of Derwentwater and Borrowdale, draws visitors from far afield. Lunch is served in the lounge, or if you prefer, in the attractive conservatory. The menu includes 'nouvelle cuisine' style dishes of flavoursome soups with home-baked soda bread followed by beautifully fresh salmon with cucumber and ginger and fresh fruit salad for dessert. Healthy eaters may lunch on a cheese, fruit and nut platter with wholemeal bread, grilled trout or even a simple open sandwich. Special orders catered for.

KEW *Restaurant* Wine & Mousaka

12 Kew Green
01-940 5696

Map 6 D3
Surrey

Lunch 12–2.30 Dinner 6–11.30
Closed Sun, Bank Holidays &
3 days Christmas
Greek cooking

Average price £8
Credit: Access, Amex, Diners, Visa

The charcoal grill at this friendly Greek restaurant creates a warm atmosphere and deliciously tempting aroma. Starters like mushrooms à la grecque lead to main dishes such as meze, stuffed green pepper and vine leaves, grilled lamb kebabs and grilled marinated poussin. Vegetarian dishes are always available and there's a slimmer's special. Wine and moussaka, too, of course, but perhaps not for healthy eaters! Desserts include fresh fruit salad and home-made yoghurt with orange blossom honey.

ENGLAND

KINGSCOTE   *Pub*   Hunters Hall Inn

Near Tetbury
Dursley
(0453) 860393

Map 5 B3
Gloucestershire

Last order 9.45pm
Closed 25 December
Free House

Typical prices: Vegetable lasagne
£2.95 Monkfish with prawns &
salad £4.25
Credit: Access, Amex, Diners, Visa

David and Sandra Barnett-Roberts are genial hosts at this traditional British inn on the A4135, between Dursley and the A46. A splendid buffet offers cold meats, flans, sliced fish and exquisitely prepared salads, including one based upon wholemeal pasta. A blackboard lists hot dishes like vegetable lasagne and seafood crumble, and there is usually at least one simple fish dish. Wholemeal bread is served, with polyunsaturated margarine on request, and there is fresh fruit salad for afters. On Friday and Saturday evenings and summer Sunday lunchtimes there's a barbecue.

KINGSTON   *Pub*   Scott Arms

Near Corfe Castle
Corfe Castle
(0929) 480270

Map 5 B4
Dorset

Last order 8.50pm
No bar food Sun eve in winter
Closed December 25
Brewery Devenish

Typical prices: Smoked mackerel
£2.20 Vegetable lasagne £2.60

There's a fine view of Corfe Castle from the garden of this creeper-clad inn. Food is no nonsense, humble yet hearty and generally home-made. You can enjoy a farmhouse vegetable soup with locally baked brown bread, and there's always a selection of tempting salads plus vegetarian dishes like lentil cakes with chilli sauce or vegetable lasagne. Filled jacket potatoes in winter. Desserts are not very healthy and nursery puds like jam roly poly are better declined. Children are welcome in the family bar.

222

LANCASTER *Quick Bite* Dukes Playhouse Restaurant

Moor Lane
Lancaster
(0524) 67461

Map 3 C3
Lancashire

Open 10–4 & 5.30–8.30 (or until
  first interval)
Closed Mon evening, all Sun &
  Bank Holidays

Typical prices: Algerian-style
  aubergine £1.70
  Baked potato & filling 90p

Watch the passing show at this informal theatre restaurant while dining on a choice of healthy dishes. Prices are extremely reasonable and the evening menu very diverse with simple wholesome dishes such as filled baked potato or cauliflower and walnut paella. The lunchtime menu offers a selection from sandwiches to grilled sole and always includes a good home-made soup. Wholemeal bread is served, with polyunsaturated margarine if preferred, and rice, pasta and pulses all make regular appearances. The puddings are not for the health conscious.

LANCASTER *Quick Bite* Libra

19 Brock Street
Lancaster
(0524) 61551

Map 3 C3
Lancashire

Open 9–6
Closed Sun, Bank Holidays &
  1 week Christmas
Vegetarian cooking

Typical prices: Risotto £1.90
  Gado gado £1.90

Unfailingly friendly staff make calling at this simple vegetarian restaurant a pleasure. Tasty soups have natural flavours enhanced by clever seasoning; there's an attractive display of salads, and daily savouries like gado gado and kidney bean and cheese bake. Featherlight wholemeal pastry and a generous filling of swedes and green vegetables makes the harvest pie a popular choice. Beverages include speciality teas and tisanes, and there's a range of bakes made with low-fat margarine.

LANCASTER *Quick Bite* Marinada's

27 North Road,
Lancaster
(0524) 381181

Map 3 C3
Lancashire

Open 12–2 & 6.30–11
Closed Sun, January 1 &
  December 25 & 26

Typical prices: Vegetable risotto
  £2.70
  Polpette alla cacciatora £3.90
Credit: Access, Amex, Diners, Visa

Traditional Italian food is not noted for being lean cuisine, but there are several dishes on the menu at this popular pizzeria that will appeal to the healthy eater. Fresh fish is always available, together with chargrilled steak or poussin. Sensible starters include minestrone, melon with Parma ham, vegetable pâté and tuna and bean salad. Main courses are based on pasta, fish, chicken and although the vegetarian menu occasionally includes fish, it does offer acceptable dishes like vegetable risotto and simple wholemeal pizzas. Decaffeinated coffee is served.

LEAMINGTON SPA *Quick Bite* Ropers

1a Clarendon Avenue
Leamington Spa
(0926) 316719

Map 5 B2
Warwickshire

Open 8am–10.30pm (Sun from
  10am)

Typical prices: Ropers salads from
  £3.80 Ropers tonic £2.95
Credit: Access, Amex, Visa

Early birds begin the day in fine style at this attractive and extremely well run establishment. There's a choice of six breakfasts including a perfect combination for the healthy eater, of fresh fruit juice, muesli with skimmed milk, yoghurt, granary toast and honey. Throughout the day the extensive brasserie menu offers a wide variety of meals, from a light snack such as chilled watercress soup with a granary roll, to a fresh salad or a full three courses. Don't miss the smoked tuna with fresh limes.

LEDBURY   *QuickBite*   Applejack Wine Bar

44, The Homend
Ledbury
(0531) 4181

Map 5 A2
Hereford & Worcester

Open 11–2.30 (Sun 12–2) &
  7–10.30
Closed Sun eve, January 1,
  December 25 & 26

Typical prices: Donner kebab
  £3.25
  Grilled sardines £3.25
Credit: Access, Diners, Visa

Pine benches and tables under hop-hung beams provide a rustic setting for meals at this popular wine bar. Call in early, for service can be slow when the place is busy, particularly during the evening sessions. There are plenty of choices for healthy eaters, from pitta bread pockets stuffed with salad, to spicy meatballs with yoghurt and apricot dressing. Vegetarians are well catered for with things like the vegetarian 'Applejack burger' and home-made cannelloni. Wholemeal bread and side salads are served with all main dishes.

LEEDS   *QuickBite*   Strawberryfields Bistro

159 Woodhouse Lane
Leeds
(0532) 431515

Map 4 D3
West Yorkshire

Open 11.45–2.30 & 6–11
Closed Lunch Sat, all Sun, Bank
  Holiday lunchtimes, & Dec 25
  & 26

Typical prices: Ratatouille £2.99
  Baked potatoes from £1.65
Credit: Access, Visa

This friendly little bistro is all things to all its diverse customers. On an extensive evening menu wholemeal pizzas coexist with prawns; red meats with ratatouille. Vegetarians will enjoy red bean moussaka and vegetarian lasagne while carnivores call for grilled sirloin steak with brown rice or baked potatoes. Composite salads include cheese, chicken, prawns and houmus. Desserts are dangerous; correctly labelled 'temptations'. A reduced lunchtime menu with ploughman's, jacket potatoes and salads.

ENGLAND

LEICESTER *QuickBite* Blossoms

17b Cank Street
Leicester
(0533) 539535

Map 5 C1
Leicestershire

Open 9.30–4
Closed Sun & Bank Holidays
   except Good Friday
Vegetarian cooking

Typical prices: Two bean goulash
   £1.40 Barley, lentil & vegetable
   bake £1.40
Luncheon Vouchers accepted

Shoppers in search of a nourishing bite will find this simply furnished restaurant in the city centre an ideal place to stop and try one of the wide selecton of beverages and bakes. There are 20 different teas, including mixed fruit and rosehip, and apple juice is warmed in winter. Midday meals make good use of pasta and pulses in dishes like courgette and red bean bake or vegetable lasagne, served with fresh salads. Wholemeal bread is always available, with polyunsaturated margarine, and fresh fruit salad or yoghurt maintains the healthy note.

LEIGHTON BUZZARD *Restaurant* Swan Hotel, Mr Swan's Restaurant

High Street
Leighton Buzzard
(0525) 372148

Map 5 C2
Bedfordshire

Lunch 12–2 Dinner 7–9.30 (Fri & Sat till 10, Sun till 9)
Closed Dinner December 25 & all December 26

Average price £18
Set L £8.50
Set D £14.50
Credit: Access, Amex, Diners, Visa

This attractive and relaxed restaurant offers competently prepared dishes such as poached darne of salmon, goujons of monkfish and traditional roasts and grills. In addition, the small but interesting vegetarian menu is proving popular and includes such items as butter bean pie. Natural yoghurt and polyunsaturated margarine are used where appropriate. The fixed price menu usually includes at least one simple unsauced dish, and fresh fruit would make a good choice for afters.

LEINTWARDINE

Quick Bite

Selda
Coffee Shop

Bridge Street
Leintwardine
(054 73) 604

Map 5 A2
Hereford & Worcester

Open 11–3.30 (November–March)
9.30–5.30 (April–June)
9–6 (July–August)
10–5.30 (September–October)
Closed Sun & Mon (Nov–Feb)

Typical prices: Welsh rarebit
£1.55 Brown rice & celery apple
crunch 95p

Selda is the medieval Latin word for shop and there has been a mercantile establishment on this site since 1610. Today it is a craft shop-cum-coffee house where Patricia Langley serves simple snacks and savouries. The Welsh rarebit is quite outstanding, served as it is with a bouquet of fresh herbs. Fresh baked trout with salad or tuna and nice rissoles make healthy main courses, as do any one of the excellent salads on offer. Try the celery, apple and cheese combination with its tangy yoghurt dressing.

LEOMINSTER

Quick Bite

Granary
Coffee House

6 South Street

Map 5 A2
Hereford & Worcester

Open 7–4.30 (Thurs & Sat till 2)
Closed Sun, Bank Holidays,
January 1, December 25 & 26

Typical prices: Baked potatoes &
filling 70p
Vegetable chilli £1.40

Be prepared to wait or share a table at this popular coffee house. From early morning, wholemeal rolls and sandwiches share the self-service counter with cakes and bakes, including flapjacks and fruit loaves. Those in search of a more substantial snack will encounter a range of salads with ham, rare roast beef or breast of chicken all with jacket potatoes. Salads include pasta, rice and pulses, as in the brown rice, lentil, mushroom and nut salad. The hot special might be vegetarian lasagne or a chicken curry.

ENGLAND

LEVINGTON · *Pub* · Ship

Near Ipswich
Nacton
(047 388) 573

Map 6 F2
Suffolk

Occasionally bar food in eves
Brewery Tollemache & Cobbold

Typical prices: Mushroom
Stroganoff £2.50
Smoked ham salad £3.50

This tiny thatched pub dates back to the 14th century. It has a splendid view of the Orwell estuary and low beams and a large inglenook give it plenty of character. The lunch menu is simple and the food very enjoyable. Salads include dressed crab, home-smoked chicken and roast beef, and ploughman's platters are made more interesting with a variety of cheeses and a choice of granary or cheese and onion bread. There's a daily hot dish such as lentil hotpot. This is served with a jacket potato and wholemeal roll or with smoked ham. Wholemeal pasta is a speciality.

LEWES · *Restaurant* · Kenwards

Pipe Passage,
151a High Street
Lewes
(0273) 472343

Map 6 D4
East Sussex

Dinner only 7.30–9.30
Closed Sun, Mon, also Tues
October–March, 10 days
Christmas & 2 weeks spring

Average price £16

Fresh herbs subtly accent many of John Kenward's dishes on a daily changing dinner menu that is both interesting and innovative. It offers several dishes suitable for healthy eaters: cucumber and mint soup, baked salmon with sorrel sauce, monkfish and oysters with dry vermouth and parsley. Soups are invariably vegetarian and there's always at least one additional vegetarian starter and a main course such as artichokes and squash with red pepper and tarragon. Fresh fruit and a good range of cheeses.

228

7 Station Street
Lewes
(0273) 477 447

Map 6 D4
East Sussex

Open 10–3
Closed Sun, Bank Holidays & 2
  weeks Christmas

Typical prices: Spicy chicken
  kebabs £2.80
  Aduki bean bake £2.60
Luncheon Vouchers accepted

A series of interconnecting rooms on different levels make up the Lunch Counter, a simply furnished self-service restaurant which caters well for healthy eaters. The cold buffet includes sliced lean beef and ham and chicken portions with a well-stocked salad bar. Those who prefer a hot meal will find plenty of choice, from spicy chicken kebabs to bean bakes, or jacket potatoes. The home-made soups have very good flavour there is always a vegetarian dish like vegetable goulash.

197 High Street
Lewes
(0273) 477879

Map 6 D4
East Sussex

Open 10–2 & 6–10.30, Sun 11–
  2.30 & 7–10
Closed December 25 & 26

Typical prices: Courgette &
  mushroom tagliatelle £2.75
  Taramasalata £1.95
Credit: Amex, Diners, Visa

Bike over to Mike's on a Sunday for the popular brunch, available from 11 to 2.30. As well as Buck's Fizz and traditional roast the menu includes a healthy alternative of muesli with low fat yoghurt plus poached eggs and cornbread. During the rest of the week there are light main courses like spinach and bacon salad or tuna and sweet-corn au gratin. Kebabs are a speciality and chargrilled steak is perennially popular. Vegetarians are catered for with dishes like kidney bean bourguignon.

ENGLAND

LICKFOLD — *Pub* — Lickfold Inn

Near Petworth
Lodsworth
(079 85) 285

Map 6 D3
West Sussex

Last order 10pm
No bar food Mon eve
Free House

Typical prices: Mushroom
  omelette £2.25
  Chicken salad £3.25
Credit: Visa

Real log fires bid the winter visitor welcome at this lovely old inn. In summer you can sit outside on the garden terraces and sample well-prepared pub grub, including wholemeal sandwiches and omelettes. Salads are seasonal, and jacket potatoes come with fillings like cottage cheese and prawn. On Friday and Saturday evenings more substantial meals are served, including grills and poached fish dishes—salmon, halibut, trout, lemon or Dover sole as available. Weekends also see the introduction of a special meat dish such as shish kebab.

LINCOLN — *Pub* — Wig & Mitre

29 Steep Hill
Lincoln
(0522) 35190

Map 4 E4
Lincolnshire

Last order 11pm
Closed December 25
Brewery Samuel Smith

Typical prices: Avocado & apple
  cocktail £1.65
  Leek & tomato pie £3.25
Credit: Access, Amex, Diners, Visa

Not for nothing is the address of this pub-restaurant listed as steep hill. It is worth the climb, however, when you can be sure of a meal at any time from 8am till late. Catch your breath in cosy surroundings while mulling over a blackboard menu that includes some good country-style soups with wholemeal bread. Healthy eaters will probably plump for the vegetarian and vegan dishes like vegetable curry, houmus salad and toast or macaroni cheese with tomato sauce.

LIVERPOOL

Quick Bite

Armadillo Restaurant

20 Mathew Street
051-236 4123

Map 3 C4
Merseyside

Open 10.30–3 & 5–10.30
Closed Sun, Bank Holidays & 1 week after Christmas

Typical prices: Celery & apple soup 80p Sea bass with orange & mushrooms £8.95
Credit: Access, Visa
Luncheon Vouchers accepted

Meaty minestrone warms the cockles at this informal self-service restaurant. Opposite the 'Cavern', a name Beatle fans will instantly recognise, it is an ideal spot for a quick lunch or relaxing evening meal. Throughout the day there's a fine array of baked goods, soups, wholemeal sandwiches and hot special dishes. Salads such as the home-made coleslaw, and the potato, chive and yoghurt bowl are always popular. After 7pm the restaurant wears a more formal face, offering dishes like sea bass stuffed with orange and mushrooms, and roast pheasant.

LIVERPOOL

Quick Bite

Everyman Bistro

Hope Street
051-708 9545

Map 3 C4
Merseyside

Open 12–11.30
Closed Sun & Bank Holidays

Typical prices: Home-made pasta with fresh tomato sauce £2.20
Baked potato 95p
Luncheon Vouchers accepted

For more than 15 years this basement bistro has served robust home-cooked fare to an appreciative army of regulars. Queue at the counter for straightforward snacks like baked spuds or choose from a wide selection of freshly made salads. More elaborate dishes might be pink trout with poppy-seed dressing or a Chinese-style dish consisting of three types of mushrooms and served with wholemeal bread or pancakes stuffed with spiced black beans. Fresh fruit is always available.

LIVERPOOL *Restaurant* La Grande Bouffe

48 Castle Street
051-236 3375

Map 3 C4

Lunch 12–3 Dinner 6–10.30
Closed Sun, January 1 &
  December 24–26

Average price £15
Set L £6.50
Pre-Theatre Menu £6.95
Credit: Access, Amex, Visa

Do not be put off by the studiously spartan decor of this basement bistro—the tables may not always be well balanced but the menus certainly are. Healthy eaters will find plenty that pleases, from lunchtime specials like fresh salmon fishcakes or courgette and mushroom lasagne to more elaborate evening offerings such as comice pear and avocado salad followed by calf's liver with braised spinach. Raw materials are chosen and cooked with care and the atmosphere is unfailingly warm and friendly. An excellent jazz pianist adds to the enjoyment after dark.

LONG MELFORD *Restaurant* Chimneys

Hall Street
Sudbury
(0787) 79806

Map 6 E2
Suffolk

Lunch 12–2 Dinner 7–10
Closed Dinner Sun & all Mon

Average price £20
Set L £9.50
Credit: Access, Visa

This lovely 16th-century building on the main road through Long Melford provides the setting for a memorable meal. Talented chef Roger Carter provides a fine selection of dishes with an unstated but apparent emphasis on healthy eating. Starters include terrine of chicken with calf's sweetbreads, braised crab claw with ginger, and a salad of asparagus and quail's eggs. Main courses are much praised and the attractive presentation is particularly notable. A fine vegetarian menu adds to the restaurant's appeal.

LOOE

Restaurant

Talland Bay Hotel Restaurant

Talland Bay
Polperro
(0503) 72667

Map 8 B3
Cornwall

Lunch 12.30–2 Dinner 7.15–9
Closed Lunch Mon–Sat October–
   April & all December 20–
   February 15

Average price £14
Set L (Sun only) £5.45 Set D £10
Credit: Access, Amex, Diners, Visa

This Cornish seaside restaurant has plenty for the health-conscious, the set menu always offers one of its three main dishes without a rich sauce. There is also a daily vegetarian dish such as vegetables on braised rice with sherry sauce. The wholemeal bread is served with polyunsaturated margarine if preferred. Pasta and pulses regularly feature on the set menu and generous portions of vegetables are crisply cooked and imaginative. The à la carte menu includes a variety of seafood, like Cornish crab and locally-caught scallops.

LOWER BEEDING

Restaurant

South Lodge Restaurant

London Road
Lower Beeding
(040 376) 711

Map 6 D3
West Sussex

Lunch 12.30–2.30 Dinner 7.30–
   10.30

Average price £25
Set D £22.50
Vegetarian Menu £19.50
Credit: Access, Amex, Diners, Visa

James Hayward's stylish menus suit the grandly pro-portioned room in which they are served. Healthy starters include poached langoustine and John Dory which chopped chervil, or lettuce, asparagus and green bean salad with pigeon breast. Loin of lamb, studded with garlic and juniper berries and carved on to aubergine and tarragon purée is in the same tradition, and a basket of fresh sorbets and sliced fruit would provide a fine conclusion. A separate five-course vegetarian menu shows unusual initiative.

ENGLAND

LOWER WOODFORD *Pub* Wheatsheaf

Near Salisbury
Middle Woodford
(072 273) 203

Map 5 B3
Wiltshire

Last order 10pm
Brewery Hall & Woodhouse
Closed December 25

Typical prices: Grilled Dover sole
& baked potato £6
Lentil soup & wholemeal roll 85p
Credit: Amex

Enjoyable bar food with more than a hint of healthy cooking is always available at this charming inn. Jacket potatoes and composite salads are regular items, and simple fish and meat dishes include grilled Dover sole and steak. Wave the chips aside in favour of a plain jacket potato. Alternatively check the blackboard for daily specials like potatoes stuffed with brown rice and crunchy vegetables or vegetable curry with pulses. Children are made very welcome. The garden, with its climbing frame and play area is perfect for them.

LUDLOW *Quick Bite* Hardwicks ★

Quality Square

Map 5 A2
Shropshire

Open 10–5
Closed Sun, & December 25 & 26

Typical prices: Mystery mushroom
casserole £2.20
Chick pea salad £2

Patricia Hardwick's cooking and baking is of excellent quality and presentation is first class. Customers are warmly welcomed, and the crisp summery restaurant in the aptly named Quality Square is well patronised. Vegetarian dishes abound, and good use is made of pasta and pulses. Don't miss the delicious Swiss cabbage, if available. Tandoori chicken caters to non-vegetarians in search of a healthy meal, and there are plenty of light bites such as wholemeal scones, granary rolls and fruit bakes.

234

LUDLOW *Quick Bite* Olive Branch

2 Old Street
Ludlow
(0584) 4314

Map 5 A2
Shropshire

Open 10–5 (Oct–May till 3, Thurs–
   Sat in Summer till 8) & Fri 10–
   2.30
Closed 2 weeks Christmas
Vegetarian cooking

Typical prices: Lentil & buckwheat
   bake & salad £2.25
   Pasta verde & salad £2.25

Tile-topped tables and wooden benches create a casual atmosphere at this bright and cheerful vegetarian restaurant. Here tired shoppers stop to re-fuel and enjoy a meal chosen from the daily changing menu. Perhaps lentil and buckwheat bake or wholemeal lasagne with spinach. There are always three salads. One might be a brown rice, corn and sunflower seed mixture, another a green salad and a third, coleslaw with nuts and apple. These items are available from late morning till lunchtime, bakes and cakes are served in the afternoon.

LUDLOW *Restaurant* Penny Anthony

5 Church Street
Ludlow
(0584) 3282

Map 5 A2
Shropshire

Lunch 12–2 Dinner 7–10
Closed Sun

Average price £15
Set L £4.50
Set D £9
Credit: Amex, Diners, Visa

Helen Clarke and owner Penny Anthony team up to turn out a range of menus to suit all sorts of situations and budgets, from the reasonably-priced tourist menu (not available on Saturday evening) and family menu to the more expensive menu de la gastronomie. Healthy diners should try such dishes as the vegetable pancakes, smoked chicken, moules marinière and seafood kebabs. Food is simply cooked, ingredients first class, presentation unfussy yet colourful. Vegetarian dishes occasionally feature.

LYNDHURST
Restaurant
Parkhill Hotel Restaurant

Beaulieu Road
Lyndhurst
(042 128) 2944

Map 5 C4
Hampshire

Lunch 12.30–2.15 Dinner 7–9
Closed December 28–January 11

Average price £20
Set L £8.25
Set D £12.25
Credit: Access, Amex, Diners, Visa

Polite and professional service is a characteristic of this fine Georgian hotel. In an attractive room with french windows overlooking parkland, healthy eaters can dine most satisfactorily. Splendid raw materials are carefully prepared for starters like marinated fresh salmon and scallops, and main courses such as grilled sole with prawns and capers. Fish isn't the only choice—there's an equally wide range of meat dishes, which can be served sans sauce. Wholemeal bread is offered, with polyunsaturated margarine if preferred, and skimmed milk is used.

MALMESBURY
Pub
Suffolk Arms

Tetbury Hill
Malmesbury
(066 62) 2271

Map 5 B3
Wiltshire

Last order 10pm
Free House

Typical prices: Filled jacket
  potatoes from £1.25
  Smoked trout £2.75
Credit: Access, Amex, Diners, Visa

Good fresh food is always available at this attractive ivy-clad inn. The composite salads are ideal for a healthy light bite. Choose from ham, chicken, beef, prawn and smoked salmon, or sample similar ingredients in a wholemeal sandwich. Jacket potatoes are popular snacks while a more substantial meal might be grilled swordfish with new potatoes and crisp vegetables or salad. Alternatively, there are hot specialities like lasagne or vegetarian curry with brown rice. Fresh fruit salads are usually available.

MANCHESTER

Restaurant

Britannia Hotel, Cromptons Restaurant

Portland Street
061-228 2288

Town plan
  Manchester
  Greater Manchester

Lunch 12.30–2 Dinner 7–11
Closed Lunch Sat & all Sun

Average price £15
Set L £5.95
Set D £13.50
Credit: Access, Amex, Diners, Visa

When it comes to healthy cooking, this opulent restaurant is ahead of the field. Particularly notable is the lunchtime 'menu légère'—designed to keep fats, oils, salt and sugar to the minimum. Natural yoghurt, fromage blanc and soy bean curd all play their part and sauces are made without reductions of butter, cream or alcohol. You might opt for a light courgette soup flavoured with fresh basil, followed by poached turkey with glazed baby onions. Imaginative desserts make the most of fresh fruits and there is a selection of low-fat cheeses served with Californian apples.

MANCHESTER

Restaurant

Market

30 Edge Street
061-834 3743

Town plan
  Manchester
  Greater Manchester

Dinner only 6.30–10.30
Closed Sun, Mon, Bank Holidays, 1 week Easter, all August & 1 week Christmas

Average price £12
Credit: Access, Amex

This atmospheric little restaurant surrounded by fashion warehouses offers some delicious dishes cooked to order by the obliging staff. The handwritten menu changes weekly and, though not extensive, includes dishes to suit most diners, including those for whom healthy eating is a priority. You might try smoked salmon and tarama timbales followed by golubsty—cabbage leaves stuffed with meat and prunes and baked in a sour cream sauce. The home-made desserts range from the light to the luscious.

MANCHESTER

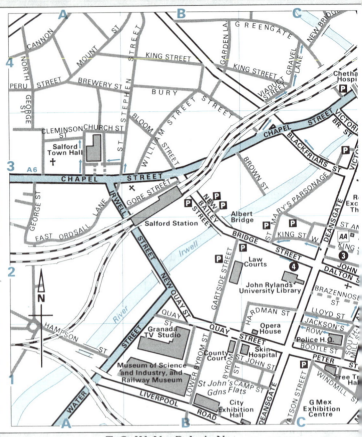

TOWN PLAN

ENQUIRIES

(tel code: 061)

Tourist Information	....	234 3157
Railway	....	832 8353
Bus	....	273 4541
Coach	....	228 3881
Airport	....	489 3000

MANCHESTER

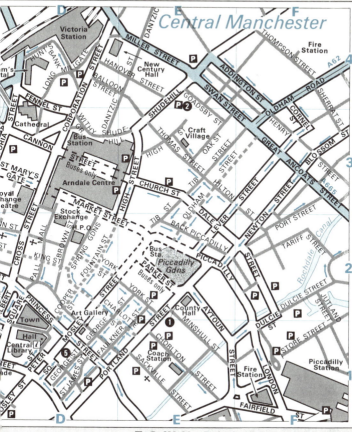

Central Manchester

TOWN PLAN

ESTABLISHMENTS LISTED

1. **Britannia Hotel,**
   Cromptons Restaurant
   Portland Street

2. **Market**
   30 Edge Street

3. **Rajdoot**
   South King Street

4. **Truffles**
   63 Bridge Street

5. **Yang Sing**
   34 Princess Street

239

ENGLAND

MANCHESTER *Restaurant* Rajdoot

St James' House,
  South King Street
061-834 2176

Town plan
  Manchester
  Greater Manchester

Lunch 12–2.30 Dinner 6.30–11.30
Closed Lunch Sun & Bank
  Holidays
Indian cooking

Average price £14
Set D from £9.50
Credit: Access, Amex, Diners, Visa

An Indian restaurant is an excellent choice for the health-conscious diner, and the Rajdoot caters even better than most with a particularly good selection of tandoori specialities. Young spring chicken marinated in yoghurt with herbs and spices and cooked over coals is a perfect choice or there is fish tikka, prawn kebab or gurda kebab (marinated lamb's kidneys). The pilau rice is excellent and chick peas and lentils appear in traditional dishes such as chana bhuna and dal. For a healthy dessert try mangoes, guavas and lychees.

MANCHESTER *Restaurant* Truffles

63 Bridge Street
061-832 9393

Town plan
  Manchester
  Greater Manchester

Lunch 12.15–2.30 Dinner 7–11
Closed Lunch Sat, all Sun, Mon,
  Bank Holidays & 2 weeks August
French cooking

Average price £20
Set L £10.95
Credit: Access, Amex, Diners, Visa

Victorian dining with French flair — that's the recipe at this smart city centre restaurant. Sauces are a speciality but healthy eaters who prefer plain cooking can choose fresh fish such as chargrilled salmon, or sirloin or fillet steak, or make a careful selection from the à la carte menu—grilled marinated pigeon breast with orange segments and red-currant sauce, perhaps, with an oat and vegetable crumble to follow. Vegetables are lightly cooked and side salads are always available.

MANCHESTER · *Restaurant* · Yang Sing

34 Princess Street
061-236 2200

Town plan
  Manchester
  Greater Manchester

Meals 12–11.15
Closed December 25
Chinese cooking

Average price £15
Credit: Access, Amex

This restaurant makes dining out Chinese-style extremely enjoyable. Despite a move to larger premises, few tables are empty, especially at night, so booking is essential. The menu is vast—over 250 items with the emphasis on Cantonese cooking. The obliging and friendly owner, Gerry Yeung, is happy to advise diners on which dishes will suit them best. Salads are not on the menu but will gladly be created from English and Chinese vegetables. There are numerous healthy dishes such as seaweed and sesame prawns on toast, or steamed sea bass.

MARLBOROUGH · *Quick Bite* · Polly

26 High Street
Marlborough
(0672) 52146

Map 5 B3
Wiltshire

Open 8.30–6 (Sat 8–7, Sun 9–7)
Closed January 1, first two Fri &
  Sat in October & 3 days
  Christmas

Typical prices: Carrot & orange
  soup £1.35 Mushroom &
  aubergine pancake £3.45
Credit: Access, Amex, Diners, Visa

This pretty little tea room is renowned for its delicious cakes, so healthy eaters should time their visit to coincide with lunch when home-made soups and salad platters with smoked trout, honey-baked gammon or light fish mousse are available. Hot specials might include cauliflower and ham bake or vegetable curry. Wholemeal bread is served, and you will find natural yoghurt in some salad dressings, and as a topping for the home-made muesli that is part of their healthy breakfast.

241

MARLOW

Restaurant

Compleat Angler Hotel, Valaisan Restaurant

Marlow Bridge
Marlow
(06284) 4444

Map 5 C3
Buckinghamshire

Lunch 12.30–2.30 (Sun till 3)
  Dinner 7.30–10 (Sat till 10.30)
French cooking

Average price £25
Set L Mon–Fri from £16, Sun
  £19.50
Credit: Access, Amex, Diners, Visa

Easily accessible from both the M4 and the M40, this riverside restaurant has a marvellous range of options for the healthy eater. Choose eight items from the finger buffet or select more substantial dishes such as cold lobster or lamb cutlets en gelée from the cold table, preceded by melon cocktail or vegetable terrine. Baked jacket potatoes or new potatoes, assorted salads and hot savouries complete the selection. The French-influenced à la carte menu includes some excellent poached fish dishes. There is also a sensibly-priced selection of vegetarian dishes.

MAWNAN SMITH

Restaurant

Meudon Hotel Restaurant

Near Falmouth
Falmouth
(0326) 250541

Map 8 A3
Cornwall

Lunch 12.30–2.30 Dinner 7.30–
  8.45
Closed late November–late
  February

Average price £20
Set L (Sun only) £10 Set D £15
Credit: Access, Amex, Diners, Visa

Seafood is an obvious and healthy choice at this spacious and serene hotel, where beautiful gardens can be glimpsed through the restaurant windows. Fresh local lobster, dressed crab and Helford oysters are available most of the year and may be ordered in advance. The dinner menu is fairly predictable with dishes like hake mornay, salmon mousse and poached whiting, but there are some occasional surprises such as nasi goreng and suprême of chicken with passion fruit sauce. Vegetarian dishes on request.

Fletching Street
Mayfield
(0435) 872200

Map 6 E3
East Sussex

Last order 9.45pm
Closed December 25
Free House

Typical prices: Macaroni &
vegetable gratin £2.25
Seafood pancakes £2.50

This quintessentially English inn has low beamed ceilings, log fires and sturdy old furniture and host Richard Leet extends a warm welcome while his wife Claudette cooks with such consistent skill that many chance callers become regular customers. Her excellent home-made chicken broth is accompanied by good granary bread. Main courses run from pancakes to seafood platters and there are always some vegetarian choices with brown rice or wholemeal pasta chalked up on a daily changing blackboard menu. Natural yoghurt is used in some dressings and polyunsaturated margarine is available on request.

If you are unsure of what to order, do remember to ask the staff for advice on food choices. Many restaurants will adapt dishes to suit your requirements or prepare special meals if given prior notice.

MELMERBY   *Quick Bite*   Village Bakery ★

Near Penrith
Langwathby
(076 881) 515

Map 3 C2
Cumbria

Open 8.30–5 (Sun and Bank
    Holidays from 9.30)
Closed Mon (except Bank
    Holidays) & Christmas–Easter

Typical prices: Seafood pizza
    £3.25
    Fruity flapjack 28p

Good food news begins with breakfast at this outstanding restaurant at the foot of the Pennines. Grapefruit or fresh orange juice is a prelude to porridge or granola and yoghurt. Boiled new-laid eggs (from free-range hens on their adjacent smallholding) follow with freshly-baked wholemeal bread. Add Loch Fyne kippers, organically grown tomatoes, mushrooms and choice teas and you have a breakfast that would be hard to better anywhere in the country. And that is just the beginning of the story. Throughout the day Andrew and Lis Whitley and their dedicated team serve a wide selection of remarkably good cakes, teabreads and bakes. Lunch might be spiced prawns with brown rice and salad, a baked jacket potato with home-baked beans or a wholemeal pizza, baked when the breads have left the brick oven. There's always a choice of vegetarian dishes, such as sunflower slice or buckwheat pancakes with ratatouille. Organically-grown vegetables — many grown next door — are frequently used and there is usually at least one simple chicken or fish dish. Desserts include carob ice cream and raspberry sorbet. Everything merits applause.

MIDHURST *Restaurant* Spread Eagle Hotel Restaurant

South Street
Midhurst
(073 081) 6911

Map 6 D3
West Sussex

Lunch 12.30–2.15 Dinner
  7.30–9.30

Average price £17
Set L & Set D £13.50
Credit: Access, Amex, Diners, Visa

Attention to detail is instantly apparent at this charming hotel restaurant where the flowers on the tables are as fresh as the ingredients chosen by the skilful chef. Try his marinated sea trout with white wine sauce for starters, or simple smoked sirloin of beef with melon. Fish is a good choice for the main course, with such options as salmon with fennel and Pernod, and brill wrapped in lettuce and served with a basil and tomato sauce. Vegetarians will enjoy the spinach parcels filled with a trio of puréed vegetables. For dessert, choose a healthy fresh fruit salad.

MONKSILVER *Pub* Notley Arms ★

Taunton
Stogumber
(0984) 56217

Map 8 C1
Somerset

Last order 9.30pm
Closed December 25
Brewery Ushers

Typical prices: Home-made pasta
  with ham & mushrooms £2.25
  Broad bean & courgette salad
  £1.75

The emphasis is on fresh ingredients of high quality at this delightful inn, where chef Sally Wardell and a dedicated team produce excellent food. The wholemeal pitta pockets, filled with salads and extras like garlic beef or cheese make a tasty snack. Also on the menu are wholesome soups, inventive salads, flans and jacket potatoes with a variety of toppings including simple natural yoghurt. The vegetarian curry is a fragrant combination of potatoes, coconut, tomatoes and freshly ground herbs—don't miss it.

ENGLAND

NEWARK *Quick Bite* **Gannets**

35 Castlegate
Newark
(0636) 702066

Map 4 E4
Nottinghamshire

Open 10–4.30
Closed Sun, Bank Holidays & 1
  week Christmas

Typical prices: Pasta bake £2.15
  Brown rice & vegetable bake
  £1.95

The name of this restaurant is no reflection on the clientele, though hearty appetites are much in evidence, doing justice to Hilary Bower's capable cooking. Wholesome teatime treats include wholemeal scones, moist carrot cake and banana loaf, while lunchtime guests can tuck in to savoury pasta and beef bake, pâtés and vegetarian specialities such as aubergine bake. Wholemeal bread is served with low fat spread and natural yoghurt and skimmed milk are used where appropriate. Desserts include light egg custard and fresh fruit salad.

NEWCASTLE-UPON-TYNE *Quick Bite* **Madeleine's**

134 Heaton Road,
Heaton
Tyneside
(091) 2765277

Map 4 D2
Tyne and Wear

Open 12–1.30 & 7–9.30
Closed Sun & 1 week Christmas
Vegetarian cooking

Typical prices: Baked potato &
  chilli beans £1.05
  Stuffed green peppers £3.50
Credit: Access, Visa

Vegans are well catered for at this unassuming vegetarian restaurant, with at least one vegan dish in each category. You might start with a simple soup and a wholemeal roll, followed by ratatouille cheese bake or Brazil nut roast with vegetable curry. Light meals include filled potatoes, marinated mushrooms and houmus. Wholemeal pasta, pulses and brown rice all feature frequently on the menu and natural yoghurt and skimmed milk are used in the cooking. Desserts include soya ice creams.

NEWPORT *Quick Bite* God's Providence House

12 St Thomas Square
Isle of Wight
(0983) 522085

Map 5 C4
Isle of Wight

Open 10–5
Closed Sun & Bank Holidays

Typical prices: Wholemeal open
Danish sandwich £1.20
Spinach lasagne £1.40

The name of this fine old house is believed to stem from the fact that it was the only house in Newport to escape a plague in the 16th century. Extended since then—the date above the door reads 1701—it is a pleasant place in which to sample simple snacks like wholemeal quiches, rolls, sandwiches and scones. From noon the restaurant assumes a split personality—roast and steak puddings downstairs and healthy light lunches upstairs, including vegetarian dishes. Afternoon teas take over at 2.30, with topped toasts, jacket potatoes, sandwiches and cream teas.

NORWICH *Quick Bite* Café la Tienda

10 St Gregory's Alley
Norwich
(0603) 629122

Map 6 F1
Norfolk

Open 10.30–5, also Fri & Sat
7–10.30 pm (Full meals only)
Closed Sun & Bank Holidays

Typical prices: Bean & tomato
stew £1.80
Rice & vegetable bake £2.20

Enthusiastic owners have made this pleasant two-floor restaurant a friendly place in which to enjoy simple tasty food. There's a definite emphasis on healthy cooking and much of their produce is organically grown in their own 3-acre market garden. Sandwiches and bakes give way at about 11.30 am to home-made soup with granary bread and savouries like smoked haddock and mushroom flan, or brown rice and vegetable bake. There's an extended menu in the evenings.

NOTTINGHAM *QuickBite* Café Punchinello

35 Forman Street
Nottingham
(0602) 411965

Map 4 E4
Nottinghamshire

Open 8.30am–10pm (Sat till
  10.30)
Closed Sun & Bank Holidays

Typical prices: Vegetarian
  shepherd's pie 95p
  Bean & fruit stew £1.60
Luncheon Vouchers accepted

Good home cooking at reasonable prices is the hallmark of this popular café just off Parliament street. Everything is made on the premises. The day begins with breakfast— fresh fruit, wholemeal toast or muffins, muesli—and proceeds through the morning coffee time to the midday selection of wholesome hot dishes. Try the kidney and mushroom casserole or the bean and fruit stew. Up to 10 bowls of help-yourself salads are always on offer, with various dressings including natural yoghurt. The dessert trolley always includes a simple fresh fruit sweet.

NOTTINGHAM *QuickBite* The Q in the Corner
at Ziggi's

3 Victoria Street
Nottingham
(0602) 506956

Map 4 E4
Nottinghamshire

Open 9.30–5
Closed Sun & Bank Holidays
  except Good Friday

Typical prices: Courgette bake
  £1.50 Lasagne & salad £1.75
Credit: Access, Visa

Situated inside a ladies' fashion store (which provides a strong incentive to maintaining a balanced diet) is this pleasant little coffee shop. In a cottage kitchen atmosphere you can enjoy Danish open sandwiches, bakes, salads and savouries. The open sandwiches, on wholemeal bread, have a variety of fillings, including cottage cheese, tuna and egg, and there are about eight salads. The light wholemeal quiches are popular and there's always a vegetarian special such as tagliatelle with vegetable sauce.

ENGLAND

10 Commerce Square,
  off High Pavement
Nottingham
(0602) 585211

Map 4 E4
Nottinghamshire

Open 12–11 (Fri & Sat till 11.30 &
  Mon till 3)
Closed Sun & Bank Holidays
  except lunch Good Friday &
  December 25
Vegetarian cooking

Typical prices: Broccoli thermidor
  £5.75 Nut rissoles £3
Credit: Access

Despite its basement setting, this vegetarian restaurant is light and airy. The menu proves just how successful an imaginative approach to vegetarian food can be, and the cooking is extremely capable. The daytime menu has starters like bean and sweet red pepper pâté and houmus with pitta bread. Light meals include lots of burgers (bean, rice and nut-based), buckwheat flan, filled baked potatoes and herb waffles, plus daily specials such as nut rissoles with sweet herb sauce. Dessert might be thick-set yoghurt with honey and nuts. The evening menu is more sophisticated.

OAKHAM   *Quick Bite*   **Oakham Gallery**

17 Mill Street
Oakham
(0572) 55094

Map 5 C1
Leicestershire

Open 9.30–5 (Sun 2–5)
Closed Mon & December 25 & 26

Typical prices: Wholewheat &
  vegetable fricassee £1.75
  Lentil pattie 80p

This attractively furnished tea-room above an art gallery is a charming place in which to sample honest home-made fare. The substantial open sandwiches are very popular with healthy eaters. Try the Rutland, with its generous topping of smoked salmon and prawns, cottage cheese and salad. Simpler sandwiches, super salads and other savouries are on sale together with wholefood dishes like wholewheat and vegetable fricassee or lentil patties with home-made tomato sauce.

OFFCHURCH Stag's Head

Near Leamington Spa
Leamington Spa
(0926) 25801

Map 5 C2
Warwickshire

Last order 10pm
Brewery Ansells
Closed December 25 & 26 eve

Typical prices: Taramasalata
£1.45 Salmon steak £4.95

Named after Offa—the Anglo-Saxon king—Offchurch is an attractive village not far from Leamington Spa. The Stag's Head specialises in steaks and offers an impressive variety, cooked simply or with sauces, and served with jacket potatoes or rice as alternatives to chips. Grilled fish is also popular—do try the fisherman's kebab or grilled salmon. Salads and ploughman's provide lighter meals and the vegetarian choices include vegetable moussaka and nut roast. Cooking is robust and dependable and service is friendly and capable.

OMBERSLEY Kings Arms

Near Worcester
Worcester
(0905) 620142

Map 5 B2
Hereford & Worcester

Last order 9pm
No bar food Sun
Brewery Mitchells & Butlers

Typical prices: Fish kedgeree
£3.10 Fresh mackerel £3.10

Any publican who fears that serving 'health' food would lose him custom should visit this inn. But come early—at lunchtime the place is packed. The roast beef salad is a palette for the palate, the meat contrasting with three types of lettuce plus apple, grapes and kiwi fruit. Fresh grilled trout or salmon steaks are always on offer and there are regular vegetarian dishes. Skimmed milk is used exclusively in cooking and bread is wholemeal. Sorbets and yoghurt-based desserts.

OSWALDKIRK — *Pub* — Malt Shovel Inn

Near Helmsley
Ampleforth
(043 93) 461

Map 4 E3
North Yorkshire

Last order 9.30pm
No bar food Mon eves (except
  Bank Holidays)
Closed December 25 eve
Brewery Samuel Smith

Typical prices: Mixed bean soup
  £1.10 Grilled lemon sole £6

Once a manor house, later a coaching inn, the Malt Shovel has considerable character. The bar snacks menu is full of interest and variety. Healthy eaters can sample simple soups such as lentil, or open sandwiches with prawns and cottage cheese, tandoori chicken or home-cooked beef or ham. For more healthy appetites there is suprême of chicken with basil and tomato, or sea trout with tarragon sauce. Perfectly cooked vegetables will be served without butter or sauce on request. Regular vegetarian dishes include cashew nut roast with mushroom sauce.

OSWESTRY — *Quick Bite* — Good Companion (Wine Bar)

10 Beatrice Street
Oswestry
(0691) 655768

Map 5 A1
Shropshire

Open 12–2.30 & 7.30–11
Closed Mon lunch, all Sun,
  December 25 & 26, & January 1

Typical prices: Kofta kebabs £2.10
  Cashew nut lasagne £3.50
Credit: Amex, Diners

Sip a spritzer at the bar while placing your order at this modest establishment near the town centre. The food is well prepared from good quality fresh ingredients and offers a wide choice of healthy dishes. Try cashew nut lasagne or kofta kebabs—spicy meatballs in pitta pockets with salad and yoghurt, or sample smoked trout with baked potato and salad. Grills satisfy more ample appetites and there are salads like prawn, avocado and nut. Vegetable specialities include stuffed courgettes.

OXFORD *Restaurant* Randolph Hotel, Spires Restaurant

Beaumont Street
Oxford
(0865) 247481

Map 5 C2
Oxfordshire

Lunch 12.30–2.15 Dinner 7–10.15
Closed Dinner December 25

Average price £17
Set L £6.25
Set D £14.10
Credit: Access, Amex, Diners, Visa

Avant garde paintings line the walls of this lofty, elegant restaurant. The menu includes traditional favourites like the chef's roast of the day and poached salmon alongside dishes influenced by nouvelle cuisine, such as chicken and avocado timbales, or trout and coriander saladette. Many of the dishes are offered in two portion sizes, a boon to the customer who always wishes a starter could be a main course and vice versa. The menu includes a vegetarian speciality such as vegetable moussaka and any of the dishes will be cooked without a sauce on request.

PARKGATE *Pub* Ship Hotel

The Parade, Near
 Neston, Wirral
051-336 3931

Map 3 B4
Cheshire

Last order 10.30pm
No bar food Sun & Mon eves
Owners Anchor Hotels

Typical prices: Avocado pear with
 shrimps £2.90 Grilled salmon
 steak & lemon £5.50
Credit: Access, Amex, Diners, Visa

Birdwatchers taking a breather favour this comfortable inn, as the picture windows in the main bar give a fine view of the feathered inhabitants of the Dee Estuary. The food holds plenty of interest too. Healthy eaters can enjoy simple fish dishes like chargrilled salmon steak, served with a jacket potato and a selection of salads. A lighter meal might be a bowl of tasty home-made soup with granary bread, or pizza. Vegetarian dishes are mainly pasta-based and there are excellent lean steaks.

Three Crowns Yard
Penrith
(0768) 66660

Map 3 C2
Cumbria

Open 9.30–4.30
Closed Sun, Bank Holidays &
  1 week Christmas–New Year

Typical prices: Honey & sesame
  cake 50p Citron pressé 50p

The Bluebell Tearoom is a browser's paradise. You could spend hours leafing through the vast collection of books which line the walls and spill over into stacks. Take sustenance at one of the little tables under the window, where you can enjoy freshly-ground coffee, leaf teas and tisanes. Pure fruit juices too, and healthy eaters can opt for citron pressé, a blend of freshly squeezed lemon juice and iced water. The wonderful cakes are made from organically grown wholewheat flour, raw sugar, free-range eggs and polyunsaturated margarine.

PITTON   *Pub*   Silver Plough ★

Salisbury
Farley
(0722 72) 266

Map 5 B3
Wiltshire

Last order 10pm
Closed December 25 eve
Free House

Typical prices: Fillet of red sea
  bream £4.95
   Dorset crab salad £4.95
Credit: Access, Amex, Diners, Visa

There is much to delight on chef Rupert Wilcox's ambitious and well-executed menu at this lovely converted farmhouse. Quick snacks include fresh pasta with fish and shellfish, and soup with a granary roll. More substantial dishes might be breast of chicken with tomato and tarragon sauce, grilled steak, and daily fish specialities. Composite salads include smoked salmon, Dorset crab and Wiltshire ham. Sorbets or a good selection of cheese to follow, with decaffeinated coffee.

ENGLAND

POOLE — *Quick Bite* — Inn à Nutshell

27 Arndale Centre
Poole
(0202) 673888

Map 5 B4
Dorset

Open 9.30–5
Closed Sun & Bank Holidays
Vegetarian cooking

Typical prices: Mushroom
  Stroganoff £1.45
  Spinach & mushroom bake £1.45
Credit: Access, Amex, Diners, Visa
Luncheon Vouchers accepted

Sensible prices and self-service make this a popular eating place. The vegetarian menu provides plenty of healthy choices, and the generous and carefully prepared salads are particularly popular. A wide selection includes Chinese leaves with cucumber and courgettes, and bean-sprouts with mixed fresh fruits. Hot dishes range from simple wholemeal pasties to the popular cheese and oatmeal roast or more sophisticated spinach roll filled with cottage cheese and walnuts. Fresh fruit salad, cakes, bakes and a good selection of speciality teas.

PORTSMOUTH (SOUTHSEA) — *Quick Bite* — Country Kitchen

59 Marmion Road
Portsmouth
(0705) 811425

Map 5 B4
Hampshire

Open 10–6
Closed Sun, January 1, Good
  Friday & December 25 & 26
Vegetarian cooking

Typical prices: Stuffed cabbage
  £1.95
  Vegetable lasagne £1.95
Luncheon Vouchers accepted

From the Country Kitchen come all manner of good things to eat, from wholemeal rolls and sandwiches to filled jacket potatoes. There are always about six salads, including one using chick peas and beans. The blackboard announces the day's soup, perhaps home-made tomato (bursting with flavour), and vegetarian specials like stuffed cabbage and vegetable lasagne. Natural yoghurt and soya milks are used, and there is a low fat spread with the wholemeal bread. Fresh fruit salad and gingery peach crumble.

POWERSTOCK *Pub* Three Horseshoes

Bridport
Powerstock
(030 885) 328

Map 5 A4
Dorset

Last order 10pm
No bar food Mon
Brewery Palmer

Typical prices: Grilled fresh plaice
£3.95
Wholewheat pancakes £3.50
Credit: Access, Visa

Grill your own meat on the garden barbecues at this Victorian pub or venture indoors for a comprehensive selection of healthy dishes, from melon filled with fresh crab to grilled Lyme Bay plaice. Fish is definitely the best catch, and baked grey mullet, poached salmon trout and grilled local lobsters are just a few of the regular seafood specials. Omelettes, wholewheat pancakes and salads, soups and sandwiches are also available and there's an additional grill menu. Finish with fresh fruit salad or a fruit crumble.

PYRTON *Pub* Plough Inn

Near Watlington
Watlington
(049 161) 2003

Map 5 C3
Oxfordshire

Last order 10pm
Free house

Typical prices: Vegetarian nut
roast £4.95
Poached trout £5.90
Credit: Access, Visa

The welcome is warm and pleasant at this archetypal country pub where good home-cooking tempts people to linger for more than just a drink. For healthy eaters the lunchtime slimmer's special—cottage cheese and pineapple with crackers and salad—is a good choice, as is the prawn platter with crusty wholemeal bread. Vegetarians will find nut roast with brown rice or vegetable lasagne (wholemeal pasta), and a range of light snacks. Also grills and simple fish dishes.

ENGLAND

5 Dome Buildings,
  The Quadrant
01-940 1138

Map 6 D3
Surrey

Open 11.30 am–11 pm (Sun till
  10.30 pm)
Closed December 25–January 1
Vegetarian wholefood cooking

Typical prices: Rice, red pepper,
  celery, cress salad £1.10
  Mediterranean courgette
  casserole £3.15
  (Minimum charge £1.95)

The menu changes twice daily at this tiny vegetarian restaurant but always includes plenty of vegan dishes and wholefoods. You might start with a piping hot bowl of barley soup with wholegrain bread, or choose a substantial salad such as the buckwheat, mixed peppers, cauliflower, cucumber and celery combination. Specials include a Mediterranean courgette casserole and a nut roast with mixed salad. Finish with a delicious dried fruit crumble or fresh fruit salad, with herb tea or decaffeinated coffee. A deservedly popular place that is frequently crowded.

RICHMOND *QuickBite* **Wildefoods Wholefood Café**

98 Kew Road
01-940 0733

Map 6 D3
Surrey

Open 9–7, Sun 12–5 (summer
  only)
Closed Sun in winter, January 1,
  Good Friday, December 25 & 26
  & 1 week in summer
Wholefood vegetarian cooking

Typical prices: Tofu stir rice 50p
  Apricot & almond slice 25p

Originally a wholefood shop and vegetarian take-away, but so many customers couldn't wait to get home to sample the fare that they provided first two, then four tables for eating-in. Soups are delicious, and snacks include crêpes, lentil balls and vegetarian burgers. Bean casseroles and brown rice stir-fries cater for hungry eaters, and wholemeal baps and sandwiches, made with polyunsaturated margarine, are also on offer. The cooking is something of a cottage industry with various people contributing.

RIPON *Quick Bite* Warehouse

Court Terrace,
Ripon
(0765) 4665

Map 4 D3
North Yorkshire

Open 9.30–5.15
Closed Sun & January 1, May 1,
December 25 & 26

Typical prices: Wholemeal quiche
& salad £2.65
Bean casserole £2.50

At the Warehouse you can make a choice from scores of good things ranging from simple wholemeal scones to hearty soups and hot savouries that are definitely in the come-again category together with an excellent selection of six to eight salads. Hot savoury specials served with baked potatoes in winter and new potatoes in summer, include minted cucumber lamb and chicken with peaches, while special vegetarian dishes like black-eyed bean casserole appear on the menu three times a week. Staff are friendly and helpful.

ROMSEY *Quick Bite* Latimer Coffee House

11 Latimer Street
Romsey
(0794) 513832

Map 5 C4
Hampshire

Open 9.15–5.15
Closed Sun & December 25 & 26

Typical prices: Jacket potato £1.50
Brown rice salad 40p

Pop into this charming establishment in the morning and you risk being seduced by a mouthwatering display of scones and home-bakes on the counter. Save yourself by going in the afternoon when you'll find home-made soup, filled jacket potatoes and several savoury flans, including bacon, tuna, and a vegetarian variety. Vegetables are not served, but there are always several salads including the popular brown rice with mushrooms, sweetcorn, pepper, pumpkin and sunflower seeds.

ROSS-ON-WYE *Quick Bite* Meader's

1 Copse Cross Street
Ross-on-Wye
(0989) 62803

Map 5 A2
Hereford & Worcester

Open 10–3 & 7–10
Closed Dinner Mon, all Sun,
  January 1 & December 25 & 26

Typical prices: Hungarian bean
  soup 95p
  Bean & vegetable rissole 80p

At least fourteen salads are regularly on offer at this simple restaurant close to the Bradley Hill Workshop. Vegetarian dishes are always available and there's at least one vegan speciality every day. The owner is Hungarian and has introduced several of his national dishes. The layered cabbage is excellent, as is the hearty bean soup. Lunchtime main courses also include simple meat and fish dishes which can be served with jacket potatoes instead of chips. The evening menu is more elaborate, with grills and goulashes in addition to old-fashioned flambés.

RYTON-ON-DUNSMORE *Quick Bite* Ryton Gardens Café

Warwick Road
Coventry
(0203) 303517

Map 5 C2
Warwickshire

Open October–March 9–4, April–
  September 9–6
Closed December 25 & 26
Vegetarian cooking

Typical prices: Vegetable curry
  £1.50 Banana surprise 85p

Ryton Gardens, the National Centre for Organic Gardening, has extensive vegetable plots, so this simple little café has a ready supply to reinforce its policy of using organically grown and additive-free raw materials wherever possible. Cakes and bakes are served all day, plus filled wholemeal rolls and omelettes. Lunch might be fennel soup followed by vegetarian cottage pie or mushroom risotto. Fruit from the centre's own trees is used in desserts. Allow time to visit the gardens and don't miss the observation beehive.

ST MICHAEL'S MOUNT *Quick Bite* Sail Loft

The Harbour, near
  Marazion
Penzance
(0736) 710748

Map 8 A3
Cornwall

Open 10.30–5.30 (weather and
  tide permitting)
Closed end October–beginning
  April

Typical prices: Home-made soup
  £1.25
  Hobbler's choice £3.50
Credit: Access, Amex, Visa

There can't be many restaurants whose opening times are dictated by the state of the tide, but this Cornish National Trust restaurant, situated as it is on St Michael's Mount, is very much at the mercy of wind and weather. Cross the causeway to taste the well-flavoured tomato and lentil soup with island-baked wholemeal bread, or try the hobbler's choice of locally caught fish. There's always a range of composite salads and a vegetarian dish such as courgette and pasta bake or hazelnut and rice hotpot, with home-made fruit squash as a healthy drink.

SALISBURY *Quick Bite* Mainly Salads

18 Fisherton Street
Salisbury
(0722) 22134

Map 5 B3
Wiltshire

Open 10–5
Closed Sun, Bank Holidays & 1
  week September
Vegetarian cooking

Typical prices: Lentil loaf £1.10
  Pineapple pavlova 75p
(Minimum lunchtime charge £1.50)
Luncheon Vouchers accepted

As the name suggests, salads are the star attraction at this bright and fresh self-service vegetarian restaurant. You'll find a wide range of interesting combinations, including lentil, leek and mushroom; pasta, peas, celery and carrot; and brown rice with raisins, peanuts and red pepper strips. The fruit salad is savoury, not sweet, and combines cabbage with apples, grapes and pineapple pieces. Also on the menu are ratatouille, flans, pizzas, and filled potatoes, plus specials like vegetable goulash.

259

ENGLAND

SALISBURY   *Quick Bite*   Mo's

62 Milford Street
Salisbury
(0722) 331377

Map 5 B3
Wiltshire

Open 12–2.30 & 5.30–11.15 (Fri &
   Sat till midnight, Sun 6–10.30pm)
Closed Lunch Sun, all January 1 &
   December 25 & 26

Typical prices: Smokey burger
   £2.55
   Mushroom croustade £3.40

The enthusiastic partners who run this restaurant have rapidly made it a popular eating place, thanks to efficiency unimpaired by informality. The mainstay of the menu is the hamburger, which can be served plain with salad. Fresh trout and barbecued chicken are other hot favourites. Salads are many and varied and baked potatoes are served with crunchy salad fillings. There is a good choice of vegetarian dishes like burghul wheat chilli and mushroom croustade. Gooey sweets are not suitable for healthy diners but fresh fruit is always available.

SANDFORD ORCAS   *Restaurant*   Holway Mill

Sherborne
Corton Denham
(096 322) 380

Map 5 A4
Dorset

Lunch 12–2 Dinner 6.30–9
Closed 2 weeks November
Vegetarian cooking

Average price £12
Set L £6
Set D £7.50

A reader's recommendation led us to this delightfully welcoming guesthouse and vegetarian restaurant. Caroline Woodward uses first-class organic produce plus her own inimitable style and imagination. Dinner (book at least 24 hours ahead) might be mushroom bisque, stuffed vine leaves with new potatoes and fennel, and poached pears with cardamom and ginger. There are always several salads and the Woodwards will happily meet special dietary requirements if adequate notice is given.

SCUNTHORPE

Quick Bite

Bees Garden
Coffee Lounge

4 Cole Street
Scunthorpe
(0724) 848751

Map 4 E4
Humberside

Open 9–5
Closed Sun & Bank Holidays

Typical prices: Wholemeal open
   sandwich £1.30
   Baked potato 90p

It never rains in this garden, for the simple reason that it is only an illusion, created by setting outdoor furniture and umbrellas on a grass-green carpet with masses of genuine plants. The open salad sandwiches are fresh and tasty with toppings like cottage cheese and turkey breast. As an alternative, try the filled baked potatoes or the main dish salads. A range of hot meals includes a vegetarian lasagne and there's a lemon poached plaice, ideal for delicate digestions. Fresh fruit to follow. Thirst quenchers include speciality teas and fresh orange juice.

SHEFFIELD

Quick Bite

Just Cooking

16–18 Carver Street
Sheffield
(0742) 27869

Map 4 D4
South Yorkshire

Open 11–3.30 (Sat from 10), also
   Fri 6–11pm
Closed Sun, Mon, Bank Holidays
   except Good Friday & 1 week
   Christmas

Typical prices: Tuna bake with
   mushrooms £2.80
   Chicken casserole £3.65

Just Cooking is the conscientious concern of partners John Craig and Brian Rosen. They take pains to ensure that ingredients are of top quality, and fuss amiably over the food. The results are memorable. You can make a meal of their super salads, which include cottage cheese and fresh pineapple, smoked mackerel and ham. Hot dishes change daily: try lamb and apricot casserole with brown rice if available—the flavours harmonise beautifully. Healthy desserts include fresh pineapple and strawberries.

SHEFFIELD *Quick Bite* Toff's Restaurant & Coffee House

23 Matilda Street,
  The Moor
Sheffield
(0742) 20783

Map 4 D4
South Yorkshire

Open 10–3 (Sat till 4.30)
Closed Sun, all Bank Holidays

Typical prices: Chicken niçoise & salad £2.95 Vegetable wholemeal quiche £1.45
Luncheon Vouchers accepted

Summery decor—white furniture, climbing plants, hanging baskets—sets the scene for lovely light meals at this restaurant close to a multi-storey car park and the Moor shopping precinct. Top marks for perfect, wholemeal pastry in tartlets with flavoursome vegetable fillings. Salads complete the light theme in combinations such as French leaves with oak leaf lettuce and pine kernels served with wholemeal bread. Another winning partnership is breast of chicken with wholemeal pasta and fresh tomato sauce or chicken with apricots and almonds in a mild curry sauce.

SHIPSTON ON STOUR *Pub* White Bear

High Street
Shipston on Stour
(0608) 61558

Map 5 B2
Warwickshire

Last order 9.30pm
No bar food Sun eve
Brewery Bass

Typical prices: Baked mackerel £3.75 Chilli bean & vegetable hot pot £3.25
Credit: Access, Amex, Diners, Visa

The bar food is highly recommended at this small family-run hotel. The standard menu includes wholesome soups with home-baked wholemeal bread, starters like avocado with crab and apple, and specials such as poached chicken breast with watercress sauce, prawn-stuffed plaice and baked mackerel with fresh herbs. There's always a hot vegetarian dish such as chilli, bean and vegetable hot pot. Snacks include pâtés, pancakes, salads and jacket potatoes all beautifully prepared and cooked.

SHREWSBURY

Quick Bite

Cornhouse Restaurant & Wine Bar

59 Wyle Cop
Shrewsbury
(0743) 231991

Map 5 A1
Shropshire

Open 12–2.30 & 6.30–10.30
Closed December 26

Typical prices: Lentil & rice bean
  soup 90p
  Gigot steak & brown rice £6.50
  (Restaurant)
Credit: Access, Visa

This handsome wine bar stands at the bottom of a steep hill near Shrewsbury city centre. Food is well above average and a daily changing blackboard menu includes very good vegetable soups such as mushroom and spinach, main courses like rack of lamb and simple sweets. A wrought-iron spiral staircase leads to the restaurant, which offers healthy eaters such dishes as plain poached salmon, cashew nut paella with brown rice and gigot steak with fresh rosemary and lemon. Side salads are always available and vegetables will be served plain if preferred.

SHREWSBURY

Quick Bite

Delanys

St Alkmunds Square,
  St Julian's Cross
Shrewsbury
(0743) 60602

Wyle Cop
(0743) 66890

Map 5 A1
Shropshire

Open 10.30–3.30 (Wyle Cop:
  9.30–5.30, Fri & Sat 7–10.30pm)
Closed Sun, Bank Holidays & 3
  days Christmas
Vegetarian cooking

Typical prices: Spinach tortilla
  £1.50
  Bean casserole £1.50
Luncheon Vouchers accepted

Simple vegetarian food, carefully prepared and competently cooked, is the secret of success here. Morning callers will find wholesome bakes like carob and pear cake and sugar-free fresh fruit slices. Lunch might be corn chowder with home-baked wholemeal bread, or a fresh vegetable bake with rosemary and cheese. Lentil burgers are also popular and there is a good range of salads. A new restaurant (Wyle Cop) has recently been opened serving more formal evening meals as well as lunches.

ENGLAND

SKIPTON — *Quick Bite* — Herbs Wholefood & ★ Vegetarian Restaurant

10 High Street
Skipton
(0756) 60619

Map 4 D3
North Yorkshire

Open 9.30–5
Closed Sun, Tues, December 25 & 26
Wholefood vegetarian cooking

Typical prices: Vegetable pancakes in a hazelnut sauce £2.45
Herbs fruit & nut platter £2.65

Herbs restaurant was opened over a bustling homeopathic shop to demonstrate how natural wholefoods could produce tasty and nourishing dishes. You might start with egg and sage pâté and a delicious wholemeal roll and proceed with cottage cheese salad or the popular fruit and nut platter. Daily specials, indicated on a blackboard menu, include items like vegetable pancakes with hazelnut sauce. Savouries and sandwiches are also on sale, and sweets include fresh fruit salad and sorbets. There are no fewer than twelve fresh juices, including redcurrant.

SOUTH WOODFORD — *Restaurant* — Ho-Ho

20 High Road, E18
01-989 1041

Map 6 D3
Essex

Lunch 12–3 Dinner 6–11.30
Closed December 25 & 26
Chinese cooking

Average price £14
Set D from £9.50
Credit: Access, Amex, Diners, Visa

Ho-Ho describes itself as an inter-regional Chinese restaurant. On the menu you will find specialities from Peking, Szechuan and many other parts of China. As this is essentially a healthy cuisine, it is not difficult to choose a suitable meal. A fine combination of flavours is to be found in the crispy seaweed with grated scallops, while the delicate sharks' fin soup would be another wise starter. Steamed sea bass with ginger and scallions is a speciality and vegetable and noodle dishes abound.

264

SOUTHWOLD Crown Hotel

High Street
Southwold
(0502) 722275

Map 6 F2
Suffolk

Last order 10pm
Brewery Adnams

Typical prices: Cod in pesto sauce
£3.65 Southwold fish soup £1.85
Set L from £8
Set D from £10
Credit: Access, Amex, Visa

A meal at this attractively restored 18th-century hotel is an enjoyable experience, thanks to a menu which makes healthy eating easy. Fish is a speciality and the Southwold fish soup is highly commended. Eat à la carte or settle for a two or three course meal with perhaps poached chicken or steamed halibut steak as the main attraction in the restaurant or try a variety of snacks at the bar. Vegetarians are not well catered for but will enjoy the fresh fruit desserts such as poached peaches with raspberries.

STAPLE FITZPAINE *Pub* Greyhound Inn

Near Taunton
Hatch Beauchamp
(0823) 480227

Map 8 C1
Somerset

Last order 10pm
Free House

Typical prices: Kipper & black
olive pâté £1.35
Grilled whole plaice £4.95
Credit: Access, Visa

This classic country inn is only four miles from Junction 25 on the M5 and is an ideal spot for a healthy meal. Home-made soup and simple fish dishes like grilled plaice or herbed trout are good choices. Steamed vegetables are served and sauces can be omitted or served separately. Both pulses and wholemeal pasta are enthusiastically included in dishes like vegetable and nut chilli and fettuccine Alfredo. Natural yoghurt and skimmed milk are used and fresh fruit salad is always on the menu.

STOKPORT *Quick Bite* Coconut Willy's

37 St Petersgate
061-480 7013

Map 3 C4
Greater Manchester

Open 10–9.30 (Sat till 11.30, Sun
 6.30–10.30pm)
Closed Sun lunch, all Mon & Bank
 Holidays
Wholefood cooking

Typical prices: Butter bean risotto
 £1.10 Lentil & apple loaf £1.10
Credit: Visa
Luncheon Vouchers accepted

This recently refurbished restaurant is conveniently situated in the centre of Stockport. Shoppers can sip fresh fruit juices, teas, tisanes, decaffeinated coffee or a glass of non alcoholic damson 'wine' while enjoying wholesome bakes made with organic flour and polyunsaturated margarine. Wholemeal pancakes, nut roasts and stir-fries are the main attractions, with a selection of attractive salads. Home-made soup is served with wholemeal bread and desserts make good use of fresh and dried fruits. Special diets catered for with advance notice.

STOKE ST GREGORY *Pub* Rose & Crown

Woodhill
North Curry
(0823) 490296

Map 8 C1
Somerset

Last order 10pm
Free House

Typical prices: Grilled whole
 plaice £3.25
 Home-made soup 85p
Credit: Access, Visa

Irene Browning's home-made and delicious soups and a chunk of her home-baked wholemeal bread make a nourishing meal at this country inn. Equally popular in the cosy beamed bar are her salads and and sandwiches, and hot savoury dishes like vegetable curry on brown rice. There's always a selection of dishes for those who prefer plain food, such as grilled lamb cutlets, liver or kidneys, grilled whole plaice or sirloin steak. Also a selection of omelettes. A daily vegetarian dish is always on the menu.

STON EASTON *Restaurant* Ston Easton Park Restaurant

Near Bath
Chewton Mendip
(076 121) 631

Map 5 A3
Somerset

Lunch 12–2 Dinner 7.30–9.30 (Sat till 10)

Average price £28
Set L £13.50 (Sun £14)
Credit: Access, Amex, Diners, Visa

A beautiful country house is home to this well-patronised restaurant where guests can enjoy dishes like charcoal grilled breast of duckling with apple and sage or saddle of venison with apricot and brandy marinade. The menu always includes an interesting and often out-of-the-ordinary vegetarian dish such as homemade pasta with Chinese, local and oyster mushrooms, or a vegetarian lasagne. Wholemeal bread is available, with polyunsaturated margarine if preferred, and fresh fruit is always on offer. Decaffeinated coffee is an alternative to ground Colombian.

STREATLEY-ON-THAMES *Restaurant* Swan Hotel ★ Restaurant

Goring-on-Thames
(0491) 873737

Map 5 C3
Berkshire

Lunch 12.30–2.30 Dinner 7.30–9.30

Average price £24
Set L £11.95
Set D £14.95
Credit: Access, Amex, Diners, Visa

Finding the finest ingredients is obviously of prime importance to chef Richard Sparrow—so important that he actually credits his major suppliers in his menu. The association clearly pays dividends in such specialities as paupiettes of Dover sole lined with spinach, bound in a sea trout and crab mousseline and laid on celeriac and langoustine sauces. There is a particularly fine selection of cheese, wonderful walnut bread, and both vegetarian and unsauced dishes on request.

STROUD   *Quick Bite*   **Mother Nature**

Bedford Street
Stroud
(0452) 78202

Map 5 B3
Gloucestershire

Open 9–4.30
Closed Sun & Bank Holidays
Vegetarian cooking

Typical prices: Lentil, cheese &
 green veg bake £1.25
 Fruit crumble 70p
 (Minimum lunchtime charge
 £1.25)

Cheeses are a speciality at this agreeable little vegetarian café at the back of a healthfood store. You'll find over 50 varieties, including several low and medium-fat varieties. Having made your choice, add a selection of salads. Try the wholewheat pasta with peppers and black olives, perhaps, or the coleslaw with caraway seeds. Organically-grown vegetables are used wherever possible in salads and savouries like vegetable crumble, lentil, cheese and green vegetable bake or Chinese sweet and sour vegetables on brown rice. Finish with a sorbet or fresh fruit salad.

STUDLEY   *Restaurant*   **Peppers**

45 High Street
Studley
(052 785) 3183

Map 5 B2
Warwickshire

Lunch 12–2.15 Dinner 6–11.30
Closed Lunch Sun and all
 December 25 & 26
Indian cooking

Average price £10
Credit: Access, Amex, Diners, Visa

India provides the inspiration and the style for this popular high-street restaurant, where the skill of the chef is evident in such dishes as spinach-rich lamb sagwala or the aromatic chana masala—spiced chick peas with ginger and fresh coriander. Tandoori chicken is always available for guests who prefer simple low-fat food, and there's a six-dish vegetarian thali. The freshly baked nan is very good as is the pilau rice. A glass of yoghurt lassi, served sweet or salted, makes a refreshing health drink.

STURMINSTER NEWTON

Restaurant

Plumber Manor Restaurant

Dorset
Sturminster Newton
(0258) 72507

Map 8 D1
Dorset

Dinner only 7.30–9.30 (Sun till 9)
Closed Mon, also Sun November–
March to non-residents, all Feb &
first 2 weeks November

Average price £20
Set D £14 & £16.50

Parma ham with fresh peach is a good way to begin an evening at this impressive and elegant restaurant. The well-balanced set menus are not extensive, but change with the seasons and offer the choice of fish, game, meat or poultry, with a vegetarian dish such as lentil Wellington. All dishes can be served with or without sauces, and there is positive discrimination in favour of both pasta and pulses. Whole-wheat bread is served and vegetables are offered without butter or sauce if preferred. Sweets are on the sinful side of sumptuous but fruit salad is always available.

SURBITON

Quick Bite

Liberty Bell

158 Ewell Road
01-390 7564

Map 6 D3
Surrey

Open 12–2.30 & 6–11
Closed Sun & 1 week Christmas

Typical prices: Tuna fish salad
£3.40 Vegetarian rösti 80p
Credit: Access, Visa
Luncheon Vouchers accepted

This attractive Edwardian-style restaurant makes an instant and pleasing impression with its stained glass panels and lofty ceilings. Service is swift and attentive and the atmosphere is relaxed and friendly. The menu runs to regulars like tuna and bean salad, followed by a selection of grills. Choose a lean burger with cottage cheese, pineapple and salad, or a simple grilled chicken breast. The daily specials provide more unusual and imaginative dishes like cauliflower niçoise followed perhaps by grilled trout.

40 Havelock Street
Swindon
(0793) 39396

Map 5 B3
Wiltshire

Open 10–6
Closed Sun & Bank Holidays
Wholefood cooking

Typical prices: Italian seafood
   salad £2.25 Vegetable pancakes
   & salad £2.50
Credit: Access

A good selection of vegetarian and fish dishes is on offer at this self-service restaurant above a health food shop. Early callers will find a range of home bakes with beverages that include teas, tisanes, barleycup and carob milk. There's also a selection of unusual fruit drinks such as strawberry and apple. From around noon the more substantial dishes appear. Vegetarians have choices like spicy chick pea casserole or cashew nut lasagne, while lovers of seafood plump for poached plaice or peppered mackerel salad. Attractive side salads too, and soya ice cream.

TEWKESBURY *QuickBite* Telfords

61 High Street
Tewkesbury
(0684) 292225

Map 5 B2
Gloucestershire

Open 12–2pm
Closed Sun, January 1 &
   December 26, 2 weeks February
   & 1 week November

Typical prices: Cheese & apple
   salad £2.95
   Baked trout £6.50
Credit: Access, Amex, Visa

A seasonally changing menu and home-grown herbs make meals special at this charming high street restaurant. There's plenty here for the healthy eater, from stylish salad combinations like smoked chicken and celery, to one-course lunches like pan-grilled chicken breast or baked trout. The home-baked wholemeal bread (served hot) is delicious. There are regular vegetarian dishes making good use of pasta, pulses and fresh vegetables. Fresh fruit salad to follow. Full evening meals also available.

THAME *Quick Bite* Mallards (Wine Bar)

87 High Street
Thame
(084 421) 6679

Map 5 C2
Oxfordshire

Open 11–3 & 6–11 (Sun 12–2 &
  7–10.30)
Closed 10 days Christmas

Typical prices: Home-made soup
  £1.50 Baked halibut £4.95
Credit: Access, Visa

Duck into Mallards at dinner time and try the peppered smoked mackerel or home-made soup with crusty French bread. Main course dishes cater for the health conscious and include such items as baked halibut with horseradish butter (the butter will be omitted on request) and grilled steak or noisettes of lamb. There's always a vegetarian dish such as lasagne or pizza on a wholemeal base and the salads are imaginative and well prepared. Vegetables are crisp and fresh and may be served sans sauce by the helpful and efficient staff.

THETFORD *Restaurant* President

St Nicholas Street
Thetford
(0842) 2133

Map 6 E2
Norfolk

Lunch 12–2 Dinner 7–9.30
Closed Lunch Sat, all Sun, Bank
  Holidays except December 25, 2
  weeks August & December 26–
  January 2

Average price £16
Set L & Set D (Mon–Fri) £8.95
Credit: Access, Amex, Diners, Visa

A remarkably comprehensive menu offers a wide choice of healthy dishes at this pleasant restaurant. Starters include chilled melon with sliced stem ginger, or if you prefer something slightly more adventurous, try spezialitat schinken, smoked spice-cured ham, thinly sliced and served with schnapps. Dover sole and poached salmon are usually accompanied by sauces, but can be served plain. There is always a vegetarian starter and main course but, sadly, no pasta or pulse dishes.

271

ENGLAND

TIDESWELL *Quick Bite* Horsmans Poppies

Bank Square, Near
  Buxton
Tideswell
(0298) 871083

Map 4 D4
Derbyshire

Open 11–2 & 6–11
Closed Mon (except Bank
  Holidays) & Tues

Typical prices: Chilli bean &
  vegetable casserole £3.85
  Houmus £1.55
Credit: Access, Visa

There's something for almost everyone at this unassuming little restaurant on Bank Square. Su Horsman, herself a vegetarian, produces delicious and unusual wholefood dishes like her famous six bean curry with brown rice or green lentil cutlets, while providing equally well for meat eaters with such items as chicken with apricots. Simple grills are only occasionally on offer and most main courses are composite dishes, so customers requiring simple unsauced food should enquire when booking. Soups and salads at lunchtime.

TIMPERLEY *Pub* Hare & Hounds

1 Wood Lane, Near
  Altrincham
061-980 5299

Map 3 C4
Cheshire

Last order 10.30pm
Brewery Marston, Thompson &
  Evershed

Typical prices: Cheese & onion
  flan £1.75
  Poached salmon & salad £4.50
Credit: Access, Amex, Diners, Visa

The cold table at this popular inn would be the envy of many an hotelier. Not only is the choice remarkably varied, but dishes are beautifully set out and attractively presented. Choose from rollmops, smoked herring, trout, a selection of cold meats and several light, savoury flans. Add salads and a slice of wholemeal bread for a simple and nutritious lunch. There are two bars—the second serving hot dishes, including grilled and poached fish. Sandwiches only at night and hot savoury dishes only on Saturdays.

ENGLAND

1 Angel Terrace
Tiverton
(0884) 254778

Map 8 C1
Devon

Open 9–5.30, Thurs 9–2.30
Closed Sun, Bank Holidays &
1 week Christmas–New Year
Vegetarian wholefood cooking

Typical prices: Kidney bean
    salad 70p
    Vegetable crumble pie 70p

Herb teas are a feature of this little restaurant tucked away at the back of a wholefood shop. There are 18 different varieties to sample, along with savouries like cheese and vegetable pasties and several salads, including one based on kidney beans and another where chick peas are the principal ingredient. At lunchtime there's an aroma of steaming hot soup in the air and flans and pizzas are also available with crudités as a healthy alternative. Fresh fruit salads are not available, but yoghurts are.

Changes in data may occur in establishments after the Guide goes to press. Prices should be taken as indications rather than firm quotes.

TIVERTON *Restaurant* Hendersons ★

18 Newport Street
Tiverton
(0884) 254256

Map 8 C1
Devon

Lunch 12.15–2 Dinner 7.15–9.45
Closed Sun, Mon, 4 days
  Christmas & last 3 weeks August

Average price £17.50
Set D £12.50
Credit: Access, Amex, Diners, Visa

It is worth making a detour from the M5 to visit this deservedly popular restaurant. Leave the hurly-burly at Junction 27, and in less than ten minutes you can be relaxing in pleasant surroundings, sipping wine by the glass and making a selection from the à la carte or fixed price menu. Nevill and Elizabeth Ambler meet all our criteria for good healthy food—they use only the freshest ingredients, purchased daily, and cook with care and consideration. The pasta is made in their own kitchen, as is the delectable wholemeal bread, and their soups are simply splendid, thanks to a superior stockpot. Lunches tend to be lighter than dinners and guests are welcome to choose a single dish for a midday meal. When fresh fish of good quality is available locally, it is cooked simply with fish stock, a little low fat spread, white wine and parsley. Vegetarians will find regular dishes like green pasta with fennel or spinach and soft cheese pancakes, and there are always at least five vegetables and salads available. Customers with special dietary needs, such as specific food allergies, will happily be catered for if advance notice is given.

82a High Street
Totnes
(0803) 865522

Map 8 C2
Devon

Open 10.30–2.15 also 6.30–9 in
  high season (Thurs–Sat in early
  & late season)
Closed Sun, Bank Holidays & first
  2 weeks January

Typical prices: Home-made pizza
  £1.25
  Cauliflower au gratin £2.55
Credit: Access, Amex, Diners, Visa

A large terrace makes a peaceful setting for summer meals at this bright and cheerful restaurant. The blackboard menu changes every two days and details some delicious home-cooked items, including hearty vegetable soups and granary bread baked on the premises. Pasta makes regular appearances in simple dishes like macaroni and tuna cheese and tagliatelle with vegetables. Other hot dishes on the menu might include home-made pizza or chicken curry and brown rice. There is always a selection of fresh seasonal salads.

TOTNES   *QuickBite*   Willow

87 High Street
Totnes
(0803) 862605

Map 8 C2
Devon

Open 9–5 (from 10 in winter), also
  Tues–Sat 6.30–10 (Fri & Sat only
  in winter)
Closed Sun, December 25 & 26,
  January 1, Good Friday
Vegetarian cooking

Typical prices: Lentil & walnut
  bake £2
  Coriander tofu dip £1.20

Customers of all ages congregate in this friendly self-service vegetarian restaurant, where high chairs and toys are provided for small children in a special family room. Ingredients are carefully selected (free-range eggs, organic vegetables, natural sweeteners, even filtered water). Pasta and pulses are used with flair and popular lunchtime dishes include courgette and mushroom crumble. In the evening, dishes like stuffed aubergine appear, together with healthy desserts like carob and tofu mousse.

TOWERSEY — *Pub* — Three Horseshoes

Chinnor Road, Near
  Thame
Thame
(084 421) 2322

Map 5 C3
Oxfordshire

Last order 10pm
Brewery Aylesbury

Typical prices: Home-made soup
  £1.50 Fresh salmon £6.95
Credit: Access, Visa

Pitch up at the Three Horseshoes and enjoy a healthy meal and a warm welcome. If there's nothing on the blackboard menu that tickles your fancy, and the fine cold buffet fails to tempt you, you may make a selection from either the regular or the vegetarian restaurant menu. Start, perhaps, with melon-filled juicy fresh fruit, graduate to poached salmon, and enjoy a decaffeinated coffee with your biscuits and cheese. Alternatively, it's back to the blackboard for soup, salad, a simple savoury, or a selection of cold meats or smoked fish.

TREBARWITH STRAND — *Quick Bite* — House on the Strand

Near Tintagel
Camelford
(0840) 770326

Map 8 B2
Cornwall

Open 10.30–9.30
Closed end October–early March

Typical prices: Spicy Greek lamb
  £3.70 Special curries & brown
  rice £5.25
Credit: Access, Visa

One of the most popular features of this family-run restaurant is Wednesday's pauper's supper, a wholesome three-course meal for under £6. It starts with a hearty soup such as parsnip and tomato, continues with a satisfying casserole, perhaps pulse or pasta based, and ends with a simple pud like fruit crumble. In summer salads are offered instead of vegetables. The regular menu is much the same with home-made pasta, vegetable dishes like bean curry, seafood crumble and turkey satay on brown rice.

TUNBRIDGE WELLS *Quick Bite* Pilgrims

37 Mount Ephraim
Tunbridge Wells
(0892) 20341

Map 6 E3
Kent

Open 10.30–8
Closed Sun, Bank Holidays &
3 days Christmas
Vegetarian wholefood cooking

Typical prices: Moussaka £1.95
Courgette casserole £2.05
(Minimum mealtime charge
£1.50)
Luncheon Vouchers accepted

Pilgrims are renowned for their pizzas, crisp wholemeal affairs with delicious toppings, prepared, like everything else at this attractive vegetarian restaurant, with care and consideration. The healthy fare also includes tasty soups, casseroles, paella, risottos and pasta and pulse dishes like lentil lasagne and lentils au gratin. In addition, there is good quality wholemeal bread (with polyunsaturated margarine if preferred) and self-service means you are able to choose from a fine array of crisp salads. For a final fling, choose fresh fruit salad, yoghurt whip or sorbet.

TWICKENHAM *Pub* Prince Albert

30 Hampton Road
01-894 3963

Map 6 D3
Middlesex

No bar food Sun
Closed December 25 eve
Brewery Fullers

Typical prices: Seafood grill £6
Lasagne £1.80

Step inside this Victorian building and you could be in a village pub. The furnishings convey a country feel, and fresh flowers and leafy plants intensify the atmosphere. Elizabeth Lunn puts a lot of thought into her lunch menus (only toasted sandwiches available in the evening). The main course might be grilled plaice or swordfish steak, or pancakes with smoked salmon. Seafood salads are also on offer and there's at least one vegetarian dish every day. Raw materials are of prime quality.

ENGLAND

TWICKENHAM — *Pub* — White Swan

Riverside
01-892 2166

Map 6 D3
Middlesex

Last order 10.30pm
No bar food Sun
Brewery Watney Combe Reid

Typical prices: Lentil & carrot
  soup & granary bread £1.20
  Wholemeal spinach pancakes
  £2.60

Shirley Sutton makes imaginative use of wholesome ingredients at this popular riverside inn. From about 1pm she serves an excellent home-made soup such as lentil and carrot, with granary bread. Light dishes include wholemeal pancakes filled with fresh spinach or brown rice and prawns, bean salads or grilled avocado, together with many more that appear on the regularly changing menu. Customers wanting a big bite should opt for shark steak, simply cooked and served with fresh tomato sauce. In the evening only filled rolls and toasted sandwiches are available.

WALLINGFORD — *Restaurant* — Brown & Boswell

28 High Street
Wallingford
(0491) 34078

Map 5 C3
Oxfordshire

Lunch 12–2.30 Dinner 7–10 (Sun 7–9)
Closed Lunch Tues, all Mon, Bank Holidays, 2 weeks March & 1 week October

Average price £17
Set D £14
Credit: Access, Amex, Diners, Visa

Consideration and a sincere desire to please are apparent as soon as you arrive at this warmly welcoming ground floor restaurant. Some dishes are available in half portions for children or as starters. Guests with special requirements are invited to make their wishes known, as happened recently when customers with food allergies acknowledged their approval in an official newsletter. The menu always includes a vegetarian dish together with an ample choice of dishes served with excellent fresh vegetables.

WARE *Quick Bite* Sunflowers

7 Amwell End
Ware
(0920) 3358

Map 6 D2
Hertfordshire

Open 10–5 (Thurs till 1.30)
Closed Sun & Bank Holidays
Vegetarian wholefood cooking

Typical prices: Pinto bean
   casserole £1.50
Sunflower risotto £1.50

The seeds of the sunflower are much in evidence at this friendly and well-run restaurant above a wholefood shop. Try the sunflower risotto, where they are combined with brown rice, corn and peas. There's always a soup, perhaps lentil or mushroom, and daily dishes such as red pepper and leek croustade, or butter bean ratatouille with green, bean and grain salads (organic vegetables are used where possible). Also filled jacket potatoes, pizzas and vegeburers. The Sunflower Special scones, filled with sugar-free jam and thick-set yoghurt, are delicious.

WAREHAM *Quick Bite* Annies

14a North Street
Wareham
(09295) 6242

Map 5 B4
Dorset

Open 10–5.30 (mid-July-mid-
   September 8 am–10 pm)
Closed Sun, Bank Holiday except
   August & 1 week Christmas
Vegetarian cooking

Typical prices: Vegetable &
   cashew curry £1.40
Mexican bean pot £1.40

Such is the popularity of Annie's vegetarian cooking that her former craft shop has been commandeered to provide extra seating space. In mid-season she serves wholesome breakfasts; otherwise the day begins at 10 with tasty bakes and biscuits. Midday brings hot dishes such as soup, omelettes, and jacket potatoes, plus a special like nut, cheese and millet rissoles. Super salads, too. The evening menu offers main courses such as buckwheat galettes with ratatouille. Fresh fruit salad is available.

WARLEY   *QuickBite*   Wild Thyme

422 Bearwood Road
Birmingham
(021) 420 2528

Map 5 B2
West Midlands

Open 12–2 & 6–10 pm
Closed Sun, Mon, Bank Holidays
   except Good Friday also
   December 25–January 2
Vegetarian cooking

Typical prices: Split pea &
   mushroom casserole £3.20
   Aubergine & cashew nut timbale
   £3.20

Like its sister restaurant, Wild Oats in Birmingham (see page 143), Wild Thyme offers a range of robust and ably cooked dishes. Start, perhaps, with subtly seasoned cashew nut pâté and wholemeal pitta bread. Main courses vary from session to session and include such interesting dishes as aubergine and nut timbale, mushroom wheatbake and beorijh (black-eye bean and mixed nut casserole). Your choice will be served with two salads chosen from over a dozen. Desserts include Middle Eastern fruit salad and fruit crumbles. Teas and tisanes to follow.

WARMINSTER   *QuickBite*   Jenner's

45 Market Place
Warminster
(0985) 213385

Map 5 B3
Wiltshire

Open 9.30–5.30
Closed Sun (October-Easter) &
   December 25-January 2
Vegetarian wholefood cooking

Typical prices: Brown lentil &
   mushroom soup 65p
   Hot spiced apple juice 55p

Cashew nut and pepper pilaff is just one of the popular dishes available at this wholefood store-cum-restaurant in the town centre. In winter visitors wander in for a glass of their special hot spiced apple juice, then stay to sample super snacks like filled wholemeal baps, pizzas or hot savouries such as chilli bean stew or vegetable crumble. Desserts include fruit yoghurts and sorbets and there is an all day selection of bakes to try with decaffeinated coffee, sparkling mineral water or fresh juices.

WARWICK

Quick Bite

Bar Roussel
(Wine Bar)

62a Market Place
Leamington
(0926) 491983

Map 5 B2
Warwickshire

Open 12–2.15 & 7–9.45
Closed Lunch Sun & all December
25 & 26

Typical prices: Tzatziki & pitta
bread £1.10
Chicken in lemon & white wine
£2.95

Lighting is low key at this spacious, modern wine bar. A cold buffet provides plenty of choice for the healthy eater, including cold turkey, beef, ham and smoked trout with a selection of crisp salads. The freshly-made quiches have fine pastry and generous vegetable fillings such as courgette and tomato, or broccoli and cheese. Tzatziki with pitta bread makes a good starter, and a blackboard lists a daily selection of hot dishes, including a vegetarian choice such as vegetable and tarragon pie or lasagne. Wholemeal bread, natural yoghurt, fresh fruit salad.

WARWICK

Restaurant

Randolph's

21 Coten End
Warwick
(0926) 491292

Map 5 B2
Warwickshire

Dinner only 7.45–10
Closed Sun, Bank Holidays except
Good Friday & 1 week Christmas

Average price £20
Credit: Access, Visa

A splendid timbered restaurant where the welcome is genuine, the food and service outstanding. Everything is perfectly cooked and beautifully presented. There is a subtle emphasis on healthy eating, and only top quality raw materials are used. Butter, cream and flour are kept to the minimum and will be omitted altogether on request. A healthy eater might start with pawpaw and mango salad, advance to calf's kidneys with wholemeal tagliatelle and mustard sauce, and conclude with fresh fruit sorbet.

WELLS   *QuickBite*   Cloister Restaurant

Wells Cathedral
Wells
(0749) 76543

Open 10–5 (Sun from 2 &
   November–February 11-4)
Closed 2 weeks Christmas

Map 8 D1
Somerset

Typical prices: Vegetable curry
   £1.75 Apricot wholemeal
   cake 55p

There can few settings as exalted as these enclosed cloisters, with their mullioned windows, marble memorials and soaring ceiling. Earthly pleasures are to be found within its walls in the shape of wholesome home-bakes and warming midday meals. Enjoy a bowl of celery or minted pea soup with wholemeal bread and butter (or polyunsaturated margarine). There are cold meats and salads to follow, or a hot dish such as vegetable curry or spicy bean casserole. Desserts are devilishly rich but there are healthier alternatives like wholemeal scones.

WELLS   *QuickBite*   Good Earth

4 Priory Road
Wells
(0749) 78600

Open 9.30–5.30
Closed Sun & Bank Holidays
Wholefood vegetarian cooking

Map 8 D1
Somerset

Typical prices: Lentil soup 55p
   Red kidney bean casserole £1.30
   Credit: Access, Amex

Healthy eating is at its best at this popular restaurant and wholefood store. Natural unrefined ingredients are imaginatively used in a wide variety of tasty snacks, from simple soups to savouries like mushroom and cashew nut pie. Salads with cunning combinations like apple, pear, celery and cabbage, are served with a variety of dressings including natural yoghurt. Drinks vary from pure unsweetened fruit juices to teas, tisanes, barleycup and decaffeinated coffee. Desserts are based on fresh fruit.

WENTWORTH   *Pub*   George & Dragon

Main Street
Barnsley
(0226) 742440

Map 4 D4
South Yorkshire

Last order 9pm
Limited bar food eves
  No bar food December 25
Free House

Typical prices: Steamed whiting
  £1.95 Pulse surprise £1.95

The 16th-century building that houses this atmospheric inn was formerly a courthouse. Cosy, comfy and very welcoming, it is an ideal place to enjoy Margaret Dickinson's wholesome home cooking. She makes fine use of wholemeal pasta, and there is also a popular brown rice, nut and sultana medley. Fish gets the healthy treatment in dishes like poached fresh salmon stuffed with prawns. Wholemeal bread is served, with polyunsaturated margarine if preferred. Salads, sandwiches and vegetarian dishes. Less hot choice evenings.

WHITBY   *Quick Bite*   Magpie Café

14 Pier Road
Whitby
(0947) 602058

Map 4 E2
North Yorkshire

Open 11.30–6.30
Closed Friday before Spring Bank
  Holiday & mid October–1 week
  before Easter

Typical prices: Magpie salad
  lunch £7 (3 courses)
  Crab salad £2.90

What else would you have in Whitby but fish? In a café overlooking the quayside it's the obvious choice, and the Mackenzie family cook it extremely well. Fried fish is their speciality but they will gladly grill sole or halibut and accommodate customers with special dietary requests. Starters include fresh grapefruit and melon and there's a wide selection of salads, with steak and grilled ham for those who don't fancy fish. Several sweets are gluten-free and there are also fat-free and dairy-free desserts.

ENGLAND

WILMSLOW *Restaurant* Stanneylands Hotel Restaurant

Stanleylands Road
Wilmslow
(0625) 525225

Map 3 C4
Cheshire

Lunch 12.30–2 Dinner 7–10
Closed Dinner Sun to non-residents, January 1 and Good Friday

Average price £18
Set L £7
Set D £17
Credit: Access, Amex, Diners, Visa

To say that a chef is inventive is not always a compliment—but in Iain Donald's case the adjective is an apt accolade. His menus are full of the most satisfactory surprises, like noisettes of lamb with basil mousse and aubergine and courgette compote, or breast of chicken with mango and avocado slices. Pulses shine in such dishes as mangetout and lentil strudel on tomato and tarragon coulis. There are some spectacular salads and both yoghurt and skimmed milk are used where appropriate. Wholemeal bread and polyunsaturated margarine are always available.

WINCHESTER *Pub* Wykeham Arms

75 Kingsgate Street
Winchester
(0962) 53834

Map 5 C3
Hampshire

Last order 8.45pm
No bar food Mon eve & all Sun
Brewery Eldridge Pope

Typical prices: Tuna & bean antipasto £2.50
Grilled River Test trout £4.35

Sandwiched between the college and the cathedral, this Georgian inn is a delightful spot. Graeme and Anne Jameson produce a variety of imaginative and tasty dishes. Healthy eaters can select sandwiches, salads, omelettes or hot dishes from the blackboard menu. For the starters try the feta cheese salad, followed by grilled fresh river trout with crisp vegetables and new potatoes. Vegetarian dishes are always available and meat-lovers should not miss the exceptionally good rump and venison steaks.

284

49 Peach Street
Wokingham
(0734) 788893

Map 5 C3
Berkshire

Open 12–2.30 & 7–10.30
Closed Sun & Bank Holidays

Typical prices: Lasagne & side
  salad £3.95
  Marrow stuffed with lentils £5.75
Credit: Access, Diners, Visa

Old advertising posters adorn the walls of this smart town-centre restaurant. Lunch might be home-made chicken and leek soup with wholemeal bread (polyunsaturated margarine on request), or a filled jacket potato and side salad. Oriental pancakes are popular, too, and there is always a vegetarian dish such as aubergine and nut bake or Italian bean casserole. Hot specials, chalked on the blackboard, include rabbit casserole and lamb curry, while seekers after simplicity can settle for a grilled steak or Dover sole.

17 The Thoroughfare
Woodbridge
(039 43) 2557

Map 6 F2
Suffolk

Open 12–2 & 7–10
Closed Sun, Mon & Bank Holidays

Typical prices: Brochette of
  monkfish £4.65
  Vegetable terrine £3.75

Sally O'Gorman cooks with flair and imagination at this informal wine bar. The menu changes every week but always includes one or two vegetarian specialities and a simple fish dish such as grilled brochette of monkfish, and king prawns with vegetables and rice and mushroom sauce if liked. Imaginative starters range from aubergine pâté to feta and courgette roulade, and a popular meat dish consists of slivers of spicy pork with cardamom and coriander, served with rice and salad.

ENGLAND

WOODSTOCK

Quick Bite

Brothertons Brasserie

1 High Street
Woodstock
(0993) 811114

Map 5 C2
Oxfordshire

Open 10.30–10.30
Closed January 1 & December 25
& 26

Typical prices: Vegetarian plat du
jour £4.50 Greek salad £4.75
Credit: Access, Amex, Diners, Visa

Fresh ingredients lead to rewarding results at this bustling brasserie on the site of a former hardware store. Kick off with crudités or soup of the day with wholemeal bread and low fat spread. Eggs florentine or smoked salmon are equally suitable for healthy eaters, who can then select a vegetarian dish, be tempted by a grilled steak or smoked chicken and avocado salad. Desserts are wonderful but rich but you can call for Greek yoghurt with honey or simply choose cheeses. Slake your thirst with citron pressé, freshly squeezed orange juice or sparkling mineral water.

WOOLHOPE

Pub

Butchers Arms

Near Hereford
Fownhope
(043 277) 281

Map 5 A2
Hereford & Worcester

Last order 10pm
No bar food December 25
Free House

Typical prices: Vegetarian lasagne
£2.75 Home-made soup 95p

This picturesque country inn is ideally situated for holidaymakers exploring the Wye valley. A small restaurant serves dinners from Wednesday to Saturday, while well-cooked bar meals are always available. The menu is simple, with salads and sandwiches sharing the bill with ploughman's platters. Home-made specials range from Moroccan spiced bean soup to chillis and curry. Vegetarians are well catered for with dishes like mushroom biryani and dhal and a very good vegetarian lasagne.

Near Bath
Frome
(0373) 830350

Map 5 B3
Somerset

Last Order 10pm
Closed 2 days Christmas

Typical prices: Salad Italienne
£2.50 Spring chicken & orange
salad £4.60

Salads and baked potatoes—that's the simple but highly successful formula at this well run pub beside the A36. Bumper bowls of dressed salad—up to 15 of them—are temptingly displayed. Combinations include egg, ham, walnuts and tomato; tomato, egg, olives, peppers and onion; and peeled prawns with oranges. A blackboard lists the daily choice of jacket potato toppings, and in addition there are filled rolls and variations on the ever-popular ploughman's. Try the fisherman's lunch, with Cornish smoked mackerel and a salad garnish. Wholemeal bread is not served but crusty french bread is always available.

We welcome complaints and bona fide recommendations on the tear-out pages for readers' comments. They are followed up by our professional team. Please also complain to the management instantly.

ENGLAND

4, The Hopmarket
Worcester
(0905) 26654

Hopmarket open 10–4 (summer
  till 4.30), Sat 10–5
Closed Sun & Bank Holidays
  (except Good Friday)

17 Mealcheapen St
Worcester
(0905) 26417

Mealcheapen Street open 10–4,
  Sat 9.30–5
Closed Sun & Bank Holidays
  (except Good Friday)

Kidderminster
6/7 Blackwell Street
Kidderminster
(0562) 743275

Kidderminster open 9.30–4.30
  (Sat till 5)
Closed Sun & Bank Holidays
  (except Good Friday)

Map 5 B2
Hereford and
  Worcester

Wholefood cooking

Typical prices: Savoury flan 95p
  Almond Slice 40p
  (Minimum lunchtime charge
  95p)
Luncheon Vouchers accepted

A central kitchen supplies all the above restaurants, but the food tastes so fresh and wholesome that it is difficult to believe it has not been prepared on site. The simple and highly successful formula is to serve wholemeal flans, salads, savouries and sweets, all made from pure natural ingredients. The range is remarkable—15 flans and the same number of top quality salads including beans and chick-peas in pineapple dressing, and sweetcorn, butter bean and broccoli. Among the savouries, stuffed eggs and sandwiches on wholemeal bread are available. The newest branch recently opened in Kidderminster.

Our inspectors never book in the name of
Egon Ronay's Guides; they disclose their
identity only after paying their bills.

WORTHING *QuickBite* Hannah

165 Montague Street
Worthing
(0903) 31132

Map 6 D4
West Sussex

Open 9.30–7 (Sat till 5)
Closed Sun

Typical prices: Lentil burgers 80p
 Fish pie £1.25

Carefully chosen raw materials make meals memorable at this well-kept restaurant. On a largely vegetarian menu, the salads are outstanding, particularly one made from a mixture of beans tossed with shredded carrot and lettuce in a light lemon flavoured dressing. Stir-fried vegetables accompany filled jacket potatoes, lentil burgers and flans, including a splendid light wholemeal shell filled with fresh flaked salmon. Wholemeal bread is served, with polyunsaturated margarine, and both skimmed milk and natural yoghurt are used. Desserts include fresh fruit salad.

WORTHING *QuickBite* Nature's Way Coffee Shop

130 Montague Street
Worthing
(0903) 209931

Map 6 D4
West Sussex

Open 9.15–5
Closed Sun & Bank Holidays
Vegetarian wholefood cooking

Typical prices: Mushroom &
 butter bean Stroganoff £1.20
 Wholemeal lasagne £1.50
 Luncheon Vouchers accepted

The salads get a special mention at this self-service wholefood restaurant. An unusually extensive selection includes the delicious combination of pear and date, together with chick pea and garlic or more substantial mixtures based on pasta and pulses. Daily savoury specials include leekaroni cheese—a pleasant variation on a familiar theme with chopped leeks tucked into a light cheese sauce. Soups, flans and filled potatoes. The drinks list includes fruit juices, decaffeinated coffee.

ENGLAND

YATTENDON *Pub* Royal Oak

The Square, Near
  Newbury
Hermitage
(0635) 201325

Map 5 C3
Berkshire

Last order 10pm
Free House

Typical prices: Lentil soup £1.95
  Plaice with herb butter £4.85
Credit: Access, Amex, Visa

Richard and Kate Smith set high standards at this award-winning village inn (it was Pub of the Year in 1985). Bar snacks are imaginative and varied and there is plenty to please the healthy eater. Starters include terrine of chicken with salad, or simple baked herrings. Several plain fish dishes are always on offer, such as fillet of brill with mussels and dill. A vegetarian dish might be home-made noodles with wood mushrooms. Natural yoghurt, crème fraîche and fromage blanc are all used in cooking and desserts include fresh pineapple with mango ice-cream.

YEOVIL *Restaurant* Little Barwick House

Barwick Village, Near
  Yeovil
Yeovil
(0935) 23902

Map 8 D1
Somerset

Dinner only 7–9
Closed Dinner Sun (to non-
  residents) & 1 week Christmas

Average price £15
Set D £13.50
Credit: Access, Amex, Diners, Visa

This comfortable Georgian dower house is popular with both residents and dinner guests. Veronica Colley is a talented cook, whose strength is simplicity. Set menus always offer a good choice and include vegetarian dishes. Healthy eaters may begin with chilled melon or fresh grilled herring with cucumber and yoghurt sauce, and choose poached brill or roast pheasant to follow. Everything is cooked to order, and fresh vegetables will be served without butter or sauce on request.

YEOVIL
Quick Bite
Trugs

5 Union Street
Yeovil
(0935) 73722

Map 8 D1
Somerset

Open 8.30–5.30
Closed Sun & Bank Holidays
Wholefood cooking

Typical prices: Mushroom &
   watercress pancakes £1.85
      Filled jacket potatoes from £1.05
(Minimum lunchtime charge £1)
Luncheon Vouchers accepted

Hooray for a children's menu that combines good nutrition with real appeal. Choices include a half jacket potato with baked beans, and melted cheese on a warm wholemeal bap. Half portions of main menu dishes are also available for young customers. Parents and other patrons are equally well catered for. There is always home-made soup, with a wholemeal roll or warm cornmeal muffins and butter or polyunsaturated margarine. Pizzas, salads and jacket potatoes vie with pitta pockets packed with good things. Fresh fruit salad or yoghurt for pud.

YORK
Quick Bite
Gillygate Wholefood Café

Millers Yard, Gillygate
York
(0904) 24045

Map 4 E3
North Yorkshire

Open 10–5 (Oct–Feb till 4)
Closed Sun, January 1 &
   December 25 & 26
Vegetarian wholefood cooking

Typical prices: Filled wholewheat
   rolls 60p
      Stir-fry vegetables & rice £2.15

This courtyard restaurant draws people by the tempting aroma of its own bakery. The breads, cakes and bakes are nutritious, thanks to wholemeal flour and fillings like tofu, not cream, for the cheesecake. At noon hot savouries like spinach lasagne are served. Quiches with fillings like carrot and onion or mushroom and pepper, and tofu burgers and baked potatoes are popular. Salads and filled wholemeal rolls. Beverages include herb teas, barleycup, decaffeinated coffee, fruit juices and sparkling natural mineral water.

HEALTHY EATING OUT
—IN—
SCOTLAND

SCOTLAND

SCOTLAND

SCOTLAND

SCOTLAND

SCOTLAND

SCOTLAND

SCOTLAND

SCOTLAND

GUIDE TO ESTABLISHMENTS

ABERFELDY — *Quick Bite* — Country Fare Coffee House

7 Bridgend
Aberfeldy
(0887) 20729

Map 2 C4
Tayside

Open 10–4.45
Closed Sun, Wed afternoon in
winter, January 1 & 2 &
December 25 & 26

Typical prices: Smoked trout &
salad £3.50
Home-made quiche £1.50

Eileen Morgan gets up early to begin the day's baking at this delightful little coffee shop in the centre of Aberfeldy. Her wholemeal bread is delicious. Try a slice with a bowl of home-made soup, or one of the four salads on offer every day. The blackboard menu carries daily specials like vegetable quiche with light wholemeal pastry, smoked trout or nut cutlets and you'll also encounter ploughman's platters. Gâteaux and cakes are a speciality 'to give the visitors a treat'. All breads, cakes and scones can be served with polyunsaturated margarine.

ACHILTIBUIE — *Restaurant* — Summer Isles Hotel Restaurant

By Ullapool
Achiltibuie
(085 482) 282

Map 1 B1
Highland

Dinner only at 7.30
Closed mid October–Easter

Average price £20
Set D £18

Nearly everything you eat is either home produced or locally caught at this fairly remote and very relaxing hotel. Set menus make the best use of such bounty. A typical four-course dinner might begin with courgette and cucumber soup followed by mushroom soufflé and salad and have as its highlight fresh turbot with prawns. Vegetables are organically grown in the hotel garden or hydroponicum, and a variety of berry fruits make summer sweets a delight. Vegetarian dishes on request. Booking is advised.

ARISAIG

Quick Bite

Old Library Lodge & Restaurant

Arisaig
(068 75) 651

Map 1 B3
Highland

Open 8.30–10, 12–2 & 6.30–9
Closed October–Easter

Typical prices: Home-made soup
& bread £1
Lentil & mushroom burger £4.75

It's worth a detour from Fort William to visit this delightful restaurant on the Argyll coast. On fine days, sit on the terrace and look over the sea to the Isles of Rhum and Eigg. The food is thoughtfully prepared, with an unstated emphasis on healthy cooking. Both natural yoghurt and skimmed milk are used and there are plenty of low-fat dishes like poached trout and chicken casserole with vegetables. Simple soups and stews are midday fare with more elaborate food including some vegetarian dishes at night.

COLBOST

Quick Bite

Three Chimneys

Near Dunvegan,
Isle of Skye
Glendale
(047 081) 258

Map 1 A2
Highland

Open 12–2 & 7–9
Closed Lunch Sun & November–
March

Typical prices: Home-made soup
& wholemeal bread £1.50
Vegetarian pancakes £4.50
Credit: Access, Visa

Holidaymakers to Skye should certainly schedule a stop at this cosy crofter's cottage restaurant. The beautiful location is rather remote, so do telephone for directions before you set out. Eddie and Shirley Spear excel in cooking food with an authentic Scottish flavour. Lunch might be a bowl of soup with freshly baked wholemeal (stoneground) bread and salad platter, with Skye prawns or smoked trout. There are also wholemeal pizzas and tarts. Evening menus are more elaborate and make marvellous use of local produce.

CULLIPOOL *Quick Bite* Longhouse Buttery ★

Isle of Luing, By Oban
Luing
(085 24) 209

Map 2 B4
Strathclyde

Open 11–5
Closed Sun & early October–mid
 May

Typical prices: Lentil soup 95p
 Wild salmon salad £4.95

The wonderful setting and incredibly beautiful views
(especially at sunset) make this superb little buttery
unforgettable. Find Longhouse by taking the ferry to the
enchanting Isle of Luing and sample the range of simple
snacks which are available all day. The subtle and sensi-
tively seasoned artichoke soup is a must, and both the wild
salmon salad and Cullipool platter (lobster, prawns, fresh
and pickled salmon and squat lobster tails) are magnificent, but even the simple open sandwiches are highly
praised. Round off the meal with fresh fruit salad.

DIRLETON *Quick Bite* Open Arms Hotel Lounge

Dirleton
(0620 85) 241

Map 2 C4
Lothian

Open 12.30–2
Closed Sun, January 1, December
 25 & 4 days second week January

Typical prices: Chicken, apricot &
 spinach terrine £1.85
 Poached haddock £3.25

The warm welcome is well known in this Scottish hotel,
and staff are eager to please. Customers who would like a
light lunch of grilled fish or meat have only to make their
wishes known, and vegan guests will be accorded the same
courtesy. There are several vegetarian specialities, plus
starters like melon, tomato and cucumber cocktail and
snacks like hot courgette and apple quiche, or smoked
salmon with prawns on brown bread. Hot dish of the day
could be poached haddock. Home-made sorbets.

DUMFRIES — *Quick Bite* — Opus Salad Bar

95 Queensberry Street
Dumfries
(0387) 55752

Map 2 C6
Dumfries & Galloway

Open 9–5 (Thurs till 2.30)
Closed Sun & Bank Holidays

Typical prices: Bean salad 35p
Orange & yoghurt cake 60p
Credit: Access

Climb the stairs to this contemporary café where the Halliday family cater for healthy appetites with a selection of snacks and light meals. Wholemeal rolls, scones and shortbread give way at lunchtime to soups, mushroom pie, cauliflower cheese and an attractive selection of salads, some simple, others, like the bean medley or pasta salad, more substantial. Brown rice and wholemeal pasta are freely used and there's a place for both natural yoghurt and polyunsaturated margarine. Vegetarians are catered for and there's an impressive range of good quality teas.

EDDLESTON — *Pub* — Horse Shoe Inn

Near Peebles
Eddleston
(072 13) 225

Map 2 C5
Borders

Last order 10pm
Closed January 1 & December 25
Free House

Typical prices: Vegetarian pâté
£1.50 Lemon sole £3.25
Credit: Access, Amex, Diners, Visa

This white-painted inn was once the village smithy. Today the only things forged on the premises are friendships, fuelled by good company and fine food. Bar snacks include fattening old favourites but you will also find plenty of healthy alternatives from salads and wholemeal sandwiches to vegetarian pâté, grilled lemon sole and walnut and aubergine lasagne. The à la carte menu offers choices like chargrilled halibut with mangetout or vegetable Stroganoff. Fresh fruit salad, sorbets, cheese platter.

EDINBURGH   *Quick Bite*   Brasserie Saint Jacques

King James Thistle
 Hotel, Leith Street
031-556 0111

Town plan Edinburgh
 Lothian

Open 12.30–2
Closed December 25 & 26

Typical prices: Danish-style open
 sandwich £2.50
 Fresh mussels £2.45
Credit: Access, Amex, Diners, Visa

Whether you choose a single starter or a three-course meal at this stylish hotel at the eastern end of Princes Street, you will be equally welcome. Danish-style open sandwiches on wholemeal bread are always popular —the rare roast beef and dill pickle topping is delicious. Other quick bites are avocado and pink grapefruit with yoghurt, fresh mussels with white wine and shallot sauce, omelettes, and pasta with pepper sauce, or you could make a meal of it with oysters followed by stuffed green peppers with chilli sauce. French or Scottish cheese to finish, or sliced fresh fruit.

EDINBURGH   *Quick Bite*   Country Kitchen

4 South Charlotte
 Street
031-226 6150

Town plan Edinburgh
 Lothian

Open 8 am–7 pm
Closed Sun & Bank Holidays
Wholefood cooking

Typical prices: Fresh chicken
 risotto £2.50
 Bean stew £1.95

An immensely popular self-service restaurant where the raw materials are carefully selected and organic produce is used wherever possible. Slimmers will find the calorie counts alongside each dish most useful and will be delighted to find delicious desserts with a very low sugar content. The menu includes many vegetable dishes, fresh fish, lean meat, home-baked wholemeal bread and very good vegetables. Salads like yoghurt with walnuts, apples, raisins and cauliflower are highly recommended.

EDINBURGH *Quick Bite* **Helios Fountain**

7 Grassmarket
031-229 7884

Town plan Edinburgh
Lothian

Open 10–6 (summer till 8)
Closed Sun & Bank Holidays
Vegetarian wholefood cooking

Typical prices: Tofu pie £2.25
 Butter beans & vegetables citron
 £1.95
Credit: Access, Visa

May the sun never set upon Helios, where the food is absolutely delicious. Whether you are swayed by the fact that this coffee house is run by anthroposophists who use only organically or biodynamically grown produce, or whether you are merely an intrigued outsider, you cannot help but be impressed. Start with a delicious and delicately flavoured soup such as pea and spinach, and graduate to a broccoli and pepper quiche or the extremely popular chestnut and pimiento casserole. Splendid desserts include carrot and cardamom cake and fresh fruit salad.

EDINBURGH *Quick Bite* **Henderson's
Salad Table**

94 Hanover Street
031-225 2131

Town plan Edinburgh
Lothian

Open 8 am–11pm (Sun 9–9 during
 Festival)
Closed Sun (except during
 Festival) & Bank Holidays
Vegetarian cooking

Typical prices: Bean hot pot £2
 Lentil stew £2
Credit: Visa

You don't have to look far to find the source of the Henderson family's supply of first-class vegetables and fruit for their basement restaurant and wine bar—it all comes from their wholefood shop upstairs. Breakfast starts at 8 am with home-made muesli, yoghurt, fresh and dried fruit together with simple cakes and bakes. Just before noon the choice widens to include soup, hot dishes like mushroom savoury and a wide selection of super salads. Hot items also in the evening. The sweets can be a bit indulgent.

SCOTLAND

299

EDINBURGH

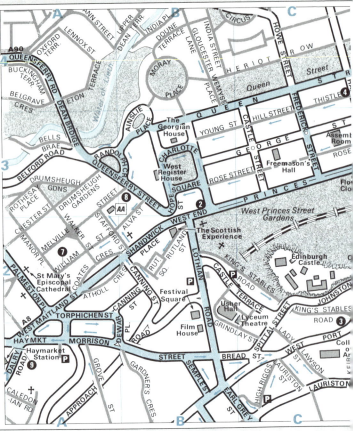

TOWN PLAN

ENQUIRIES

(tel code: 031)

Tourist Information	332 2433
Railway	556 2451
Bus	556 8464
Coach	556 8464
Airport	333 1000

EDINBURGH

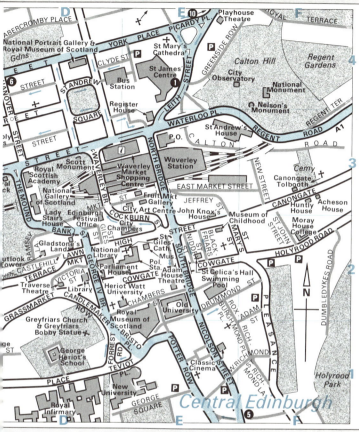

TOWN PLAN

ESTABLISHMENTS LISTED

1. **Brasserie Saint Jacques**
   King James Thistle Hotel,
   Leith Street

2. **Country Kitchen**
   4 South Charlotte Street

3. **Helios Fountain**
   7 Grassmarket

4. **Henderson's Salad Table**
   94 Hanover Street

5. **Kalpna**
   2 St Patrick Square

6. **Laigh Kitchen**
   117a Hanover Street

7. **Lune Town**
   38 William Street

8. **No 10**
   10 Melville Place

9. **Verandah Tandoori**
   17 Dalry Road

10. **Waterfront Wine Bar**
    1c Dock Place, Leith

EDINBURGH *Quick Bite* Kalpna ★

2 St Patrick Square
031-667 9890

Town plan Edinburgh
Lothian

Open 12–2 & 5.30–11
Closed Sun, January 1 &
December 25 & 26
Indian vegetarian cooking

Typical prices: Dosa masala £2.50
Kalpna thali £5
Credit: Access, Visa

Kalpna means imagination, an ingredient present in every dish served at this wonderful vegetarian restaurant, where flavours are blended with rare subtlety and style. It offers exceptional value for money, a fact which has not escaped students from the nearby University. Hard to highlight specific dishes among the many healthy choices, but the dosa masala, a rice pancake with spiced vegetable filling, is excellent. Main courses might be a light vegetable and nut curry or spinach and curd cheese in a spicy sauce. Super sorbets and unusual Indian sweets.

EDINBURGH *Quick Bite* Laigh Kitchen ★

117a Hanover Street
031-225 1552

Town plan Edinburgh
Lothian

Open 8.30–4 (till 7.30 during
Festival)
Closed Sun & Bank Holidays

Typical prices: Tuna fish pâté 65p
Stovies £1.60

The Laigh Kitchen is a basement restaurant along the lines of a traditional eighteenth century coffee house and Joan Spicer has lots to offer. Though quite rightly famous for its baked goods, wholemeal scones and oatcakes are not the only attraction for the healthy eater. There is a fine range of salads, including citrus with onion and cheese, which may be teamed with jacket potatoes or slim slices of quiche. Hearty broths take the chill off wintry days, and there's a regular hot special such as chicken risotto or kedgeree.

EDINBURGH *Restaurant* Lune Town

38 William Street
031-225 9388

Town plan Edinburgh
  Lothian

Meals 12–2.30 & 6–12, Sat
  2pm–1am, Sun 4–11.30
Closed January 1
Chinese cooking

Average price £12
Set L & Set D from £7
(Minimum charge £5.50)
Credit: Access, Amex, Diners, Visa

Smiling service and carefully cooked Cantonese food make this restaurant a popular meeting place. Fresh raw materials, cooked carefully so that the flavours complement each other, make for memorable meals. The dim sum are excellent and the siu-mai, steamed prawn and pork balls, highly recommended. Soups are subtle and main courses for healthy eaters include steamed prawns, abalone with vegetables and lemon chicken. Vegetables are fresh and crisp, noodles cooked to perfection and sweets like lychees or fresh fruit salad make fine endings.

EDINBURGH *Restaurant* No. 10

10 Melville Place
031-226 3579

Town plan Edinburgh
  Lothian

Lunch 12–2 Dinner 6–11
Closed Lunch Sat & Sun, Dinner
  Sun in winter, all December 26
  and January 1–3

Average price £15
Credit: Access, Amex, Diners, Visa

This simple yet well-presented restaurant serves mainly French-style dishes. Many are named after politicians and it is interesting to speculate on whether the names appearing under 'Cabinet cuts' represent wishful thinking! The health conscious can opt for such specialities as raw French beans with mushroom, anchovy and herb dressing, moules marinière or steak tartare. Vegetarian dishes on request. Puddings, aptly called 'capital gains', are generally rich and creamy, but there is a good fruit salad.

EDINBURGH

Restaurant

Verandah Tandoori

17 Dalry Road
031-337 5828

Town plan Edinburgh
 Lothian

Lunch 12–2.30 Dinner 5–11.45
Bangladeshi cooking

Average price £12
Set L & Set D £10
Credit: Access, Amex, Diners, Visa

Care is the cornerstone of this popular tandoori restaurant at the Haymarket end of Dalry road. Only the freshest raw materials and spices are used and chef and partner Kaisar Miah is at pains to please his many customers. He is always willing to meet a request for a dish cooked simply, or with specific ingredients. Particular attention is paid to vegetarian dishes such as the fairly fiery Madras sambar or the medium-hot vegetable karai. There is also a vegetarian thali. Meat eaters will find numerous healthy dishes among the Bangladeshi specialities.

EDINBURGH

Quick Bite

Waterfront Wine Bar

1c Dock Place, Leith
031-554 7427

Town plan Edinburgh
 Lothian

Open 11 am–midnight (Thurs–Sat till 1 am)

Closed Sun, January 1 & 2, & December 25 & 26

Typical prices: Courgette & coriander soup 70p
Barbecued salmon steak £5.20

A dockside haunt immensely popular with visitors and locals alike, the Waterfront consists of a cheerfully cluttered main bar, several small rooms with a nautical flavour and a conservatory overlooking dockland. There's also a terrace for al fresco meals. From noon–9 pm, six days a week, light meals like squid salad, Dunbar crab and bouillabaisse are served with wholemeal bread. The barbecue grill operates between 6 and 9.30 pm and delivers more delectable seafood such as sole with lemon and coriander.

ERISKA

Restaurant

Isle of Eriska
Restaurant

Ledaig, By Oban
Ledaig
(063 172) 371

Map 2 B4
Strathclyde

Lunch 12.45–1.45 (Sun 1–1.45)
　　Dinner 7.30–8.30
Closed December-mid February

Average price £23
Set L from £4 (Sun £16.50)
Set D £21
Credit: Access

Locally-grown vegetables and home-produced eggs all help to make this a traditional Scottish restaurant where healthy eating is an integral part of every day. Lunch and dinner are set menus. Wholemeal bread is baked on the premises as are wholemeal scones for tea, and Sheena Buchanan-Smith makes her own yoghurt and uses it with flair to lighten some of her special sauces and sweets. All sauces are served separately and the vegetables are crisp and full of flavour. There are no vegetarian dishes on the set menu, but these are available on request.

FALKIRK

Quick Bite

Healthy Life

2a Park Street
Falkirk
(0324) 37186

Map 2 C4
Central

Open 9–3.30 (Sat till 4.30)
Closed Sun & Bank Holidays
Vegetarian cooking

Typical prices: Lentil & pasta bake
　　£1.25
　　Lentil dahl £1.25

Much to the delight of regular customers, Eileen Clason has returned to this simple counter-service restaurant after an absence of some years. Her imaginative approach to healthy eating is immediately apparent in the excellent range of salads, including celery, date and apple, and coconut and fruit. Jacket potatoes have interesting fillings like mashed turnip and hot dishes include a tasty cashew nut risotto. There's also a selection of filled wholemeal rolls and nutritious fruit breads.

GLAMIS

Strathmore Arms Restaurant

Main Street, By Forfar
Glamis
(030 784) 248

Map 2 C4
Tayside

Open 12.15–2, also Easter–
October 2.30–6
Closed Mon (January–Easter) &
1 week January &4 days after
Christmas

Typical prices: Kedgeree £2.95
Fruit crumble 75p
Credit: Access, Amex, Diners, Visa

Proximity to Glamis Castle guarantees this well-run pub some trade, but were it to be transferred to a location devoid of any other attraction, it would doubtless remain popular, thanks to good quality Scottish fare at reasonable prices. The popular summer buffet has plenty of healthy dishes, including a wide selection of cold meats and immaculately presented salads. Winter warmers include herrings in oatmeal, country chicken casseroles and vegetarian dishes such as brown rice pilaff. Grilled haddock is a simple alternative. Finish with fresh fruit salad or crumble.

GLASGOW

Pub

Babbity Bowster

16 Blackfriars Street
041-552 5055

Map 2 C5
Strathclyde

Last order 10pm
Free House

Typical prices: Poached Tay
Salmon £5.80 Vegetarian
Stroganoff & salad £3.15
Credit: Access, Amex, Visa

The old Merchant District of Glasgow is enjoying a renaissance, with many once derelict buildings being lovingly restored. One such is this splendid 18th-century town house designed by Adam, and today a vibrant centre for the arts, both visual and culinary. A café-bar serves breakfasts and early morning snacks and from noon the restaurant takes over. A healthy meal might begin with a salad, continue with Poached Tay salmon and conclude with Orkney oatcakes and a low-fat Brie. Vegetarian dishes, too.

GLASGOW *Quick Bite* Café Gondolfi

64 Albion Street
041-552 6813

Map 2 C5
Strathclyde

Open 9.30 am–11.30 pm
Closed Sun & Bank Holidays

Typical prices: Lentil soup 90p
Spicy marinated herring £3.25

There's something for everyone at this extremely popular café-restaurant. Quick bites include really tasty home-made soups served with first-rate wholemeal bread. A not-to-be-missed speciality is the gravadlax, salmon marinated in dill and mustard and served on an open sandwich. Pasta dishes include a vegetable lasagne and wholemeal tagliatelle, and healthy eaters might enjoy spicy marinated herring or chicken and smoked salmon parcels. Natural yoghurt and skimmed milk are used in sauces and dressings and desserts include fresh fruit salad.

GLASGOW *Quick Bite* Ubiquitous Chip

12 Ashton Lane, off
  Byres Road
041-334-5007

Map 2 C5
Strathclyde

Open 12–2.30 & 5.30–11
Closed Sun, January 1, December
  25 (& December 31 after 9 pm)

Typical prices: Vegan bean soup
  50p Chicken casserole & brown
  rice £2.95
Credit: Access, Amex, Diners, Visa

Don't let the name mislead you — the ubiquitous chip was given the chop a long time ago at this delightful restaurant with its charming covered courtyard. There is a main, ground floor restaurant where a healthy choice might be leek and lemon soup, salmon with cucumber sauce and a choice of salads including celery and apple in yoghurt, followed by fresh fruit salad or dried fruit compote. Upstairs in the lunch bar, there are excellent wholewheat flans, grilled squid or langoustines, and a variety of salads.

GULLANE *Restaurant* Greywalls Restaurant

Muirfield
Gullane
(0620) 842144

Map 2 C4
Lothian

Lunch 12.30–2 Dinner 7.30–9.30
Closed November–mid April

Average price £25
Set D £19.50
Credit: Access, Amex, Diners, Visa

The great Edwardian architect, Sir Edwin Lutyens, designed Greywalls with the front entrance as the focal point, drawing guests irresistibly from the gate towards a splendid front door. Inside there's a fine rather gracious restaurant, where chef Andrew Mitchell caters to healthy appetites with starters like chilled trout terrine with oatcakes or beef consommé with garden vegetables. Your main course might be breast of chicken filled with wild salmon, poached in its own juices, or a simple grilled fillet steak. Elaborate desserts include a lime and ginger granita.

INVERGARRY *Restaurant* Inn on the Garry Restaurant

Invergarry
(080 93) 206

Map 1 B3
Highlands

Lunch by arrangement only Dinner
7–8 (7–9 in summer)
Closed November–March

Average price £15
Set D £10

At this hotel restaurant on the road to Skye fish is a clear favourite. Guests will appreciate simple dishes such as baked cod with lemon and rosemary or poached salmon. For starters, a traditional Scottish soup, perhaps, or lightly scrambled egg with smoked salmon. Generous portions of perfectly cooked vegetables are another plus, but unfortunately vegetarians are not well catered for on the restaurant menu. There is, however, a salad bar, and wholemeal bread with polyunsaturated margarine is always available.

INVERSION *Quick Bite* Brookes Wine Bar ★

75 Castle Street
Inverness
(0463) 225662

Map 1 C2
Highland

Open 12–10 pm, Sun 12.30–2.30
& 6.30–10.30
Closed Sun in winter (October 1–
April 30)

Typical prices: Poached trout £3
Dried fruit salad £1.50

The food, service and ambience are exemplary at this chic wine bar opposite Inverness Castle. Start with a subtly flavoured soup such as courgette and fennel, then pick one of the hot dishes like salmon tagliatelle in dill sauce, or, if you prefer, something like cold poached wild salmon, thinly coated in aspic from the inviting selection at the cold table. Superb salads include very good ratatouille and home-made coleslaw. Both pasta and pulses have a place in the chef's repertoire and the wholemeal bread is delicious. Desserts include a wholesome dried fruit salad.

INVERSION  Dunain Park Hotel Restaurant

Inverness
(0463) 230512

Map 1 C2
Highland

Lunch 12–2 Dinner 7–9
Closed Lunch Sat & 1 week
Christmas

Average price £17
Set L £7
Set D £15
Credit: Access, Amex, Diners, Visa

Ann Nicoll cooks with competence and care in this attractive Georgian house. The five-course dinner menus are vehicles for a variety of well-chosen local ingredients. Herbs from the restaurant's own garden add interest to healthy dishes such as pasta with cucumber, peppers and mushrooms in yoghurt sauce. There are plenty of simple chicken and fish dishes such as breast of chicken, steam-baked in stock, or salmon marinated in lime and baked in home-made breadcrumbs. Desserts include fresh fruit.

SCOTLAND

KILDONAN Three Rowans Tea Shop & Restaurant

Near Edinbane,
Isle of Skye
Edinbane
(047 082) 286

Map 1 A2
Highland

Open 10–5.30 (Sun 12–5.30) &
  from 7
Closed Sat & end Oct–week
  before Easter, except weekend
  dinners by arrangement

Typical prices: Hazelnut roast
  £4.75
  Winkles & kailkenny £2.75

Wednesday night is folk night at this friendly spot by Loch Snizort. Lunch is a simple meal of stuffed pancakes or perhaps curried rice, served somewhat surprisingly with a jacket potato. Some Scottish specialities are available, too, including freshly gathered winkles with a local potato, cabbage and herb dish called kailkenny. In the evenings choose soup or Skye scallops, followed by poached rainbow trout, or a vegetarian dish such as hazelnut roast or Edam cheese fondue. Salads are not usually served, but local vegetables are used as far as possible.

KINGUSSIE *Quick Bite* Wood 'n' Spoon

3 High Street
Kingussie
(054 02) 251

Map 1 C3
Highland

Open 10–9.30 (Sun from 12.30)

Typical prices: Venison burger
  £2.25 Cold macaroni salad £1
Credit: Visa

There's plenty of room for walkers and tourists in this large self-service restaurant. Simple unsophisticated snacks are the order of the day. A cold table displays competently baked quiches, and tasty salads such as cauliflower and green bean, and macaroni, celery and yoghurt. Hot items include vegetarian dishes such as risotto as well as things like baked trout with lime and dill and venison burgers. Healthy eaters should steer clear of the tempting puddings and pick fresh fruit instead.

KINLOCHBERVIE *Restaurant* Kinlochbervie Hotel Restaurant

By Lairg,
Kinlochbervie
(097 182) 275

Map 1 B1
Highland

Lunch 12–1.45 Dinner 7.30–8.30

Average price £20
Set D £15.95
Credit: Access, Amex, Diners, Visa

Abundant seafood and garden fresh salads make this modern hotel a good choice for a healthy meal, whether it be lunch in one of the bars or dinner in the dining room. Pub snacks include smoked salmon salad, prawn open sandwiches and very good macaroni cheese. For dinner, the obvious choice has to be fresh fish. Try the poached salmon with watercress sauce or monkfish kebabs. If you prefer, there are vegetarian dishes available on request and cooked with care. Desserts include fresh fruit salad and a large range of delicious sorbets.

LOCHGAIR *Pub* Lochgair Hotel

By Lochgilphead
Minard (0546) 86333

Map 2 B4
Strathclyde

Last order 9pm
Closed end October–mid March
Free House

Typical prices: Grilled
langoustines £4
Vegetable curry £2.40

On the shores of Loch Fyne, this unpretentious hotel is a favourite place for local fishermen. Fish is, not surprisingly, a speciality, and above average bar food includes poached or grilled trout, salmon, haddock and langoustines. The wholemeal sandwiches are offered with polyunsaturated margarine and vegetables will be served simply, sans sauce or butter, on request. Soups, sandwiches and savouries augment the menu and there is also a place for pasta and pulses. Vegetarian dishes, fresh fruit salad.

LONGFORMACUS *Restaurant* Horn House Hotel

Duns
Longformacus
(03617) 219

Map 2 D5
Borders

Dinner only from 7 pm
Closed to non-residents Mon–
  Thurs

Average price £15
Set D £12.50

Horn House is to the many allergy sufferers in Britain a haven, where everything, from the scrubbed wooden floors and cotton bedspreads to the carefully cooked food is tailored to their individual needs. The dining room is open to the public for dinner at weekends and it is well worth the scenic drive. Organic vegetables are used, and meat comes from naturally reared or wild animals. Set dinners include main dishes as diverse as smoked breast of pheasant, steamed trout, roast woodpigeon, and wholemeal macaroni and vegetable casserole. Fresh fruit platters to follow.

NEW ABBEY *Quick Bite* Abbey Cottage

By Dumfries
Dunscore
(038 782) 361

Map 2 C6
Dumfries & Galloway

Open 10–5
Closed October–Easter &
  weekdays Easter–Spring Bank
  Holiday

Typical prices: Lentil soup 60p
  Wholemeal vegetable pizza
  £1.80

Fresh and tasty snacks are available all day at this unpretentious coffee house-cum-craft shop. Start with home-made lentil soup and granary bread and follow with a wholemeal vegetable pizza or a baked potato stuffed with tuna. There's a small selection of salads and several plain or toasted sandwiches made with granary bread and topped with polyunsaturated margarine if preferred. Fillings run from simple salad to lean roast beef. On a fine day take tea in the attractive garden overlooking Sweetheart Abbey.

PEEBLES — *Quick Bite* — Sunflower

4 Bridgegate
Peebles
(0721) 22420

Map 2 C5
Borders

Open 10–5.30 (Wed in winter till
2.30)
Closed Sun, Bank Holidays &
Christmas–New Year
Wholefood cooking

Typical prices: Broccoli &
mushroom pancake with tomato
sauce £2.40 Cauliflower, Stilton
& walnut flan £1.95

Several rooms (including one for non-smokers) make up this rambling restaurant. The menu is simplicity itself: there's a range of sandwiches, filled baked potatoes and salads, all based largely on permutations of egg, ham and cheese. From noon the menu broadens to include soup with home-made (and very good) wholemeal bread, and wholefood dishes like cauliflower, Stilton and walnut flan or a lentil bake with tomato or mushroom sauce. No fresh fruit except in savoury salads or in the form of fresh fruit juices. Try the herb teas.

ST ANDREWS — *Quick Bite* — Brambles

5 College Street
St Andrews
(0334) 75380

Map 2 C4
Fife

Open 10–4.30
Closed Sun & Mon, 2 weeks
September & 2 weeks Christmas
Wholefood cooking

Typical prices: Greek spinach,
mushroom & pasta pie £1.20
Banana loaf 55p
(Minimum lunchtime charge £1)

Jean Hamilton's excellent cooking attracts shoppers, students and healthy eaters to her attractive pine-furnished café. Drop in mid morning for delicious home-made oatcakes plus other wholesome bakes and filled rolls waiting on the self-service counter. Lunchtime brings wonderfully inventive salads plus hot savouries such as haddock, leek and mushroom crumble. There's always a daily vegan choice. Jean doesn't serve meat and she uses the very freshest organic produce.

ST ANDREWS *Quick Bite* Pepita's Restaurant

11 Crails Lane
St Andrews
(0334) 74084

Map 2 C4
Fife

Open 9.30am–11pm, Sun
10.30am–10pm
Closed 2 weeks Christmas

Typical prices: Greek salad £1.80
  Courgette bake £3.30
(Minimum evening charge £2)
Credit: Access, Amex, Visa

Undergraduates from St Andrews University mix with shoppers and visitors at this atmospheric little restaurant off the market square. Lunch simply on a pizza or choose the ham salad with coleslaw-topped baked potato. Hot savouries are described on the blackboard and there's always a vegetarian dish of the day. An expanded menu operates during the evening when a meal might consist of Greek salad, baked rainbow trout in vine leaves with ratatouille and a jacket potato, and fresh fruit salad or lemon sorbet. Service is friendly and cheerful.

TARBERT *Pub* West Loch Hotel

Loch Fyne
Tarbert
(08802) 283

Map 2 B5
Strathclyde

No bar food eves
Closed November
Free House

Typical prices: Grilled fresh
  herring £3.50
  Fresh local prawns & salad £4.60
Credit: Access

Local seafood is a speciality of this fine old inn on the main road to Campbeltown. Starters include smoked mackerel and mushroom salad with yoghurt dressing, fresh whiting portugaise and prawn bisque. Follow perhaps with poached fillet of turbot in lettuce leaves or grilled lobster. Home-made soups are always on the menu as well as vegetarian dishes like baked stuffed aubergine. Healthy eaters could also try the marinated pork and prune kebab with orange rice. Vegan dishes on request.

TARBET

Quick Bite

Tigh-na-Mara Seafood Restaurant

Scourie, By Lairg
Scourie
(0971) 2151

Map 1 B1
Highland

Open 12–8
Closed Sun (except July & August)
and early October–Easter

Typical prices: Portuguese
sardines £2.75
Vegetable lasagne £2.85

This simple restaurant in a remote little settlement is renowned for its super seafood. Salmon is farmed locally, cooked simply with ground pepper and parsley, and served hot or cold with new potatoes and rough-cut salad. It makes a mouthwatering meal. Or there is fresh local crab or halibut when available and smoked salmon and smoked mackerel add to the selection. On cold days there are hearty soups served with chunks of wholemeal bread, and the menu always includes a vegetarian dish such as vegetable lasagne.

TAYVALLICH

Restaurant

Tayvallich Inn

By Lochgilphead
Tayvallich
(054 67) 282

Map 2 B4
Strathclyde

Lunch 12–2 Dinner 7–9
Closed Dinner Sun & all Mon–
Thurs November–April, January
1, December 25 & 2 weeks end
January–February

Average price £14
Credit: Access, Visa

Clams from the Sound of Jura, Craignish mussels, wild salmon and local lobster are among the splendid seafoods on the menu at this comfortably casual pub restaurant. The healthy eater can dine extremely well on starters like octopus vinaigrette or gravadlax, and main courses such as clams with ginger and walnuts or grilled fillet steak and prawns. Lightly steamed vegetables will be served without sauce if preferred, and desserts include fresh fruit salad and tangy sorbets. Bar lunches also available.

TROON
Restaurant

Piersland House Hotel Restaurant

Craigend Road
Troon
(0292) 314747

Map 2 B5
Strathclyde

Lunch by arrangement only
Dinner 7–9.30

Average price £20
Set D £12.50
Credit: Access, Amex, Diners, Visa

The welcome is warm at this panelled restaurant. Chef Ian McGregor's menus are short but well constructed. Fish is first choice for the health conscious with local scallops and salmon sharing the billing with sole jardinière. Pasta and rice dishes are conspicuous by their absence but will be prepared on request. The same can be said for vegetarian dishes. Grilled lamb chops and steaks are cooked to order. Wholemeal bread is served with polyunsaturated margarine, if preferred, and both natural yoghurt and skimmed milk are used in cooking where appropriate.

TURRIFF
Pub

Towie Tavern

Auchterless
Turriff
(08884) 201

Map 1 D2
Grampian

Last order 9pm
No bar food Sun & Mon eve & Mon lunch Nov–Feb
Closed 2 weeks Jan–Feb
Free House

Typical prices: Seafood & broccoli lasagne £3.45
Mushroom & almond pâté £2.30
Credit: Access, Visa

Surrounded by beautiful Scottish countryside this pebble-dash pub restaurant on the A947 Aberdeen to Banff road is constantly busy and booking is a must at weekends. Mrs Rattray does most of the cooking and her imaginative menus make good use of local produce, wholegrains, polyunsaturated fats and skimmed milk. You might sup tomato soup with delicious oatmeal bread, then try vegetable and cashew nut Merati, grilled chicken breast, or seafood and broccoli wholemeal lasagne. Vegan dishes.

TURNBERRY  Turnberry Hotel Restaurant

Strathclyde
Turnberry
(065 53) 1000

Map 2 B5
Strathclyde

Lunch 1–2.30 Dinner 7.30–10
Closed end November–end
  February

Average price £25
Set L £11.50
Set D £21
Credit: Access, Amex, Diners, Visa

In terms of healthy eating, this attractive restaurant is well above par. Local ingredients include turbot, scallops, lobster, salmon and sea trout. The Ayrshire beef and lamb are very good and this hotel is also well known for its game dishes. Wholemeal pasta appears regularly and most of the soups are pulse-based. There are plenty of simple yet stylish dishes such as paper thin raw fillet of lamb in the carpaccio style, or suprême of chicken with lemon. The vegetarian menu includes vegetable cutlets with sharp fruit sauce.

ULLAPOOL *Quick Bite* Ceilidh Place

West Argyll Street
Ullapool
(0854) 2103

Map 1 B2
Highland

Open 9 am–9 pm
Closed Nov 1–February 28

Typical prices: Grilled sole £6.75
  Vegan loaf 45p
Credit: Access, Amex, Diners, Visa

Hard to fault this happy place, whose owners provide comfortable accommodation and make memorable meals. Fish is a speciality, and their Lochinver sole is very good. Vegetarian dishes include cracked wheat and mushroom casserole, bean moussaka and vegetable curry. The wholemeal bread is commended for its very good flavour and nutty texture. Low-fat spread is offered and both yoghurt and skimmed milk are used in cooking where appropriate. Book for dinner in high season.

WESTER HOWGATE

 QuickBite

Old Howgate Inn,★ Coach House

Near Penicuik
Penicuik
(0968) 74244

Map 2 C5
Lothian

Open 11.30–2.30 (Sun from 12.30)
& 6–10 (Sun from 6.30)
Closed January 1 & December 25

Typical prices: Smørrebrød of
Danish caviar with raw egg yolk
£2.30
Cold meats with salad & a baked
potato £5.80
Credit: Access, Amex, Diners, Visa

Danish dishes delight at this centuries-old coaching inn. Start with a simple consommé and then move to the superb smørrebrød — open sandwiches on nutty rye bread. Two or three make an ample meal. There are 36 to choose from, including roast beef with tomatoes and olives, Danish herring with crème fraîche, and smoked trout with spinach pâté. The non-meat varieties include pickled mushrooms, and quail's eggs garnished with sliced tomatoes. More substantial dishes include fresh lobster salad and pickled salmon with scrambled egg and sautéed spinach, while to finish you could try fresh orange segments with orange sorbet, or a selection of Danish cheeses.

If you are unsure of what to order, do remember to ask the staff for advice on food choices. Many restaurants will adapt dishes to suit your requirements or prepare special meals if given prior notice.

HEALTHY EATING OUT
—IN—

WALES

WALES
WALES
WALES
WALES
WALES
WALES
WALES
WALES

GUIDE TO ESTABLISHMENTS

ABERAERON

Quick Bite

Hive on the ★ Quay

Cadwgan Place
Aberaeron
(0545) 570445

Map 7 B3
Dyfed

Open 10.30–5, (July–beginning
 September 10–9)
Closed end September–Spring
 Bank Holiday

Typical prices: Pasta, apple &
 green pepper salad 60p
 Lamb kebabs with brown rice &
 Greek salad £4.25

Attentive staff cope well with the swarms of summer
visitors that gather at this delightful quayside café-restaurant. Honey from the Holgate family's own hives is used
in many of the tasty cakes and bakes. The sandwiches are
super and may be enjoyed with lemon tea, decaffeinated
coffee or fresh fruit and vegetable juices. The buffet, which
operates from 12–2 and 6–9 includes salad platters,
savoury pancakes and evening specials like grilled Welsh
lamb chops or fresh local crab. Local, organically grown
vegetables are used where possible.

ABERYSTWYTH

Quick Bite

Connexion

19 Bridge Street
Aberystwyth
(0970) 615350

Map 7 B2
Dyfed

Open 10–4.30 & 6.30–10.30
Closed Sunday & December 25

Typical prices: Nut roast & jacket
 potato £3.95
 Tuna pizza £2.90
Credit: Access, Visa
Luncheon Vouchers accepted

Thanks to owner Janet Fuerst's enthusiasm and drive, this
restaurant has become a popular place for students and
families alike. Seating is in booths separated by screens,
and food is simple and satisfying. You can settle for soup,
salad, pizza, or order chargrilled chicken or T-bone steak
(available evenings only). Vegetarians are well catered for
and there's always a vegan dish. Specials include stuffed
aubergines or peppers, lobster salad and smoked salmon,
and local fish will be poached or baked on request.

BODFARI   *Pub*   Dinorben Arms Inn

Near Denbigh
Bodfari
(074 575) 309

Last order 10.15pm
Closed December 25
Free House

Map 7 C1
Clwyd

Typical prices: Poached salmon
    salad £4.75
     Mushroom omelette £2.95
Credit: Access, Visa

Serve yourself with a healthy meal at the popular lunchtime smorgasbord. A wide range of cold meats, fresh and soused fish, salads and cheeses is on display, with seasonal fruits and wholemeal bread. Conventional pub grub such as soups, sandwiches and jacket potatoes is available too, along with specials like poached salmon, grilled trout and omelettes. In the evening the smorgasbord becomes a starter bar, and there's a carvery from Wednesday to Saturday evenings. Vegetarians are limited to omelettes, salads and smorgasbord selections.

CARDIFF   *Quick Bite*   Armless Dragon ★

97 Wyverne Road,
   Cathays
Cardiff
(0222) 382357

Open 12.30–2.30 (Full evening
    meals 7.30–10.30)
Closed Lunch Sat, all Sun, Bank
    Holidays & Christmas week

Map 7 C4
Mid Glamorgan

Typical prices: Lentil & mushroom
    pie £5.20 Poached fresh fish of
    the day £6.20
Credit: Access, Amex, Diners, Visa

Despite its fanciful name, the Armless Dragon looks rather ordinary from the outside. Inside, it is anything but. David Richards originally specialised in macrobiotic cooking and although he has now broadened his repertoire and joined forces with Mark Sharples, that fresh and fundamentally healthy approach to food is still apparent in such stupendous starters as laverballs with mushrooms and main courses that range from poached hake in samphire sauce to a vegetarian platter with excellent wholemeal rolls.

CARDIFF — *Quick Bite* — Sage

Unit 3, Wellfield
  Court, Roath
Cardiff
(0222) 481223

Map 7 C4
Mid Glamorgan

Open 9.30–5
Closed Sun, & 1 week at Christmas
Vegetarian wholefood cooking

Typical prices: Cauliflower soup
  75p Aubergine parmesan £1.95

In ancient times sage was termed 'the healer'. Certainly you will feel a lot better for a visit to this charming little vegetarian restaurant, where wholefood dishes are served in a relaxed and friendly environment. Sit outside when the sun shines and enjoy a tisane or dandelion coffee with a slice of carrot and cinnamon cake. Linger till lunchtime and you'll find a choice of vegetarian and vegan dishes, including soups, savouries such as leek and aduki bean casserole and a selection of inviting salads. All cooking is done with sunflower oil and natural yoghurt is used.

CARDIGAN — *Restaurant* — Rhyd-Garn-Wen

Cardigan
(0239) 612742

Map 7 A3
Dyfed

Dinner only 7.30–9.30
Closed October–Easter

Average price £16
Set D £12.50
Credit: Access, Amex

This small, select restaurant is worth searching out but ask for directions when you book. Susan Jones takes pleasure in planning dishes her guests will enjoy. Vegetarians who order ahead will find a selection of five or six special dishes, balanced for relative food values, at the fixed price of £12.50. There is also spinach roulade, wild rice with peppers, peas, beans and spices, houmus or salads. Wholemeal bread is made daily. If unsauced dishes are preferred, a carefully prepared garnish will be provided.

CARMARTHEN

Quick Bite

Waverley Restaurant

23 Lammas Street
Carmarthen
(0267) 236521

Map 7 B3
Dyfed

Open 9–4 (Thurs till 2)
Closed Sun, Thurs afternoon &
  Bank Holidays
Vegetarian wholefood cooking

Typical prices: Nut & lentil
  burgers 40p
  Lentil shepherd's pie £1.10

Nut burgers are the top seller at this simple café at the back of a wholefood store. Try them with a selection of salads, including celery and bean, and sweetcorn and fruit. Susan Anderson is a dedicated and enthusiastic cook and everything is fresh and attractively presented. Several quiches—with wholemeal pastry and generous fillings—are always available. Specials change every day, and could include mushroom Stroganoff, vegetable curry and brown rice, and stuffed peppers. Non-dairy spreads are available with the wholemeal bread, and sunflower oil is used.

CHEPSTOW

Pub

Castle View Inn

16 Bridge Street
Chepstow
(029 12) 70349

Map 7 C3
Gwent

Last order 9.30pm
Free House

Typical prices: Fresh Wye salmon
  salad £4.95
  Chilli bean casserole £2.85
Set D from £8.45
Credit: Access, Amex, Diners, Visa

Conveniently sited close to the M4 and M5 crossroads, this charming hotel offers a good selection of fresh local produce. Salmon and trout from the River Wye find their way on to the menu in a wide variety of delicious dishes, from simple starters to salads and flans. Try poached salmon with a light cucumber and dill sauce for a perfect light meal. Also on the bar menu are omelettes, casseroles and wholemeal sandwiches. Grills are served in the restaurant and there's a first rate vegetarian menu.

WALES

323

CHEPSTOW — *Restaurant* — Willow Tree

'The Back', Chepstow
 River Bank
Chepstow
(029 12) 6665

Map 7 C3
Gwent

Meals 11–5 & Dinner from 7.30
Closed Sun eve, all Mon &
 December 25 & 26

Average price £15
Set D £13.95
Credit: Access, Visa

No weeping at this Willow—the food is outstanding. Healthy eaters are positively pampered with starters like mushrooms baked with lemon and garlic, carrot and coriander soup or moshe galah, a very tasty pasta and vegetable dish served with wholemeal bread. The main course might be a country chicken casserole, Greek lamb with cucumbers in yoghurt or poached trout with water-cress sauce. Puds are appetite's temptation, but Jeremy Hector's home-made sorbets make it easy to resist the richer options. Morning coffees and light lunches.

CRICKHOWELL — *Quick Bite* — Cheese Press

18 High Street
Crickhowell
(0873) 811122

Map 7 C3
Powys

Open 9.30–5.30 (September–
 Easter till 5) Sun 10.30–4.30
Closed Sun (January–Easter) &
 December 25 & 26

Typical prices: Vegetarian pasta
 bake £1.95
 Chick pea soup 85p
Credit: Access, Amex

This small and unpretentious café behind a gift shop is understandably proud of the fact that it serves only fresh food prepared from natural ingredients. Delectable bakes are displayed on the self-service counter and from about 11.30 the short lunch menu offers home-made soup and lentil and mushroom pâté, filled jacket potatoes and some imaginative salads, made, where possible, from organically grown vegetables. There's always a vegetarian dish—courgette and pasta bake, perhaps—and fresh fruit salad.

CRICKHOWELL

Pub

Nantyffin Cider Mill Inn

Crickhowell
(0873) 810775

Map 7 C3
Powys

Last order 10pm
Closed December 25
Free House

Typical prices: Smoked haddock
  kedgeree £2.75
  Cottage cheese & pineapple
  salad £3.10
Credit: Access, Visa

At the junction of the A40 and A479, 1½ miles west of Crickhowell, stands this handsome pink-washed inn, run by licensee Barbara Ambrose. She's a particularly fine pastrycook, so pies are a speciality, but healthy eaters will find other options, like home-baked ham and lean roast beef salads or cottage cheese and pineapple platter. There's always home-made vegetable soup with wholemeal bread and in winter simple casseroles with jacket potatoes and carefully cooked vegetables. Vegetarians will find dishes like wholemeal tagliatelle with walnuts and cheese.

HAY-ON-WYE

Quick Bite

Granary

Broad Street
Hay-on-Wye
(0497) 820790

Map 7 C3
Powys

Open 10–6 (9am–9pm July 15–
  end August)
Closed December 25 & 26

Typical prices: Home-made soup
  £1 Vegetarian bake £2.50
Credit: Access, Amex, Diners, Visa

Good home-cooked meals at very attractive prices make this stone-walled café a popular year-round meeting place. There are plenty of healthy options including fresh seasonal salads. The three fish salad—a summertime speciality served with Scandinavian crispbread—is very popular, while other guests settle for rare Hereford beef salads or home-cooked ham. There are always several vegetarian dishes such as Tibetan roast, a tasty nut loaf with burghul wheat, barley, spinach and red wine.

HAY-ON-WYE

Quick Bite

Lion's Corner House

39 Lion Street
Hay-on-Wye
(0497) 820175

Map 7 C3
Powys

Open 11–3
Closed Sun, December 25 & 26 &
  all January & February

Typical prices: Baked cod & new
  potatoes £3.50 Omelette & salad
  & new potatoes £2.50
Credit: Access, Amex, Diners, Visa

This atmospheric corner restaurant provides a varied and interesting lunchtime menu that might have been designed for healthy eaters. Start with soup and a wholemeal roll, or try the vegetarian terrine with toast and salad. The main course might be baked cod fillet with new potatoes, or a spinach and cottage cheese flan. There is almost always an omelette or two, and a pasta or pulse dish. Also vegetarian dishes and simple choices for those who like their food good and plain. Organic vegetables with advance notice. More elaborate evening meals.

HAY-ON-WYE

Pub

Old Black Lion

Lion Street
Hay-on-Wye
(0497) 820841

Map 7 C3
Powys

Last order 10pm
Free House

Typical prices: Home-made soup
  £1 Wholemeal pancakes £1.45
Credit: Access

Named after the Lion Gate, the ancient entry to Hay-on-Wye, this former coaching inn is a popular meeting spot. A good selection of quality bar snacks is available both at lunchtimes and in the evenings. Bar-meals of home-made, hearty soup and lighter wholemeal quiche are well worth sampling. Wholemeal pancakes, filled baked potatoes and substantial casseroles add further interest, and there's a good choice of vegetarian specialities. Healthy diners can also eat in the restaurant.

KEESTON *Quick Bite* Keeston Kitchen

Near Haverfordwest
Camrose
(0437) 710440

Map 7 A3
Dyfed

Open 10.30–2, (Sun from 12.30) &
 7–10
Closed Mon (except July &
 August) & 1st week January

Typical prices: Salade niçoise
 £2.75 Local trout £5.35
Credit: Access, Visa

Evening is the best time to visit this friendly farmhouse-style establishment, for this is when Phil Hallett entertains on the guitar while his wife Clare conducts in the kitchen. Home-cooked food in friendly surroundings is what the menu promises and this is precisely what you will find. Start, perhaps, with cauliflower soup, proceed to grilled trout with prawns, or poached chicken with mushrooms, celery, carrots and courgettes, and conclude with decaffeinated coffee. Brown rice is offered as an alternative accompaniment with all meals. Take away available.

LLANBERIS *Restaurant* Y Bistro

43 High Street
Llanberis
(0286) 871278

Map 7 B2
Gwynedd

Lunch by arrangement only Dinner
 7.30–9.30
Closed Sunday (except preceding
 Bank Holiday Mondays),
 December 25 & 26, January 1 &
 3 weeks January

Average price £14
Set D £10.50
Credit: Access, Amex, Diners, Visa

'Options' would be an appropriate name for this restaurant, where the set menu is available with a sliding scale of prices. Healthy eaters can stick to the low-fat specialities thoughtfully underlined on the menu. You might start with marinated chicken or gazpacho, followed by lamb kebabs or grilled local fish with a platter of vegetables. Regular vegetarian dishes include a Stroganoff with mushrooms, sunflower seeds and onions. Canapés at the bar, side salad, wholemeal bread and coffee with petits fours.

LLANFIHANGEL CRUCORNEY

Pub

Skirrid Inn ★

Near Abergavenny
Crucorney
(0873 890) 258

Map 7 C3
Gwent

Last order 9.30pm
Closed December 25
Free House

Typical prices: Filled jacket
potatoes £1.20
Grilled local salmon £7.50
Credit: Amex, Diners

This pub, said to be the oldest in Wales, has been offering hospitality since the 12th century. The friendly Foster family serve excellent pub grub in a pleasant environment. The lengthy menu has plenty of choice for healthy eaters, from poached eggs with laverbread to lightly grilled fresh salmon, Dover sole and turbot. Also home-made soups, smoked tuna, fresh asparagus or baby corn plus pasta, pulses and vegetarian dishes. Given 24 hours notice the Fosters will gladly create a balanced 3-course vegetarian meal of the customer's own choosing.

LLYSWEN

Pub

Griffin Inn

Llyswen
(087 485) 241

Map 7 C3
Powys

Last order 9pm
No bar food Sun eve
Free house

Typical prices: Home-made soup
£1.15 Grilled fresh sardines
£2.75
Credit: Access, Amex, Diners, Visa

At this attractive inn, summer visitors relax in the garden; winter guests head for the lounge bar's log fire. Bar food changes daily, and includes options for healthy eaters. Always a selection of half a dozen salads with home-baked ham, roast beef and locally smoked salmon. The same ingredients can be sampled in sandwiches. Hot dishes include vegetarian paella, bean and pasta bakes and fresh salmon in season. Fresh fruit, sorbets, home-made yoghurt and muesli ice cream are always available.

MACHYNLLETH

Quick Bite

Centre for Alternative Technology

Llwyngwern Quarry
Machynlleth
(0654) 2400

Map 7 B2
Powys

Open 10–5
Closed January 1 & December 25
Vegetarian wholefood cooking

Typical prices: Quarryworker's
    lunch £1.20
    Pasta bake & salad £1.75

Allow plenty of time for your visit to the Centre for Alternative Technology for there is plenty to see, from solar energy exhibits to a blacksmith's forge recycling waste metal. There's also a maze, children's play area and organic garden that provides most of the vegetables used in the wholefood restaurant. Enjoy excellent salads, vegetarian pâtés, home-baked bread, or lunch, between 12.30 and 2.30, on more substantial specials like chick pea and fruit curry, or pasta bake with mixed beans. There are weekend wholefood cookery courses.

MACHYNLLETH

Quick Bite

Quarry Shop

13 Maengwyn Street
Machynlleth
(0654) 2624

Map 7 B2
Powys

Open 9–3 & 3.30–5 (Thurs till 2)
Closed Sun (except Bank Holiday
    weekends) & December 25 & 26
Vegetarian/vegan cooking

Typical prices: Lentil burgers
    £1.20 Fruit trifle 75p

An offshoot of the Centre of Alternative Technology (and utilising some of their produce), this pine-furnished self-service restaurant caters well for both vegetarians and vegans. There are always four bowls brimful of well-balanced salads, together with simple specials like lentil burgers with tomato sauce and bean goulash. Both goat's and natural yoghurt are used and low-fat spreads are available with wholemeal bread. Muesli is served with skimmed milk, and there is a range of wholesome bakes.

NEWPORT · *Quick Bite* · Cnapan ★

East Street
Newport
(0239) 820575

Map 7 A3
Dyfed

Open 10.30–5
Closed Tues & November–March
(except Sun Lunch)
Wholefood cooking

Typical prices: Vegetable lasagne
£3.50 Laverbread with seafood &
lemon filling £3.50
Credit: Access, Visa

This lovely old listed house is the domain of the Lloyd and Cooper families, well-known for their tasty wholefood lunches and dinners with a Welsh flavour. Eluned Lloyd is a former dietitian, so healthy eaters need have no qualms about tucking in to delicious dishes like vegetable lasagne with yoghurt topping or oat-based fisherman's pie. Hearty home-made soups are served with chunky wholemeal bread (ask for polyunsaturated margarine if you prefer it) and fresh salads are splendid. More elaborate evening meals make much of fresh local fish, meat and vegetables.

NEWPORT · *Quick Bite* · Happy Carrot Bistro

5 Chartist Tower,
  Upper Dock Street
Newport
(0633) 66150

Map 7 C3
Gwent

Open 10–4
Closed Wed, Sun & Bank Holidays
Vegetarian cooking

Typical prices: Beanfreaks
vegetarian curry £2.50
Happy carrot cake 70p

Most of the Happy Carrot is below ground level behind the Beanfreaks Health Food Centre. It is well worth seeking out for good home cooking without frills. Start with a steaming bowl of chunky vegetable soup with a wholemeal roll, then indulge in houmus, falafel, vegetable curry or a simply delicious vegetarian burger with salad. Have the salad solo if you prefer or try the filled jacket potatoes. Plain yoghurt or bakes like the carrot cake to follow, and ginseng tea to add a spring to your step on departure.

The Precinct
Newtown
(0686) 25395

Map 7 C2
Powys

Open 9–4.30
Closed Sun & Bank Holidays
except Good Friday

Typical prices: Mixed bean bake
£1.50 Vegetable risotto £1.50

Patron power has changed the menu over the years at this bright and cheery restaurant in the Ladywell shopping centre. The two Js, Jean Bowen and Jasmine Ball, have responded admirably to a growing interest in healthier food by gradually adding more low-fat, high-fibre dishes to their menu and serving fewer traditional dishes such as beef curry and cottage pie. Today you are likely to see nourishing vegetable soups, vegetable flans, bean bakes and jacket potatoes. There's a tempting salad bar and wholemeal bread is always on offer. Sunflower oil used in all cooking.

PENLLYNE *Pub* Fox at Penllyne

Near Cowbridge
Cowbridge
(044 63) 2352

Map 7 C4
South Glamorgan

No bar food eves
Closed Sun & December 25 & 26
Free House

Typical prices: Baked sea bass
with herbs £8.50
Grilled calf's liver with avocado
£4.95
Credit: Access, Amex, Visa

The Fox is famous for its fresh fish. Depending on what is available, you may find on the menu chargrilled trout, baked sea bass with fennel or Cardigan lobster. One of their many specialities is a delicious kebab with alternate chunks of steak and peeled king prawns. Starters include smoked salmon and melon with Parma ham, and there are lean dishes like barbecued breast of chicken. Fresh pasta is always popular and there's a daily vegetarian dish. Lunch is served in the bar, evening dinners in the restaurant.

WALES

331

PENTWYNMAWR Three Horseshoes Inn

High Street,
  Newbridge
Pentwynmawr
(0495) 243436

Map 7 C3
Gwent

Last order 10pm
No bar food Sun
Brewery Whitbread

Typical prices: Wholewheat
  macaroni cheese £2.95
  Open sandwich £1.20

This jewel of an inn on the A472, with its splendid Welsh stone interior, has been lovingly restored by the Reynish family. The same perfectionism is applied to the nicely named Cottage Bar meals. The crispy mushroom bake, served with a substantial side salad, is a delight, and Peter Reynish makes a very good cottage pie. There are composite salads and a novel French ploughman's lunch consisting of a robust soup, pâté, bread and a salad garnish. Go easy on the pâté but enjoy the rest. Grilled steak is also available and vegetarians are well looked after.

SWANSEA *Quick Bite* Home on the Range

174 St Helen's Avenue
Swansea
(0792) 467 166

Map 7 B3
West Glamorgan

Open 11.30–3 & 6–10
Closed all Sun, Mon & Tues eve,
  Bank Holidays & 10 days
  Christmas

Typical prices: Vegetable & pasta
  bake £1.95
  Beef ragout & salad £2.25
Set D £6

Good home cooking is offered at this jolly community restaurant near St Helen's rugby ground. Lunch is a simple affair, with dishes set out on the counter or described on a blackboard. There is always a range of flans, several salads and a vegetarian dish of the day, perhaps lentil patties with yoghurt dressing, or brown rice and aduki bean bake. Evenings offer very reasonable three-course meals: tuna and haricot bean salad, chicken and almonds, fresh fruit crumble.

TALSARNAU   *Restaurant*   Maes-y-Neuadd Hotel Restaurant

Harlech
(0766) 780200

Map 7 B2
Gwynedd

Lunch 12.30–1.45 (Sun only)
  Dinner 7.30–9
Closed Lunch Mon–Sat except by
  arrangement & January 5–29

Average price £15
Set L £7.50
Set D £12.75
Credit: Access, Visa

It's pleasing to find several Welsh regional specialities on the four-course menu at this stylish restaurant. Try the fresh herrings stuffed with leeks, tomato and parsley or the pineapple and melon starter with an optional red wine sorbet, followed perhaps by Welsh lamb or chicken suprême with hazelnuts and orange. Wholemeal pasta and brown rice dishes regularly find their way on to the menu in such guises as spiced almond risotto or vegetable lasagne. The bread is wholemeal. Simple fish dishes like poached halibut with cucumber sauce extend the range.

TY'N-Y-MAES   *Quick Bite*   Snowdonia National Park Lodge

Bethesda
Bethesda
(0248) 600548

Map 7 B2
Gwynnedd

Open 11–4.30 & 7–9

Typical prices: Vegetable quiche
  £1.60 Chilli bean casserole £4.95
Credit: Access, Amex, Visa

Health is the raison d'être for this attractive lodge, where residents can avail themselves of a wide range of health and beauty treatments. Snacks, light lunches and dinners, open to non-residents, are served and the daily menus are well balanced and wholesome. The food makes wide use of organically grown vegetables and naturally reared meats. Calorie counters are catered for, naturally, but a typical meal might equally well be houmus, pink-roasted lean lamb, and fresh fruit with grapefruit sorbet.

HEALTHY EATING OUT
—IN THE—
CHANNEL
ISLANDS

CHANNEL
ISLANDS
CHANNEL
ISLANDS
CHANNEL
ISLANDS
CHANNEL

GUIDE TO ESTABLISHMENTS

ST AUBIN'S HARBOUR

Pub

Old Court House Inn

Jersey
(0534) 46433

Map 8 D3
Jersey

No bar food eves & Sun
Closed February
Free House

Typical prices: Avocado salad
£2.75 Lemon sole £6
Credit: Access, Visa

Yachtsmen moored in St Aubin's Harbour are not the only ones splicing the mainbrace at this popular waterfront inn. Three bars—one in the shape of a galleon—provide a variety of victuals in the form of hearty soups, salads, grills and the seafood that is a local speciality. Whether you dine on oysters or lobster, address a whole crab or select a simple grilled sole, plaice or platter of Pacific prawns, they will be carefully cooked. Starters include crudités and fresh artichoke and avocado salad and there's a vegetarian menu.

ST HELIER

Restaurant

Grand Hotel, Victoria's

Esplanade
Jersey
(0534) 72255

Map 8 D3
Jersey

Lunch 12.30–2.15 Dinner 7–10.30
Closed Sun, Good Friday & May
  Bank Holiday.

Average price £18
Credit: Access, Amex, Diners, Visa

Like many of the better Channel Island restaurants, Victoria's has an extensive international repertoire, with so wide a choice it isn't difficult to make a healthy selection. Simple chicken and fish dishes include grilled Jersey plaice, Dover sole, lemon sole, lobster, crab and scampi. Pulses are used imaginatively, and there is a good selection of vegetarian dishes including ratatouille-filled pancakes, wholemeal spaghetti with shallots, mushrooms and yoghurt, and a high fibre salad.

AN OFFER FOR ANSWERS
A DISCOUNT ON THE NEXT GUIDE

Readers' answers to questionnaires included in our Guides prove invaluable to us in planning future editions, either through their reactions to the contents of the current Guide, or through the tastes and inclinations indicated. Please send this tear-out page to us *after you have used the Guide for some time*, addressing the envelope to:

> Egon Ronay's Guides, Second Floor
> Greencoat House, Francis Street, London SW1P 1DH
> United Kingdom

As a token of thanks for your help, we will enable respondents to obtain the next Guide post free from us at a 33⅓% discount off the retail price. We will send you an order form before publication, and answering the questionnaire imposes no obligation to purchase. All answers will be treated in confidence.

This offer closes 31 July 1987.

PLEASE TICK

1. Are you ...   male? ☐   Under 21? ☐   46–65? ☐
                  female? ☐   21–30? ☐   over 65? ☐
                               31–45? ☐

2. Your occupation ....
Full time ☐ Part time ☐ Unemployed ☐ Retired ☐

3. Do you have any children?   Yes ☐   No ☐

4. In which area of the U.K. do you live?
   North East ☐   South East ☐   Wales ☐
   North West ☐   London ☐   Scotland ☐
   Midlands ☐   South West ☐   Ireland ☐

5. Do you refer to this Guide ...
   four times a week? ☐   once a week? ☐
   three times a week? ☐   once a month? ☐
   twice a week? ☐   less often? ☐

6. How many people refer to this Guide apart from yourself?
   At home .... At work ....

7. Do you own any other Egon Ronay Guides? Please state year.
   Hotel & Restaurant ☐ 19..........   Pub ☐ 19..........
                                        Just a Bite ☐ 19..........

8. How often do you eat out ...
   (a) Socially? (b) During your working day?
   (c) Business entertaining?

	(a)	(b)	(c)		(a)	(b)	(c)
More than once a week	☐	☐	☐	Once a fortnight	☐	☐	☐
Once a week	☐	☐	☐	Once a month	☐	☐	☐
				Less often	☐	☐	☐

Continued overleaf ...

A DISCOUNT ON THE NEXT GUIDE

9. How much, on average, would you expect to spend per person when you are eating out. Please write in.
   (a) Socially? £ ....(b) During your working day? £ ....
   (c) Business entertaining? £ ....

10. Which kind of restaurant do you visit *most* often when you are eating out? (a) Socially (b) Work (c) Entertaining

	(a)	(b)	(c)		(a)	(b)	(c)
Inn or pub bar	☐	☐	☐	French restaurants	☐	☐	☐
Ethnic restaurant, eg. Chinese, Indian, etc	☐	☐	☐	Italian restaurants	☐	☐	☐
				Café/tea room	☐	☐	☐
Vegetarian/wholefood restaurant	☐	☐	☐	Hamburger, pizza or pasta	☐	☐	☐
Restaurant in a hotel or pub	☐	☐	☐	Club or disco	☐	☐	☐
				Wine bar	☐	☐	☐

11. Which menu comes closest to the one you would choose when eating out? Please choose one from each selection.
   ☐ Melon ☐ Steak ☐ Sorbet
   ☐ Soup ☐ Fish or poultry ☐ Cheese
   ☐ Prawn Cocktail ☐ Non-meat meal ☐ Gateaux

12. Do you ever inquire...
   ☐ What the ingredients are?
   ☐ Whether dishes are available without butter or sauce?
   ☐ Whether skimmed milk is available?
   ☐ Whether polyunsaturated or low-fat spread is available?

13. Do you link healthier foods with slimming?
   ....

14. Do you believe that there is a link between what one eats and one's health? If so, which of these comes closest to your own position?
   ☐ I attempt to choose healthier foods when eating out.
   ☐ I only consider healthier food when eating at home.
   ☐ I attempt to stick to healthier food both at home and when eating out.

15. What other fields would you like us to survey or what improvements do you suggest?
   ....
   ....
   ....
   ....
   ....
   ....

16. Please *print* your name and address here if you would like us to send you a pre-publication order form for the next Guide.
   Name ....
   Address ....
   ....
   ....

READERS' COMMENTS

Please use this sheet for complaints about establishments or for recommending new establishments which you would like our inspectors to visit.

Please post to Egon Ronay's Guides, Second Floor, Greencoat House, Francis Street, London SW1P 1DH.

Name and address of establishment	Your recommendation or complaint

N.B. We regret that owing to the enormous volume of readers' communications received each year we shall be unable to acknowledge these forms, but they will certainly be seriously considered.

Name of sender (in block letters)

....

Address of sender (in block letters)

....

....

READERS' COMMENTS

Please use this sheet for complaints about establishments or for recommending new establishments which you would like our inspectors to visit.

Please post to Egon Ronay's Guides, Second Floor, Greencoat House, Francis Street, London SW1P 1DH.

Name and address of establishment	Your recommendation or complaint

N.B. We regret that owing to the enormous volume of readers' communications received each year we shall be unable to acknowledge these forms, but they will certainly be seriously considered.

Name of sender (in block letters)

....

Address of sender (in block letters)

....

....

INDEX
(A–Z LIST OF ESTABLISHMENTS)

Coach & Horses, Honley, p.214
Cobbett's, Botley, p.146
Coconut Willy's, Stockport, p.266
Coffee Pot, Belbroughton, p.138
Collin House Hotel Restaurant, Broadway, p.163
Combe House Hotel Restaurant, Gittisham, p.203
Compleat Angler Hotel, Valaisan Restaurant, Marlow, p.242
Connexion, Aberystwyth, p.320
Contented Sole, Burnham-on-Crouch, p.165
Cook's Delight, Berkhamsted, p.165
Cooling's Wine Bar, Exeter, p.198
Corner Stones, Bradford-on-Avon, p.149
Cornhouse Restaurant & Wine Bar, Shrewsbury, p.263
Corse Lawn House, Corse Lawn, p.182
Cottage Tea Room, Ashford-in-the-Water, p.125
Country Fare Coffee House, Aberfeldy, p.294
Country Kitchen, Edinburgh, p.298
Country Kitchen, Portsmouth (Southsea), p.254
Country Life, W1, p.65
Cranks (Great Newport Street), WC2, p.65
Cranks (Tottenham Street), W1, p.66
Cranks in Covent Garden, WC2, p.66
Cranks Health Food Restaurant, W1, p.67
Cranks Health Food Restaurant, Dartington, p.188
Crown Hotel, Southwold, p.265
Crown Inn, Hawk Green, p.211
Crowns, Haslemere, p.210

D
Daly's Wine Bar, WC2, p.67
Dedham Vale Hotel, Terrace Restaurant, Dedham, p.190
Defune, W1, p.68
Delanys, Shrewsbury, p.263
Delhi Brasserie, SW7, p.68
Di's Larder, SW11, p.69
Dining Room, SE1, p.69
Dinorben Arms, Bodfari, p.321
Diwana Bhelpoori House, NW1 & W2, p.70
Dorchester, The Terrace, W1, p.71
Dove at Corton, Corton, p.182
Draycott's (Wine Bar), SW3, p.71
Dukes Playhouse Restaurant, Lancaster, p.223
Dunain Park Hotel Restaurant, Inverness, p.309
342 Dynasty, Birmingham, p.140

E
Earth Exchange, N6, p.72
East West Restaurant, EC1, p.72
Eat Fit, Kendal (also Preston), p.218
English House, SW3, p.73
Equatorial, W1, p.73
L'Escargot, W1, p.74
Everyman Bistro, Liverpool, p.231

F
Fallen Angel, N1, p.74
Farmhouse, Chester, p.173
First Out, WC2, p.75
Flitwick Manor Restaurant, Flitwick, p.201
Flossies, Bournemouth, p.146
Fodder, Hereford, p.212
Food for Friends, Brighton, p.154
Food for Health, EC4, p.75
Food for Thought, WC2, p.76
Forrest Wine Bar, Cheltenham, p.171
Fox at Penllyne, Penllyne, p.331
Franco's, Basingstoke, p.132
Frederick's, N1, p.76
French Connection, Brighton, p.155
Friends Bistro, Great Yarmouth, p.207
Frith's, W1, p.77
Fullers Arms, Brightling, p.153

G
La Galleria Wine Bar, Birmingham, p.140
Gannets, Newark, p.246
Gar's, Brighton, p.155
George & Dragon, Wentworth, p.283
Gillygate Wholefood Café, York, p.291
Girl on a Swing, Gosforth, p.204
Gingers, Birmingham, p.141
Goblets Wine Bar, Broadway, p.163
God's Providence House, Newport, p.247
Good Companion (Wine Bar), Oswestry, p.251
Good Earth, NW7 & SW3, p.78
Good Earth, Esher, p.197
Good Earth, Wells, p.282
Govindas, W1, p.79
Gran Paradiso, SW1, p.79
Granary, Hay-on-Wye, p.325
Granary Coffee House, Leominster, p.227
Grand Hotel, Victoria's, St Helier, Jersey, p.336
La Grande Bouffe, Liverpool, P.232
Grange Bridge Cottage, Grange-in-Borrowdale, p.204
The Greys, Brighton, p.158
Green Apple, Bakewell, p.129

·M A P · S E C T I O N·

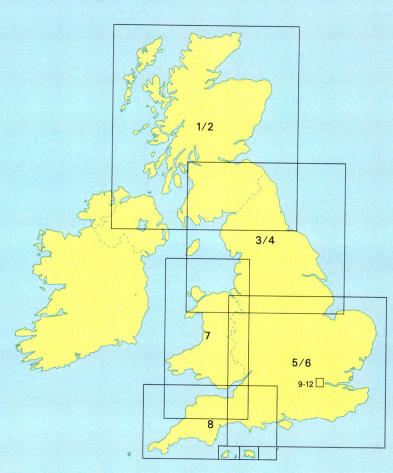

1/2

3/4

7

5/6

9-12

8

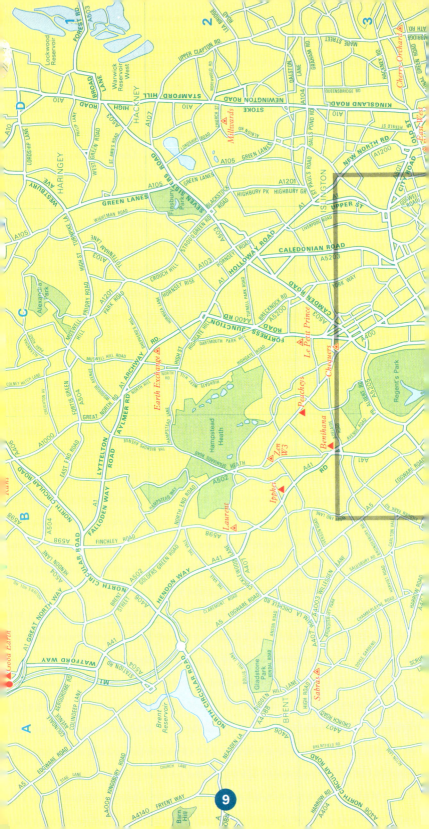

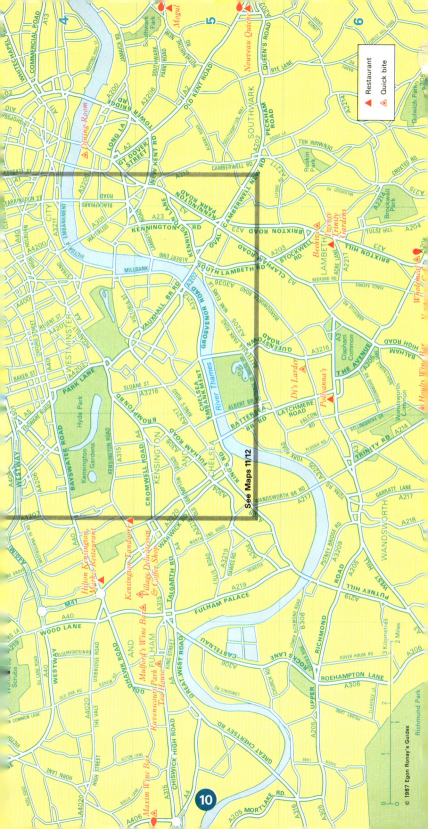

Legend

▲ Restaurant
△ Quick Bite

Map labels:

1 · 2 · 3
A · B · C · D

Youngs
Fallen Angel
Frederick's
Almeida Theatre Wine Bar
Younges
Suruchi
ALDERSGATE STREET
St Paul's Cathedral
Slender's Café
City-Miyama
LUDGATE HILL
UPPER STREET
CITY ROAD
GOSWELL ROAD
A50
GT. ST
EAST
OLD ST
HOLBORN VIADUCT
BLACKFRIARS BRIDGE
Food for Health
Daly's Wine Bar
RIVER THAMES
PENTONVILLE ROAD
FARRINGDON ROAD
ROSEBERY AVENUE
CLERKENWELL ROAD
SHOE LANE
HIGH HOLBORN
VICTORIA EMBANKMENT
Somerset House
Lincoln's Inn Wine Bar
STRAND
Cranks in Covent Garden
FLEET STREET
CALEDONIAN ROAD A5203
KINGS CROSS ROAD
GRAY'S INN ROAD
THEOBALD'S ROAD
KINGSWAY
Food for Thought
Cranks
Thesis-Jones
Cranks
First Out
Ajimura
Neal Street
ALDWYCH
Cranks
CHARING CROSS ROAD
Poons
Loons
Sisters Centre
YORK WAY
King's Cross Station
PANCRAS ROAD
St Pancras Station
EUSTON ROAD
WOBURN PLACE
SOUTHAMPTON ROW
British Museum
GOWER STREET
Aryu
OXFORD STREET
Mandeer
Frith St
Poons
YORK WAY
A5200
St Pancras Way
ROYAL COLLEGE STREET
Camden Brasserie
Pasta Underground
CAMDEN ST.
CAMDEN HIGH ST.
Nontas
PARKWAY
Kalamaras
Raj Bhelpoori House
Dicana Bhelpoori House
EVERSHOT ROAD
Euston Station
HAMPSTEAD ROAD
Diwana Bhelpoori House
Raei Shankar
Sagaramutha
TOTTENHAM COURT ROAD
Gurkhas Tandoori
Cranks
Reeves Wine Cellar
Ibyu
Govinda's
Ariyang
REGENT ST.
Cranks Health Food Restaurant
Palms
Ikeda
Kitchen Yakitori
REGENT STREET
Hobbs
Country Life
Bentley's Wine Bar
ALBANY STREET
PORTLAND PLACE
Topkapi
Woodlands
Nakamura
WIGMORE STREET
OXFORD STREET
Defune
Nanten
Itumi
Soseki
Chaopraya
Bubbles Wine Bar
One Two Two
Justin de Blank
PARK
Grosvenor House
Regent's Park
Boating Lake
MARYLEBONE ROAD
BAKER STREET
GLOUCESTER PLACE
SEYMOUR ST.
PLACE
Asuka
Raw Deal
Manna
Odette's Wine Bar
PRINCE ALBERT ROAD
Primrose Hill
PARK ROAD
WELLINGTON ROAD
ST. JOHN'S WOOD ROAD
EDGWARE ROAD
SUSSEX GARDENS
MAIDA VALE
Paddington Station
PRAED STREET
BISHOP'S BRIDGE ROAD
WESTBOURNE GROVE
Diwana Bhelpoori House
BAYSWATER ROAD
FINCHLEY ROAD A41
HARROW ROAD
A4091
EDGWARE ROAD
CASTELLAIN ROAD
A5 KILBURN HIGH RD.

11

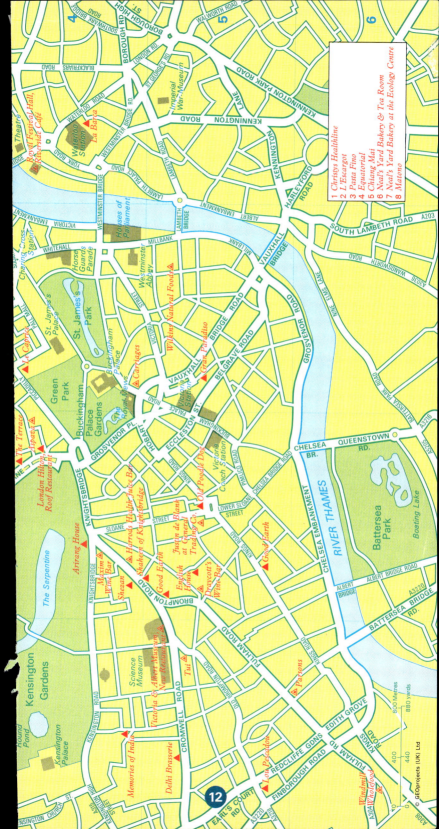